ENDANGERED PEOPLES
of Latin America

BELIZE

GUATEMALA

HONDURAS

Bay Islands

EL SALVADOR

NICARAGUA

| 0 | 100 | 200 mi. |

| 0 | 100 | 200 | 300 km. |

M E X I C O

COSTA
RICA

*Archipelago
de san Blas*

P A N A M A

Central America Inset

VENEZUELA

GUAYANA

SURINAME

FR. GUAYANA

COLOMBIA

EQUADOR

P E R U

B R A Z I L

B O L I V I A

PARAGUAY

C H I L E

A R G E N T I N A

URUGUAY

N

| 0 | 500 | 1000 mi. |

| 0 | 500 | 1000 km. |

AnthroGraphicsLab

ENDANGERED PEOPLES
of Latin America

Struggles to Survive and Thrive

Edited by Susan C. Stonich

The Greenwood Press
"Endangered Peoples of the World" Series
Barbara Rose Johnston, Series Editor

GREENWOOD PRESS
Westport, Connecticut • London

Library of Congress Cataloging-in-Publication Data

Endangered peoples of Latin America : struggles to survive and thrive / edited by Susan C. Stonich.
     p. cm.—(The Greenwood Press "Endangered peoples of the world" series, ISSN 1525–1233)
     Includes bibliographical references and index.
     ISBN 0–313–30856–X (alk. paper)
     1. Indians, Treatment of—Latin America. 2. Indians—Social conditions. 3. Indians—Government relations. 4. Indigenous peoples—Latin America. 5. Latin America—Ethnic relations. 6. Latin America—Politics and government. I. Stonich, Susan C. II. Series.
E65.E57 2001
323.1'19808—dc21   00–035371

British Library Cataloguing in Publication Data is available.

Library of Congress Catalog Card Number: 00–035371
ISBN: 0–313–30856–X
ISSN: 1525–1233

First published in 2001

Greenwood Press, 88 Post Road West, Westport, CT 06881
An imprint of Greenwood Publishing Group, Inc.
www.greenwood.com

Printed in the United States of America

The paper used in this book complies with the Permanent Paper Standard issued by the National Information Standards Organization (Z39.48–1984).

10 9 8 7 6 5 4 3 2 1

Contents

Contents

Series Foreword

Barbara Rose Johnston

Two hundred thousand years ago our human ancestors gathered plants and hunted animals in the forests and savannas of Africa. By forty thousand years ago, *Homo sapiens sapiens* had developed ways to survive and thrive in every major ecosystem on this planet. Unlike other creatures, whose response to harsh or varied conditions prompted biological change, humans generally relied upon their ingenuity to survive. They fashioned clothing from skins and plant fiber rather than growing thick coats of protective hair. They created innovative ways to live and communicate and thus passed knowledge down to their children. This knowledge, by ten thousand years ago, included the means to cultivate and store food. The ability to provide for lean times allowed humans to settle in larger numbers in villages, towns, and cities where their ideas, values, ways of living, and language grew increasingly complicated and diverse.

This cultural diversity—the multitude of ways of living and communicating knowledge—gave humans an adaptive edge. Other creatures adjusted to change in their environment through biological adaptation (a process that requires thousands of life spans to generate and reproduce a mutation to the level of the population). Humans developed analytical tools to identify and assess change in their environment, to search out or devise new strategies, and to incorporate new strategies throughout their group. Sometimes these cultural adaptations worked; people transformed their way of life, and their population thrived. Other times, these changes produced further complications.

Intensive agricultural techniques, for example, often resulted in increased salts in the soil, decreased soil fertility, and declining crop yields. Food production declined, and people starved. Survivors often moved to new regions to begin again. Throughout human history, migration became the common strategy when innovations failed. Again, in these times, culture was essential to survival.

For the human species, culture is our primary adaptive mechanism. Cultural diversity presents us with opportunities to draw from and build upon a complicated array of views, ideas, and strategies. The Endangered Peoples of the World series celebrates the rich diversity of cultural groups living on our planet and explores how cultural diversity, like biological diversity, is threatened.

Five hundred years ago, as humans entered the age of colonial expansion, there were an estimated twelve to fourteen thousand cultural groups with distinct languages, values, and ways of life. Today, cultural diversity has been reduced by half (an estimated 6,000 to 7,000 groups). This marked decline is due in part to the fact that, historically, isolated peoples had minimal immunity to introduced diseases and little time to develop immunological defenses. Colonizers brought more than ideas, religion, and new economic ways of living. They brought a host of viruses and bacteria— measles, chickenpox, smallpox, the common cold. These diseases swept through "new" worlds at epidemic levels and wiped out entire nations. Imperialist expansion and war further decimated original, or "indigenous," populations.

Today's cultural diversity is further threatened by the biodegenerative conditions of nature. Our biophysical world's deterioration is evidenced by growing deserts; decreasing forests; declining fisheries; poisoned food, water, and air; and climatic extremes and weather events such as floods, hurricanes, and droughts. These degenerative conditions challenge our survival skills, often rendering customary knowledge and traditions ineffective.

Cultural diversity is also threatened by unparalleled transformations in human relations. Isolation is no longer the norm. Small groups continually interact and are subsumed by larger cultural, political, and economic groups of national and global dimensions. The rapid pace of change in population, technology, and political economy leaves little time to develop sustainable responses and adjust to changing conditions.

Across the world cultural groups are struggling to maintain a sense of unique identity while interpreting and assimilating an overwhelming flow of new ideas, ways of living, economies, values, and languages. As suggested in some chapters in this series, cultural groups confront, embrace, adapt, and transform these external forces in ways that allow them to survive and thrive. However, in far too many cases, cultural groups lack the time and means to adjust and change. Rather, they struggle to retain the right to simply exist as other, more powerful peoples seize their land and resources and "cleanse" the countryside of their presence.

Efforts to gain control of land, labor, and resources of politically and/or geographically peripheral peoples are justified and legitimized by ethnocentric notions: the beliefs that the values, traditions, and behavior of your own cultural group are superior and that other groups are biologically, culturally, and socially inferior. These notions are produced and reproduced in conversation, curriculum, public speeches, articles, television coverage, and other communication forums. Ethnocentrism is reflected in a language of debasement that serves to dehumanize (the marginal peoples are considered sub-human: primitive, backward, ignorant people that "live like animals"). The pervasiveness of this discourse in the everyday language can eventually destroy the self-esteem and sense of worth of marginal groups and reduce their motivation to control their destiny.

Thus, vulnerability to threats from the biophysical and social realms is a factor of social relations. Human action and a history of social inequity leave some people more vulnerable than others. This vulnerability results in ethnocide (loss of a way of life), ecocide (destruction of the environment), and genocide (death of an entire group of people).

The Endangered Peoples of the World series samples cultural diversity in different regions of the world, examines the varied threats to cultural survival, and explores some of the ways people are adjusting and responding to threats of ethnocide, ecocide, and genocide. Each volume in the series covers the peoples, problems, and responses characteristic of a major region of the world: the Arctic, Europe, North America and the Caribbean, Latin America, Africa and the Middle East, Central and South Asia, Southeast and East Asia, and Oceania. Each volume includes an introductory essay authored by the volume editor and fifteen or so chapters, each featuring a different cultural group whose customs, problems, and responses represent a sampling of conditions typical of the region. Chapter content is organized into five sections: Cultural Overview (people, setting, traditional subsistence strategies, social and political organization, religion and world view), Threats to Survival (demographic trends, current events and conditions, environmental crisis, sociocultural crisis), Response: Struggles to Survive Culturally (indicating the variety of efforts to respond to threats), Food for Thought (a brief summary of the issues raised by the case and some provocative questions that can be used to structure class discussion or organize a research paper), and a Resource Guide (major accessible published sources, films and videos, Internet and WWW sites, and organizations). Many chapters are authored or coauthored by members of the featured group, and all chapters include liberal use of a "local voice" to present the group's own views on its history, current problems, strategies, and thoughts of the future.

Collectively, the series contains some 120 case-specific examples of cultural groups struggling to survive and thrive in a culturally diverse world. Many of the chapters in this global sampling depict the experiences of indigenous peoples and ethnic minorities who, until recently, sustained their customary way of life in the isolated regions of the world. Threats to survival are often linked to external efforts to develop the natural resources of the previously isolated region. The development context is often one of co-optation of traditionally held lands and resources with little or no recognition of resident peoples' rights and little or no compensation for their subsequent environmental health problems. New ideas, values, technologies, economies, and languages accompany the development process and, over time, may even replace traditional ways of being.

Cultural survival, however, is not solely a concern of indigenous peoples. Indeed, in many parts of the world the term "indigenous" has little relevance, as all peoples are native to the region. Thus, in this series, we define cultural groups in the broadest of terms. We examine threats to survival and the variety of responses of ethnic minorities, as well as national cultures, whose traditions are challenged and undermined by global transformations.

The dominant theme that emerges from this sampling is that humans struggle with serious and life-threatening problems tied to larger global forces, and yet, despite huge differences in power levels between local communities and global institutions and structures, people are crafting and developing new ways of being. This series demonstrates that culture is not a static set of meanings, values, and behaviors; it is a flexible, resilient tool that has historically provided humans with the means to adapt, adjust, survive, and, at times, thrive. Thus, we see "endangered" peoples confronting and responding to threats in ways that reshape and transform their values, relationships, and behavior.

Emerging from this transformative process are new forms of cultural identity, new strategies for living, and new means and opportunities to communicate. These changes represent new threats to cultural identity and autonomy but also new challenges to the forces that dominate and endanger lives.

Introduction

Susan C. Stonich

It is extremely problematic to generalize about the peoples and lands of Latin America. Diverse histories together with equally varied biophysical environments have created an astounding array of landscapes and cultures. No one schema can capture the considerable heterogeneity in peoples, economies, or governments. Latin America is also characterized by great differences in wealth and human well-being according to commonly used measures of income, poverty, education, and health (see Table 1). While national level statistics may be helpful in some instances, international boundaries often mask cultural differentiation or disparities in wealth and well-being. For example, the way of life (and the standard of living) of most of the people in southern Mexico is more like that in Guatemala than in northern Mexico. Aggregate data on national or per capita income suggest that certain countries in the region, such as Chile and Argentina, are significantly more wealthy than others, such as Nicaragua, Honduras, and El Salvador. They also show that, in general, poorer countries tend to have significantly lower life expectancy and literacy rates than do richer countries. However, differences in wealth, education, and well-being among socioeconomic classes within individual countries are considerable throughout the region. That is, there are extremely rich people (with access to good jobs, education, and health care) even in the poorest countries, and considerable pockets of poverty exist in the richer countries.

To make things more complicated, there is no standard or universally accepted geopolitical definition of Latin America. This volume uses one of the more widely accepted definitions in which Latin America is understood to include the heterogeneous group of countries of Mexico, Central America, and South America. This region extends from the Rio Grande River that forms the border of the United States and Mexico to the large island of Tierra del Fuego, at the southern tip of Chile. In between are vast dif-

Table 1
Important Human Indicators for Latin America, 1997

	Total population (millions) 1997	Annual population growth rate (%) 1975-1997	Urban population (%) 1997	Gross Domestic Product (GDP) (US$ billions) 1997	Real GDP (per capita) 1997	Population living on US$ 1/day (%) 1989-1994	Life expectancy at birth (years) 1997	Adult literacy (%) 1997
Latin America*	490,400	2	74.2	2,018,400	6,868	n.a.	69.5	87.2
Mexico	94.3	2.1	73.8	403	8,370	14.9	72.2	90.1
Central America								
Belize	0.2	2.4	46.4	0.6	4,300	n.a.	74.7	75
Costa Rica	3.7	3	50.3	9.5	6,650	18.9	76	95.1
El Salvador	5.9	1.7	45.6	11.3	2,880	n.a.	69.1	77
Guatemala	10.5	2.6	39.4	17.8	4,100	53.3	64	66.6
Honduras	6	3.2	45	4.5	2,220	46.5	69.4	70.7
Nicaragua	4.7	2.9	63.2	2	1,997	43.8	67.9	63.4
Panama	2.7	2.1	73.8	8.2	7,168	25.6	73.6	91.1
South America								
Argentina	35.7	1.4	88.6	325	10,300	n.a.	72.9	96.5
Bolivia	7.8	2.3	62.3	8	2,880	7.1	61.4	83.6
Brazil	163.7	1.9	79.6	820.4	6,480	28.7	66.8	84
Chile	14.6	1.6	84.2	77.1	12,730	15	74.9	95.2
Colombia	40	2.1	73.6	95.7	6,810	7.4	70.4	90.9
Ecuador	11.9	2.5	60.4	19.8	4,940	30.4	69.5	90.7
Guyana	0.8	0.6	48	0.8	3,210	n.a.	64.4	98.1
Paraguay	5.1	3	53.9	10.2	3,980	n.a.	69.6	92.4
Peru	24.4	2.2	71.6	63.8	4,680	49.4	68.3	88.7
Suriname	0.4	0.6	50.3	n.a.	5,161	n.a.	70.1	93.5
Uruguay	3.3	0.7	90.7	20	9,200	n.a.	73.9	97.5
Venezuela	22.8	2.7	86.5	87.5	8,860	11.8	72.4	92

*Includes the Caribbean.

Source: *Human Development Report 1999*, United Nations Development Programme. New York, 1999.

ferences in biophysical environments as well as among the many peoples who inhabit the region. On a map, Mexico resembles a large cone pointing to the southeast, with the Sierra Madre mountain ranges converging just south of the present day capital of Mexico City. The present location occupied by Mexico City also was the site of the great political centers of prehistoric and colonial Mexico—Teotihuacán, Tenochtitlán, and the Spanish colonial capital. Many large mountainous regions are found south of Mexico City and continue into Guatemala. Many of these were the sites of the great pre-Columbian city-states of Mesoamerica, including the several Mayan city-states, which linked highland and lowland civilizations throughout the region. Farther south is the Central American isthmus, a land bridge that links North and South America. Although extremely narrow at some points, it is extremely heterogeneous in terms of topography, climate, soils, flora, and fauna, as well as peoples. Many Central American environments, natural resources, and diverse peoples are threatened today. South of the Central American country of Panama, the Andes Mountains contain a series of highland basins where large numbers of Andean peoples live. In contrast, the Amazon basin to the east forms a more sparsely inhabited tropical region that is home to many threatened indigenous peoples and environments.[1]

Latin American history can be divided into several time periods each characterized by significantly different political and economic institutions as well as by various threats to native peoples.[2] The first is the prehistoric period, characterized by indigenous polities and economies that ranged from small autonomous groups of foragers, to village-dwelling agriculturalists, to more complexly organized and larger city-states such as the Maya, to empires such as the Aztec and the Inca. Second is the period of exploration, conquest, and colonization that began with the discovery of the Americas by Europeans and ended with the beginning of the wars of independence from Spain in the early 1800s. Less than three decades after the discovery of the Americas, Hernán Cortés completed the conquest of Mexico with the destruction of the Mexica (Aztec) capital of Tenochtitlán in 1521. Shortly thereafter, in 1533, Francisco Pizarro captured the Inca capital of Cuzco located in modern Peru. This period was a "search for wealth" to use the phrase coined by anthropologist Eric Wolf in his monumental book *Europe and the People Without History*.[3] During this time, not only were native populations devastated, many countries became economically dependent on the export of a few natural resource-based commodities—gold, silver, lumber, cattle, and agricultural crops such as indigo and sugar—a dependence that persists today. In addition, the profits generated by Latin America's mineral and agricultural wealth accrued to only a few people—another pattern that continues to the present. A further contemporary situation with a foundation during this initial period of European involvement was the establishment of the dual pattern of extremely large and small landholdings—the latifundia (the large estates owned by the elite [haciendas and plantations]) and the *minifundia* (the extremely small holdings owned by non-elite mestizos and others).

The third period of Latin American history is often referred to as the period of caudillo politics (political bosses), which lasted approximately from the end of the wars of independence (1810–1820) into the 1930s. During the end of this time period, considerable industrialization took place in some of the more economically progressive countries, which became the wealthiest countries of the region (Chile, Argentina, Brazil, Mexico, Colombia, and Venezuela). Rural peoples, especially indigenous peoples, in these countries were affected by the trend toward privatization of Indian *ejidos* (communally held and managed land) and the decimation of many indigenous communities in Mexico, Guatemala, El Salvador, Bolivia, Peru, Ecuador, and elsewhere.

During the following period, roughly between the 1930s and the early 1980s, Latin American governments attempted to expand their industrial bases, often along with considerable economic protectionism. Beginning in the early 1980s, Latin America began undergoing a period of neoliberal economic reform by which the countries of Latin America have sought further integration into the global economy. The economies of the countries of the region have been opened; formerly government-controlled services and enterprises have been privatized; international, extraregional, and regional trade agreements—such as the North American Free Trade Agreement (NAFTA) between Mexico, the United States, and Canada; and the southern common market, MERCOSUR, between Argentina, Brazil, Paraguay and Uruguay—have been negotiated to advance globalization.

The earliest period of European invasion, conquest, and colonization caused excessive suffering and death among the native populations of Latin America. It disrupted and often destroyed indigenous peoples' food production, economic, political, and social systems. Many indigenous peoples disappeared entirely and forever during this period, as much from the destruction of their social, political, and economic systems as from the effects of newly introduced European diseases. In spite of the devastating impact of the initial period of conquest, followed by 500 years of domination through a series of colonial and state governments, many of Latin America's indigenous peoples and cultures survived. The current period of economic globalization, however, is often referred to as the "Second Conquest" because of its potential threat to destroy forever indigenous cultures throughout the region.

Today, indigenous peoples make up a minority of the total population of Latin America, numerically as well as politically (see Table 2). In a few countries, however, such as Guatemala, Bolivia, Peru, and southern Mexico, native peoples make up a significant percentage of the national population. Today, Latin America is an extremely ethnically diverse region that is home to indigenous/native, mestizo/ladino, white/European, Afro-Latin American, and other groups including those with East Indian, East Asian, and Middle Eastern heritage. As Table 2 shows, the ethnic makeup varies significantly among countries.

In most countries of the region, indigenous peoples commonly occupy the more remote and isolated areas that tend also to be the areas with the greatest biological diversity, including the tropical rainforests of the Amazon and Central America. Throughout the region, the number of culturally distinct indigenous peoples tends to be high in the most biologically rich and ecologically significant ecosystems. At the same time, however, native peoples also constitute an increasing number of urban dwellers as their indigenous homelands are threatened by outside interests and they are com-

Table 2
Ethnic Composition of Latin America

	Mestizo or Ladino (%)	Indigenous, Native or Indian (%)	White or European (%)	African-Latin American, Black or Creole (%)	Other (%)
Mexico	60	30	9		1
Central America					
Belize	44	19		30	7
Costa Rica*	96*	1	96*	2	1
El Salvador	94	5	1		
Guatemala	56	44			
Honduras	90	7		2	1
Nicaragua	69	5	17	9	
Panama	70	6	10	14	
South America					
Argentina			85		15
Bolivia	30	55	15		
Brazil			55	7	38
Chile		3	95		2
Colombia	58	1	20	21	
Ecuador	55	25	10	10	
Guyana		4	2	43	51
Paraguay	95	3	2		
Peru	37	45	15	3	
Suriname		3		41	56
Uruguay	8		88	4	
Venezuela	67	2	21	10	

*Contains both mestizo and white/European.

Source: Paul B. Goodwin, Jr. *Global Studies–Latin America*, Eighth Edition. Guilford, Conn.:
  Dushkin/McGraw-Hill, 1999.

pelled to migrate to the cities. While indigenous peoples usually are part
of the poorest segment of Latin American society, by no means are Latin
America's "poor" and "indigenous peoples" synonymous. In many places,
such as Nicaragua, Honduras, El Salvador, and parts of Mexico, the
"poor" are largely composed of national ethnic majorities (mestizos or lad-

inos). In other countries, including Brazil and Ecuador, Afro-Latin Americans make up a disproportionate share of the poor.

Today, indigenous peoples of the region face considerable threats to their material and cultural survival. Many native peoples currently are resisting the so-called Second Conquest and are struggling to survive culturally as well as materially in contemporary Latin America. One of the primary means of struggle has been the political actions of a growing number of indigenous and grassroots organizations that are attempting to negotiate with nation-states and corporations for various legal rights (especially land rights) and protection. Many of these efforts also function to protect and, in some cases, rejuvenate indigenous traditions and cultures as well as increase the incomes, health, education, and well-being of the region's native peoples. Moreover, many of the current threats to, and the struggles of, indigenous peoples are shared by the multitudes of the region's poor mestizos, ladinos, and Afro-Americans, and other marginalized groups such as women and children. For example, according to many measures of human well-being—including income, poverty, health, literacy, and education— Honduras' poor ladino majority is more similar to the indigenous Mayans in neighboring Guatemala than to "rich" Hondurans.

Contemporary threats to Latin America's indigenous and other marginalized peoples during the present period of globalization are the focus of this volume. While the examples in this book concentrate on contemporary Latin America, most of the chapters show how the region's history contributes significantly to current conditions and demonstrate the need to consider the region's past in order to improve its future.

LATIN AMERICA'S SHARED PROBLEMS

Given its tremendous heterogeneity, the most obvious common denominators in Latin America may be its shared problems. Changes in the global economy since the 1970s have played a considerable role in structuring current social, economic, and political conditions in Latin America as well as contributed significantly to related problems. The pace of globalization (along with its companion, modernization) has been uneven, but no major segment of Latin America has been untouched by it. The threats, if not the impacts, of these changes are being felt socially, economically, politically, technologically, and culturally. Traditional patterns of human settlement are being altered; there is an increasing migration from rural to urban areas; new technologies of exploiting the environment are being introduced; and new industries and other institutions are appearing on the landscape. Rapid and often distressing changes have provoked political violence and revolution in many places including Mexico, Peru, Central America, Colombia, Venezuela, and Brazil.

Economic Growth Along with Increasing Unemployment and Continuing Poverty

The 1980s often are referred to as the "lost decade" in Latin America because virtually all countries in the region experienced severe economic recessions. Between 1982 and 1989 the real gross domestic product (GDP) grew an average of 1.4% annually, but per capita GDP declined by approximately 1% per year.[4] During the 1980s, the region experienced increasing rates of unemployment, declines in real wages and earning power, and increases in levels of poverty. By the end of the decade, 30% of the urban families in Latin America were living in poverty—50% in El Salvador, Guatemala, Honduras, and Nicaragua.[5]

The crippling economic crisis of the lost decade led most of the region's national governments to accept the structural adjustment measures imposed by international financial institutions such as the International Monetary Fund (IMF) and external creditors. Structural adjustment profoundly affected most people because national governments were compelled to cut spending by eliminating public sector jobs (e.g., teachers, health care professionals, garbage collectors, and administrators) and by reducing social, educational, health, and other services. Government measures also included accepting the dominant economic development model that promoted economic growth per se with little regard for the human and environmental consequences. Many large-scale development programs exacerbated social, economic, and political problems, as well as environmental degradation which most of the region's societies experienced to some extent earlier. Adjustment policies reinforced these problems, emphasized inequalities, and set the stage for political polarization.

Despite more than a decade of economic reforms aimed at furthering globalization throughout the region, a new report released by the International Labor Organization (ILO), an agency of the United Nations, raises serious concerns about the social and economic justice of globalization.[6] The report concludes that, even though Latin America experienced a moderate economic recovery during most of the 1990s, the benefits of economic growth have not been equitably distributed. The report maintains that impoverished families continue to suffer disproportionately from the paucity of job opportunities and a growing deterioration in the quality of employment that is available.

Unemployment in the region increased in the last several years when the private sector did not fill the void created by the large cuts in public sector employment. According to the report, presented by the director general of the ILO, the unemployment rate in Latin America in 1999 rose to 9.5%, surpassing the peak jobless rates during the economic and debt crisis of the 1980s—despite a decade of economic reform and modernization. Throughout the 1990s, more than 85% of all *new* jobs created in the region (and 59% of all nonagricultural jobs) were in the lower quality, so-called informal sector. The informal sector comprises temporary and part-time jobs such as street vendors, food sellers, babysitters, maids, laundresses, car washers, and shoe shiners. Wages, benefits, and levels of social protection are nonexistent or much lower in the informal sector than in the formal economic sector, and workers in the informal sector are almost never protected by any laws nor are they usually able to join recognized unions to protect their interests. As a result of recent trends, workers' buying power in Latin America fell dramatically over the past decade, dropping to 27% below what a salary bought in 1980 for minimum wage earners.

Women and younger workers have been especially hard hit by these recent economic trends. Youth unemployment rates commonly are double the national averages and triple for workers between the ages of fifteen and nineteen. Women's unemployment rates are between 10% and 60% higher than men's rates. The report also expresses a "growing concern" about child labor, which affects from 15% to 20% of the children in the region between the ages of ten and fourteen, and its potential to perpetuate high rates of poverty if left unchecked. The ILO report raises serious questions about the potential of economic globalization to benefit all sectors of society equitably and significantly reduce levels of poverty throughout the region.

Rural and Urban Poverty

Although urban areas exhibit high rates of poverty, it is the rural families who are most negatively affected and whose living conditions have deteriorated the most significantly in recent years. Estimates based on case studies conducted in rural areas by two United Nations agencies, the Economic Commission for Latin America and the Caribbean (ECLAC) and the Food and Agriculture Organization (FAO), suggest that an average of 70% of Latin America's rural families live in poverty.[7] Growing rural poverty remains one of the paramount factors stimulating rural to urban migration as the rural poor flock to towns and cities looking for work—usually available (if at all) only in the informal sector. Latin America ceased being predominantly rural during the 1960s. By 1990 only 28% of the region's population continued to live in rural areas. Current estimates are that in 2000, the rural population makes up only about 25% of the total population of the region.[8]

Environment and Health

The critical social and economic changes that have occurred in the region point to the intimate connection among economy, environmental conditions, and human health. As a result of declining health budgets and inadequate sanitation measures in many countries, diarrheal and parasitic diseases are a leading cause of high mortality and morbidity among certain groups, especially the poor, women, and children. Simultaneously, the rapid growth of urban centers has elevated health risks from increased exposure to toxic chemicals that contaminate the air, water, soil, and food.

The urban population of Latin America is increasing by about 3% annually. In 1985, 250 cities in the region had 100,000 or more inhabitants. By 2000, an estimated 450 cities will fall into that category, including about 100 cities with populations of one million or more and 15 with more than 4 million residents.[9] Deteriorating living conditions are a characteristic typical of most large cities in the region, especially in newer squatter settlements and in older downtown areas. Families that migrate to the cities from rural areas often are unable to find adequate housing or employment. Poor living conditions, including scarcity of potable water, sewerage, and solid waste disposal, intensify as population densities increase and public services (including health) continue to decline.

The production and use of chemicals by the growing number of export-oriented industrial processing plants (*maquiladores*), located in so-called Free Trade Zones throughout the region, also significantly increase environmental health problems, as do the increased number of accidents, noise, and congestion. Because the region as a whole is committed to globalization and economic growth, the upward trend in environmental problems affecting human health will persist and will probably accelerate.

Growing rural poverty and established links between environmental decline and diminished human health in rural areas suggests that people living in rural areas are also at risk. Rural people are significantly less likely than urban residents to have access to a safe and sufficient water supply, sewerage and waste disposal systems, adequate housing, and health services. In addition, because the rural poor increasingly are dependent on off-farm income, much of which is earned as agricultural laborers, they continually face the risks of exposure to toxic pesticides. Recent studies of the region demonstrate that the excessive use of pesticides is placing farmworkers in jeopardy and is contaminating soils, surface, and groundwater.[10] Moreover, as some disease vectors (such as mosquitoes) have become resistant to pesticides, the incidence of diseases such as malaria is rising.

Hunger and Food Security

In part because of ongoing economic crises, exacerbated by major natural disasters, political unrest, and wars in some countries, the overall rise in food prices in recent years has outstripped increases in wages in many countries, resulting in a drop of real purchasing power to buy food. Because levels of food consumption are linked to real income levels, food consumption has deteriorated in some countries, especially among the poor. In addition, national level data on food production suggest that per capita food production declined in approximately half of the countries in the region during recent decades while the per capita daily availability of calories diminished in about a quarter of the countries.[11]

Overall information on national food production and the per capita availability of calories or protein reveal only part of the reality. Recent analyses of hunger and food security demonstrate how hunger and malnutrition can coexist with growth in agricultural production, especially if crops are destined for export to foreign markets. International and national class interests and power relationships have meshed with donor and debt strategies to create food and nutritional deficits in many communities. The authors of a recent compilation of studies of hunger and food security in Mexico and Central America point to several factors that have generated regional food insecurity: extreme socioeconomic and political inequality, war and the large-scale displacement of peoples, responses to ongoing economic crises, overemphasis on export agriculture, overreliance on food imports, poorly developed mechanisms for distributing food to those most in need, and the degradation of the natural resource base resulting from dominant development strategies.[12]

Environmental Degradation

Continuing economic crises, population growth especially in urban areas, and the desperate need of rural people to sustain their families have all stimulated government efforts to increase foreign exchange earnings and economic growth, often through intensified exploitation of the region's natural resources. These efforts in turn have led to a staggering rate of environmental destruction. Widespread deforestation, erosion, desertification, and destruction of watersheds are among the consequences. Expansion of export crops in areas that are the most appropriate and have the greatest potential for agriculture has forced hundreds of thousands of smallholders off the land and has contributed to growing landlessness in rural areas. Those who remain find themselves relegated to marginal, steep-sloped lands that are easily degraded. Severe soil erosion and other forms of environmental degradation have decreased crop yields at a time when peasant farmers face severe economic hardships. The marginalization of peasant producers has generated hunger, reduced national food production, and systematically destroyed the environment and natural resource base. The health of the natural environment has become a critical dimension of present and future food security in many countries of the region.[13]

Environment and Indigenous Peoples

Throughout Latin America, governments pressed by continuing economic crises are struggling to increase income by expanding the exploitation of natural resources within their national territories. Simultaneously, increasingly impoverished peasant farmers likewise are attempting to survive by migrating to previously more isolated frontier areas—the few remaining areas inhabited by indigenous peoples. These economic strategies, along with the growth in road building, lumbering, agribusiness, hydroelectric projects, mining and oil operations, unregulated and planned colonization, and the expropriation of genetic materials (and the associated cultural knowledge), pose an augmented threat to indigenous peoples. They also are a major source of conflict between indigenous peoples and national governments. Aggravating the situation of indigenous peoples throughout the region are the numerous political and military conflicts—which a geographer has termed the "Third World War"—which have increasingly been associated with economic development initiatives.[14] In Central America, for example, the Miskito of Honduras and Nicaragua, caught between the Contras and the Sandinistas (and exploited by both) during the 1980s, now face threats to the control of their homelands by national development efforts to extract natural resources from their territories, and by the resettlement of impoverished ladino families from other parts of Nicaragua and Honduras (see chapters 6 and 7). In this context, a potentially positive trend for the Miskito, and other native peoples in the region, is the emergence of indigenous organizations that are attempting to maintain control of the environmental and natural resources under their domain and, in turn, their own cultures and destinies. Their efforts have been significantly enhanced by growing support from international environmental and human rights organizations.

THREATS AND RESPONSES

The case studies included in this volume are specific examples of the various cultural and material threats currently faced by indigenous and other groups at risk in Latin America. These include threats to cultural survival, to local economies and local environments, to health and nutrition, and to control of land and other natural resources. These threats come through a variety of mechanisms, including economic globalization and modernization, dominant economic development strategies—agriculture, shrimp farming, lobster diving, tourism, mining, even real estate development—and the colonization of frontier areas. Individual cases focus on particular groups, indigenous peoples, mestizos, ladinos, Afro-Latin Americans, who are struggling to sustain their cultures, lives, and livelihoods. A few of the cases examine how different groups at risk sometimes must negotiate (or choose not to negotiate) conflicts with each other.

Far from presenting a bleak picture of the future of the peoples at risk, however, the cases demonstrate the creative, innovative, and powerful responses to these threats currently being engaged in by diverse peoples throughout the hemisphere. These include responses at the individual and family level: agricultural intensification and production for markets, greater reliance on wage work, seasonal wage labor migration, rural to urban migration in search of work, and migration to frontier areas (see chapter 2). They also include group strategies, especially organization for political action. From Mexico to Chile, indigenous peoples as well as other disadvantaged groups, including peasants, fisherfolk, and women, have established local organizations that have become one of the most important elements of their survival strategies. Native peoples have enhanced their efforts to control the dominant powers that have exploited them for the last 500 years. The strengthening of ethnic and cultural identities has been an important foundation for these efforts, not only for indigenous groups but also for mestizos and Afro-Americans (see chapters 3, 5, 8, 9, and 12). In most countries, the various indigenous, peasant, and urban groups have formed national networks and organizations to promote the welfare of their communities and attain other goals and objectives. Increasingly, local and indigenous groups have joined with their compatriots in other countries in international and even global networks; for example, the Industrial Shrimp Action Network discussed in chapter 4. These international and global networks often include support from groups outside of Latin America.

Beyond the widespread movement to organize locally, nationally, regionally, and globally, the responses of particular indigenous and local cultures to renewed oppression and threats from nation-states and corporate interests have varied considerably. These strategies for cultural survival have ranged from the peaceful and generally effective political negotiations of the Kuna and Ngobe with the government of Panama (see chapters 8 and 9) to armed rebellion as in the case of the Maya Zapatistas of Chiapas, Mexico. Some cases are characterized by a degree of violent confrontation as in the examples of the Tz'utujil Maya (chapter 10), the artisanal fisherfolk of the Gulf of Fonseca (chapter 4), the English-Speaking Bay Islanders (chapter 5), and the Quechua of Peru (chapter 13). Strategies for cultural survival also include innovative and, to date, relatively successful efforts such as the creation and comanagement of forest reserve areas such as those by the Awa of Ecuador (chapter 11) and the Maya of Quintana Roo (chapter 1) which may have application to other groups in other areas. Finally, strategies also include the use of new spatial technologies (Geographic Information Systems and Global Positioning Systems) as in the participatory mapping project of the Rio Plátano Biosphere Reserve described in chapter 7.[15] However, as in the other instances, the use of innovative, new technologies is not an end in itself, but rather a means of political action aimed at providing the Miskito, Garifuna, and others the power to affect their own destinies.

NOTES

1. Sheldon Smith and Philip D. Young, *Cultural Anthropology: Understanding a World in Transition* (Boston: Allyn and Bacon, 1998), 412.

2. This classification is based on that of Smith and Young presented in chapter 12 of their introductory textbook in cultural anthropology (see Smith and Young, *Cultural Anthropology*, 414–56). Readers are encouraged to consult that book for an excellent summary treatment of this subject.

3. Eric Wolf, *Europe and the People Without History* (Berkeley: University of California Press, 1982).

4. World Resources Institute in collaboration with the United Nations Environment Program and the United Nations Development Programme, "Latin America—Resources and Environment Review," in *World Resources: 1990–91* (New York: Oxford University Press, 1990), 33–48.

5. Pan American Health Organization, *Health Conditions in the Americas.* Scientific Publication no. 524 (Washington, D.C.: Pan American Health Organization, 1990).

6. International Labor Organization, *Decent Work and Protection for All: Priority of the Americas.* Report of the Director General, International Labor Organization. (Geneva, Switzerland: International Labor Organization, 1999). http://www.oitamericas99.org.pe/

7. Pan American Health Organization, *Health Conditions in the Americas.* Scientific Publication no. 549 (Washington, D.C.: Pan American Health Organization, 1994).

8. United Nations Development Programme, *Human Development Report 1999.* (New York: United Nations Development Programme, 1999).

9. Pan American Health Organization, *Health Conditions in the Americas.* Scientific Publication no. 549.

10. Lori Ann Thrupp, *Bitter Harvests for Global Supermarkets: Challenges in Latin America's Agricultural Export Boom* (Washington, D.C.: World Resources Institute, 1995).

11. Scott Whiteford and Anne E. Ferguson, eds., *Harvest of Want: Hunger and Food Security in Central America and Mexico* (Boulder, Colo.: Westview Press, 1991).

12. Ibid.

13. Michael Painter and William H. Durham, eds., *The Social Causes of Environmental Destruction in Latin America* (Ann Arbor: University of Michigan Press, 1995).

14. Bernard Nietschmann, "The Third World War," *Cultural Survival Quarterly* 11, no. 3 (1987): 1–15.

15. See also Peter Poole, *Indigenous Mapping and Biodiversity Conservation: An Analysis of Current Activities and Opportunities for Applying Geomatic Technologies* (Landover, Md.: Corporate Press, 1995).

MEXICANS

GULF OF MEXICO

Yucatan
Peninsula

Cancun

Cozumel

YUCATAN
QUINTANA ROO

Tulum

YUCATAN
CAMPECHE

Mayan Zone

Sian Ka'an
Biosphere
Reserve

Felipe
Carrillo Puerto

M E X I C O

CAMPECHE
QUINTANA ROO

Ciudad Chetumal

Rio Hondo

C A R I B B E A N   S E A

BELIZE

GUATEMALA

N

0   40 mi.

0   60 km.

Gulf of Mexico

M E X I C O

Yucatan
Peninsula

AnthroGraphicsLab

Chapter 1

The Mayans of Central Quintana Roo

David Barton Bray

CULTURAL OVERVIEW

The People

From 1850 to 1901, a group of Yucatec Maya known as the *Cruzob* or "people of the Cross" refused to be displaced by or incorporated into expanding sugar plantations, defied the Mexican nation, and established a rebel state in the forests in the interior of Quintana Roo, at the time a remote region in the eastern Yucatán Peninsula of Mexico. These rebel Maya were descendants of one of the greatest civilizations of the Western Hemisphere. Before the Spanish conquest, the ancient Maya erected great stone buildings and pyramids, practiced intensive forms of agriculture, used a form of hieroglyphic writing, and conducted astronomical reckonings in the vast rain forests of what is today southern Mexico and northern Central America. The descendants of these Maya occupy a nearly continuous territory in southern Mexico, Guatemala, and Belize.

The contemporary Mayan people can be defined as a language family, a cultural group, and the occupants of a geographic space. In Mexico, they include the Yucatec Maya who gave birth to the rebel group discussed in this chapter, a small group of Lacandan Maya of the lowland rain forest of Chiapas, and the far more populous Tzotzil and Tzeltal Maya of the Chiapas highlands, many of whom have migrated into the lowlands, as well as scattered groups elsewhere. In Guatemala, they include the Quichean peoples of the eastern and central highlands and the Mamean peoples of the western highlands. Other groups live in Belize. The millions of contemporary Maya have generally similar sorts of subsistence patterns, textiles, and other cultural patterns but proudly differentiate themselves from each other by distinctive textile designs and other practices.

3

The rebel Yucatec Maya came to terms slowly and grudgingly with the reality of their participation in the Mexican nation; as late as the 1930s they were attempting to negotiate foreign diplomatic alliances through visiting U.S. archaeologists. "The Mayan Zone" of Quintana Roo still maintains a distinct cultural identity as the mostly heavily indigenous region of the modern Mexican state of Quintana Roo. The Maya today live in a precarious equilibrium between a declining traditional agricultural lifestyle and the economic opportunities offered by the booming tourist centers of Quintana Roo. Standing in between those two options is a third way, that of intensifying their management of the dry tropical forest habitat which has sheltered and supported them for 150 years. In the last fifteen years they have made significant strides in the sustainable management of their forest resources, particularly in the management of mahogany (*Swietenia macrophylla*). In order for the forest to become a genuine economic alternative, however, there are new demands to manage it more intensively without permanently degrading the resource for their children.

The Setting

Today Quintana Roo, formed out of a federal territory in 1973, is best known as the home of Cancún, a resort destination favored by U.S. college students. Long before the beaches of Cancún became world famous, other features of Quintana Roo's geology determined the course of its development. Quintana Roo, like the rest of the Yucatán, is mostly a flat limestone shelf, much like southern Florida in the United States. The limestone is heavily pitted with myriad sinkholes, some of them quite large, called cenotes. Quintana Roo's only river, the Río Hondo, forms the southern boundary with Belize; the rest of the water in the state moves through underground channels, accessible only through the cenotes. In most places, only a thin layer of soil has formed over the limestone which, combined with a five-month dry season, has limited the density and height of the forest. Because the forests receive about 1,200 millimeters (47 inches) of rain a year, ecologists call them "dry" or, at best, "semihumid" tropical forests. The canopy may only reach as high as 30 to 35 meters (98 to 115 feet) as opposed to 45 to 50 meters (148 to 164 feet) for wetter forests on better soils. Nonetheless, these forests have a rich biodiversity with as many as 100 tree species, 1,257 different kinds of plants, and 151 vertebrate species. One survey of late secondary forest (an advanced state of succession from an original clearing) in central Quintana Roo yielded a total of ninety-eight tree species from thirty-three families. Predominant trees include the sapodilla tree (*Manilkara zapota*); whose sap (called chicle), which was traditionally used to make chewing gum; the ramon (*Brosimium alicastrum*), used for forage; and mahogany (*Swietenia macrophylla*), valued for centuries as one of the finest woods available for use in furniture and inlays.[1]

4

Traditional Subsistence Strategies

The Mayan milpa or cornfield is more than just a place to plant corn; traditionally such crops as beans, squash, chiles, and yucca are interplanted. Corn was developed as a food crop for humans in Mexico and, as one would expect for such an ancient practice, it has developed a complex system of practices and beliefs around its cultivation. Traditionally, and to a significant degree still today, clearing land, planting, tending, and harvesting mark the principal stages of the agricultural cycle and occupy much of the Mayas' time, energy, and concern. The type of agriculture practiced is known as slash and burn because it is based on clearing and burning forestlands, planting for a few years until soil fertility is exhausted, and then clearing a new patch of forest. The technique depends on having substantial areas of forest so that whole villages can continue finding new forest soils in which to plant. When anthropologist Alfonso Villa Rojas visited the region in the 1930s, he found each farmer cultivating nearly 6 hectares (15 acres) to support his family for a year.[2] The Maya also traditionally planted vegetables and herbs in large wooden boxes next to the house and raised chickens, turkeys, and pigs. The forest was a source of game, particularly deer and white-collared peccary, wild fruits, medicinal herbs, and building materials.

Social and Political Organization

The power of the Cruzob, or Talking Cross cult, also marked Maya social organization. Until well into the twentieth century, and to some extent today, the Maya organized themselves around the model of the Yucatec militias, out of which they sprang as a military force in 1848. Since the 1930s, they have also organized their communities according to the regulations of Mexico's agrarian reform laws. These laws call for the communities to select their leadership democratically, usually for three-year periods.

Although some Maya have always lived throughout the eastern Yucatán, it is central Quintana Roo that is known as the Mayan Zone because of its density of population and the historical presence of the Cruzob as a major demographic infusion in a mostly unpopulated area. However, the rest of the state has passed from having a Maya majority to a shrinking minority, overwhelmed by the explosive growth of tourism and immigration into the state. By 1995 only 26% of the population of Quintana Roo spoke an indigenous language. Even today, however, the two *municipios* (counties) that make up central Quintana Roo, Felipe Carillo Puerto and José María Morelos, are an average of 75% Mayan; the two *municipios* to the north, Lázaro Cárdenas and Solidaridad, also have substantial Mayan populations. The largest absolute number of Maya are found in the *mun-*

icipio where Cancún is located, although they constitute only 17% of the population there. The Maya have larger families than average, with live births of 4.32 compared to an average of 3.6 for the rest of the state. Twenty-six percent of the population is illiterate, and only 38% of the population has completed primary school. Mexico's status as an advanced developing nation has meant that most villages today have running water and electricity. The Mayan Zone includes only one town with more than 10,000 inhabitants; the rest of the population lives in small hamlets widely dispersed over the landscape. In 1990 there were 244 population nucleations, with almost all of them having fewer than 500 inhabitants.[3]

Religion and World View

Although Mayan culture and religion are undergoing changes, traditional beliefs still have a very strong presence. In the Mayan conception, the world of the supernatural dominates everything; they feel continually overseen by one of the many saints and spirits that emerged from the syncretism between ancient Mayan beliefs and the Catholicism brought by the conquering Spaniards. Because the Mayan deities are demanding, people perform frequent ceremonies, rituals, and prayers to keep them satisfied. The Maya of this region have been strongly marked by the emergence of a unique cult in the nineteenth century, the cult of the Talking Cross. Although diminished in importance today, the cult and other elements of nineteenth-century Yucatec history have left their mark on local Mayan social and political organization. The emergence of the Talking Cross cult resulted in features that significantly differentiated the Maya of Central Quintana Roo from other Maya and their belief systems. For example, the image of the cross displaced the images of the saints important elsewhere, and the high priest of the Talking Cross displaced the village priest's functions.

THREATS TO SURVIVAL

You have come to pick a quarrel with me; the letter says that the Queen will send troops against me. If the English want to fight, let them come, in thousands if they like. If this is the case, say so, and I will dispose of you at once.
—The Talking Cross, addressing captured British soldiers, 1861[4]

The Mayan people as a whole have survived the collapse of their ancient civilizations at the end of the first millennium and the conquest of the Spanish halfway through the second millennium. One hundred and fifty years before the end of the second millennium, in 1850, one group of Maya passed through a third major threat to their survival, one that marks them

6

to this day. These Maya were the protagonists of an armed uprising known to historians as the Caste War of Yucatán because, during the colonial period, Maya were denied all rights as members of a scorned "caste" or lower stratum of society. Many Maya were forced into near slavery on sugarcane plantations in northwestern Yucatán, and Maya in the eastern peninsula, who had seen their fate, declined the work. As one anthropologist described it,

The Indians who, for whatever reason, refused to attach themselves to the sugar plantation (or were lucky enough to avoid getting rounded up) found themselves being pushed further into the bush with each passing year. As the plantations took over the best lands of the rich frontier region the Mayan's position was becoming more and more desperate.[5]

They also protested unfair taxes, including payments for religious sacraments, debt peonage, lack of access to agricultural land, and the frequent physical abuse they received. The Maya had firearms and military experience because they had been pressed into service in civil wars between Yucatecans who quarreled over whether to continue to be part of Mexico, declare independence, or affiliate with the United States. The Maya rose up in 1848 and almost took the capital city of Merida before retreating.

By 1850 they had lost militarily and were witnessing deadly fratricidal conflict among their leaders. Nearly 10,000 retreated into the unpopulated wilderness of eastern Yucatán. The Maya were shattered militarily, disorganized, and demoralized. In an effort to revitalize their opposition, the defeated but defiant Maya established a religious sect that has endured to this day; the Talking Cross. The followers believed that the cross spoke to them, interpreted events, and dictated courses of action. The cross was used to lead the Cruzob into battle, and authorities in Merida and Belize found themselves exchanging letters with the Talking Cross. There is historical evidence that the Mayan leaders used ventriloquists to induce belief in the cross in their followers, but in 1863 an internal uprising against the leaders associated with the cross exposed the hoax. Nonetheless, the cross remained a powerful force in Mayan religious and political life, and even if it ceased to talk, a belief in written notes from the cross survived well into the twentieth century. The rebel Maya functioned as a state in many senses. They successfully rejected the political authority of Mexico; at different times they negotiated for arms, fought with, and sought recognition from the British in Belize; and as late as the 1930s, they solicited political assistance for a possible political alliance with the United States through archaeologist Sylvanus Morley.

Another striking aspect of Cruzob culture was the fact that they reorganized themselves along the lines of the Yucatec militia in which many had served between 1839 and 1847, replete with generals, majors, lieutenants, and other military ranks, and a company structure. In 1867 there were reports of an army of 11,000 men, equipped with rifles and munitions captured from the Yucatecans. As late as the 1930s, Villa Rojas found the system of organization by companies had become a part of the way of organizing kinship and other social relations with, for example, marriages taking place outside the company.

The Caste War came to a formal end on May 4, 1901, when General Ignacio Bravo occupied the Cruzob capital of Chan Santa Cruz (today called Felipe Carillo Puerto) bringing railroad tracks and telegraph lines with him. However, the Maya continued to wage guerrilla warfare from their forest villages, intensifying attacks on convoys and commercial traffic by 1912. Due to the demands of the Mexican Revolution, Chan Santa Cruz was abandoned by the Mexicans in 1912. The Maya showed what they thought of the benefits brought by civilization and reisolated themselves from the outside world by destroying the railroad tracks and cutting the telegraph and telephone lines. In 1915 the Cruzob met with the president of Mexico and established somewhat more peaceful relations with the Mexican government.

Even though they survived the onslaught of the Mexicans, the Maya could not protect themselves against the diseases of the outside world. Smallpox and influenza swept through the population in the years before 1920, eliminating whole villages, and perhaps reducing the population by half. Only in the 1930s could the Mexican government begin to establish schools in many of the communities and to issue Mayan land titles under Mexico's agrarian reform laws.

The traditional Mayan economy revolved around the cornfield and subsistence uses of the forest. Beginning in the 1920s, however, the forests were subjected to progressively more commercial uses, uses in which the Maya have participated. By 1920 a boom in chewing gum popularity taught the Maya a new use for the sapodilla tree whose sap was the basis for gum. In the 1970s and earlier, small companies began paying pitiful amounts to log mahogany and Spanish cedar (Cedrus odorata) on their lands, and Mexico's national railroad began buying railroad ties hacked out of beautiful tropical hardwoods. Later, the soaring demand for thatching materials used in the resorts of the Cancún-Tulum corridor intensified the exploitation of palm fronds (Palmae Mexicano). The federal and state governments also became steadily more involved in various efforts to organize, to institute political controls, and to deliver services to the Mayan Zone. In the 1970s, many of the communities of the area were organized into "unions" or peasant organizations, which were focused into the production and marketing of railroad ties. This effort quickly fell into the hands of corrupt Mayan leaders who were in collusion with government officials, and the railroad-tie producers did not receive the full value of their product.

The organization has brought change. Before the peasants didn't know what forest production was; the buyers were the ones who knew and told us what to do. Now the (community) is the owner because the peasant is organized and knows his work. (Abundio Canché, former president of the Mayan Zone Organization)[6]

It was into this situation that a notable new organizing effort began among the Maya—one which has delivered a greater degree of control over their forests than previously existed, but which is now bringing new and daunting challenges as well. In the mid-1980s, foresters and organizers from the state government of Quintana Roo, the federal government of Mexico, and foreign consultants from the German government banded together with a new vision of community forest management for Quintana Roo. The assumption of this program, known as the Forest Pilot Plan (FPP), was that the only way to stop the deforestation that was then sweeping over Quintana Roo was for the communities to manage the forests directly themselves. The forest must provide an economic alternative for them that could compete with agriculture and cattle raising. The promoters of the FPP worked mostly with mestizo (mixed Spanish and Indian) colonists in southern Quintana Roo, but they also sent a small team to work with Maya in the central part of the state. Although that team received very little support from the FPP, it remained to carve out a new production alternative for some of the communities. With the help of the organizing team, twenty-three communities formed the Organization of Forest Production Communities of the Mayan Zone (Mayan Zone Organization). Following the FPP methodology, the communities voluntarily declared substantial areas of their forest lands to be "permanent forest areas," areas never to be converted into any other land use, such as agriculture or cattle. Instead, the communities would manage these permanent forest areas for timber and non-timber forest products, seeking to find enough value in them to warrant maintaining the standing forest. They also established small sawmills and furniture workshops in several communities and captured the profits from several stages of the production chain.

The members of the Mayan Zone Organization, representing about 15% of the total population of the area, served as a model for alternative development in the region. The role of university-trained forestry professionals was key in the founding of the organization and continues to be crucial today, although a new generation of Mayan leadership and forest technicians is starting to emerge. The principal management focus in the early years was on the sustainable harvesting of mahogany and cedar. Unfortunately, most of the other products of the forest, the lesser-known tropical species used for railroad ties, chicle, and palms and by wildlife, were not put under any systematic management plan. Nonetheless, some of the communities accomplished something rare in the world—community management of forests for commercial timber production. Timber production, even

9

on a small scale, is a complicated industrial process that involves substantial investments in production and processing equipment, as well as close coordination. It requires the establishment of a community enterprise dedicated to sustainable logging. This accomplishment has won the Mayan Zone a degree of international recognition, which is richly deserved. However, it has also become clear that mahogany management alone is not sufficient to save the Mayans from a series of threats to their continued ability to live in and off the forest.

In the forest there are animals: pheasant, turkey, deer . . . we also collect medicinal herbs: cinnamon, cuyo, copal, tankasché and fruits like zapote, guaya and palms like guano. That's why the young people have to preserve the forest, because it's what they are, and the only thing they have. (Jacinto Cob, of the community of Laguna Kaná, Mayan Zone, Quintana Roo)[7]

The threats stem from a series of crises in production, and from the growth of nontraditional employment opportunities in the Cancún area. The first crisis is the precipitous decline in the extent and productivity of the basis of Mayan culture, the milpa. In the 1940s, Maya typically planted almost 6 hectares (15 acres) of corn; in the 1970s and in the 1980s it was down to less than 5 hectares (12 acres), and today most plant less than 3 hectares (7.5 acres). The productivity per hectare has also plummeted. The price of chicle has been stagnant for years, and there is only one government-controlled buyer. More recently, the market for railroad ties has been highly unstable; in one recent year, there were no buyers at all. Increasingly severe droughts are also resulting in more damaging fires, whose smoke drifts across the southern United States. Over the decades of logging, both by contractors in the early period and more recently by the communities, the forests have become impoverished. Mistakes in the reforestation practices for the first ten years have also damaged the ability of the forest to recover its commercial productivity. Wildlife is being hunted out around many communities. The limitations of the FPP model are becoming obvious fifteen years after its founding. Only a handful of the FPP communities have enough mahogany to be commercially viable. All the rest have only stands of the harder-to-market lesser-known species, and they must look for other ways to reap value for the forest. For them, the FPP has not yet offered a solution.

Finally, there is both the threat and the opportunity of service-sector employment. Many of the Mayan men, particularly the young ones, now spend part of the year working as bricklayers on the high-rise hotels of the Cancún-Tulum corridor. Furthermore, the expansion of this strip, the "Riviera Maya" in the publicity campaigns of Mexico's tourism planners, is bringing luxury tourism within one hour from them. On the southern coast of Quintana Roo, the plans are on the drawing boards to develop a lower-density "Costa Maya" which will also present both economic opportunities and cultural threats to the survival of the Cruzob. Directly to the east, the urgency of conservation was responsible for the creation of the 528,000-hectare (1,304,000-acre) Si'an Kaan Biosphere Reserve, an enormous protected wetland which covers some of the traditional hunting grounds of the nearby communities.

Perhaps the most intractable crises brought by the modern world to the Maya are alcoholism and television viewing. By one estimate, a considerable amount of the income that comes from forest and service-sector activities is spent on alcohol. The acompanying problems of health, abuse of family members, and lost income are serious social problems in most Mayan communities. Organizations such as Alcoholics Anonymous have begun to appear in some of the larger villages. The spread of Protestantism in many communities, whose adherents usually give up drinking, has helped to mitigate this problem to some degree, but it is a source of cultural change among the normally nominally Catholic Maya. The presence of television sets in many homes has been blamed for a decline in home gardens. Family members find spending time in front of the television more pleasurable than tilling soil under the blazing sun. The exposure to the full range of distractions offered by the modern world by those who leave the village to work is another source of unpredictable cultural change.

RESPONSE: STRUGGLES TO SURVIVE CULTURALLY

Now, THE LAND HERE HAS BEEN DIVIDED by the Mexican masters. . . . They don't like us; they don't give us any respect. They don't AID US like they should. . . . A long time ago, long ago, we were all VERY IGNORANT. ALL IGNORANT. Our eyes were closed . . . Now, in the time we are living, WE ARE ALL "peasants of the Mayan zone". All our eyes are open. All of them.
—Narration collected by anthropologist Allan F. Burns, 1971[8]

In the second half of the nineteenth century, anthropologist Paul Sullivan quoted documentary sources describing the forests of central Quintana Roo as "a place of desolation and death . . . inhabited only by birds, wild beasts and Maya Indians more fearsome than the wild beasts themselves" and "an excellent place to keep away from."[9] Today, these same forests are increasingly impoverished of their biological diversity, surrounded by the institutions of the modern world, and the increasingly beleaguered Maya have an uncertain future as a shrinking minority with few skills needed by the modern world. Many will leave and become urbanized, but increasing efforts are being made to find new and innovative ways to manage their tropical forests sustainably, giving them a chance to exercise more control

Mayans in the village of Santa María conduct a land-use planning workshop, August 1998. Courtesy of David Bray.

of the pace of change and remain in their communities. In agriculture, the fear of fire, the declining productivity of the milpa, and the limited availability of new forest areas for planting have created new pressures to end or modify the millennia-old practice of slash-and-burn agriculture. The alternatives run the gamut from organic agriculture, which can develop richer soils allowing the farmers to continue cultivating in the same spot, to various forms of agroforestry, a practice that combines agricultural crops, fruit crops, and tree crops.

With the support of the Mayan Zone Organization, small groups within the communities are now experimenting with making compost and planting "green manures," nitrogen-fixing plants that can be turned under to enrich the soil. The goal is to extend the rotation from the current two to three years to from five to six years, and possibly build up some areas of richer soils that could tolerate permanent agriculture. When a plot is finally abandoned, it will be planted in fruit trees, timber trees, and shade-tolerant crops. In shorter-term plots, the tree crops will be planted at the same time as the corn to create an enriched secondary succession immediately after several corn crops are harvested. In timber, those communities that have mahogany have begun the process of seeking "certification" for sustainably managing their forests. Under this process, outside evaluators visit the community and analyze the forest and logging practices. If they are found to be sustainable by agreed-upon criteria, the communities can receive a "green seal" that allows them to access high-value niche markets of consumers willing to pay a premium for wood products from sustainable forests.

The communities have also improved their reforestation practices and are experimenting with new methodologies. For the first ten years of the FPP, the communities primarily replanted mahogany seedlings in the small gaps left by the selective logging. However, several years ago, a Mexican tropical ecologist, who works closely with the Mayan Zone Organization, began to study survival rates of the seedlings. She found that survival rates were quite low in the logging gaps, but much higher in logging roads and log storage areas. This discovery caused the organization to begin replanting in the larger areas favored by the sun-loving mahogany seedlings. The communities have also established mini-plantations of mahogany and cedar that can be planted and taken care of by the children in the communities, as a savings account for their own future.

For the majority of communities, however, the most important timber product remains railroad ties. Logging for railroad ties is an extremely low value and wasteful use of what frequently are very beautiful tropical hardwoods. A railroad-tie producer may be able to extract only one or two ties from an entire tree and receives only $9 for each railroad tie. An alternative being explored is the production of carved wooden artisan objects, including animals of the forest, bowls, children's blocks, and other useful and decorative objects. Workshops have already been established in several communities, and some products are already being sold to the tourist shops in Cancún. As many as 200 artisan objects could be carved out of the timber used for railroad ties, giving enormously more value to the wood and to the forest. As another use for the tropical hardwoods, a sawmill outside of Felipe Carillo Puerto is currently being reconditioned by the organization to begin producing dried and sawn lumber. Women in several villages have established a thriving business in embroidering shirts and blouses with designs based on the plants and animals of the forest, the lowest impact use of the forest of all. A program in reproductive health is also in the process of being established for these women artisans. In an effort to mitigate the increasing scarcity of deer, white-collared peccary, and game birds around many of the communities, initiatives have been made in the captive breeding of wild animals. In several communities, small stone corrals now harbor breeding stocks of white-collared peccary, preferred by the Maya over domestic pork. Other exotic efforts include the cultivation of orchids and ornamental plants under natural forest canopy.

Finally, the Mayan Zone Organization has begun initial studies for a carbon sequestration project, possibly the most novel and ambitious alternative development initiative to date. This initiative would position the Mayan Zone Organization, and eventually the entire Mayan Zone, to cash in on the global ecosystem services offered by their forests. As research on the causes and consequences of global warming and global climate change proceed apace, much attention has been focused on the role of growing forests to absorb the enormous amounts of carbon ejected into the atmosphere every year by automobiles and factories. New international mechanisms are now being developed to allow polluting manufacturers to compensate for their carbon emissions by investing in reforestation and forest management in Third World countries, working with entities such as the Mayan Zone Organization. The organization could thus receive additional payments for the reforestation and agroforestry initiatives it has already undertaken and expand in the future.

FOOD FOR THOUGHT

All of these efforts and more will be necessary if the Maya are going to be able to continue to live in the forests that have harbored them for 150 years, and their ancestors for many centuries before that. In this process, the Maya must move from depending solely upon the traditional knowledge that sustained them for so long, to an increasingly sophisticated set of management tools that draw both on traditional values and practices and the most advanced scientific concepts of ecosystem management. The Maya of central Quintana Roo are only one group within the millions of Mayan peoples, speaking many different languages, who today live in southern Mexico, Guatemala, and Belize. Their historical role as the protagonists of the Caste War of Yucatán, their adoption of the now-faded cult of the Talking Cross, and their fierce resistance to incorporation into Mexico, which lasted for the first third of the twentieth century, make them a unique case among contemporary Maya. A tradition of resistance and survival will not take them far into the twenty-first century without serious modifications. The Mayans must take on a challenge that continues to baffle highly educated conservationists and foresters—how to manage sustainably a tropical forest for both income and biodiversity conservation. The Maya will have to learn many new things in order to regain the forest as a buffer and filter, allowing them to choose those aspects of the modern world they want and reject those they do not want.

Questions

1. How is the rebellion of the Maya of central Quintana Roo different from or similar to other uprisings of economically or politically oppressed peoples in history?
2. Why do you think the Maya would have violently rejected such modern inventions as the railroad and telegraph?

3. Why would it be difficult for the forest to compete as a source of income with luxury hotels in Cancún?

4. What does it mean for tropical timber to be 'certified'? Would you pay more money for a desk made from certified timber?

5. What does it mean to have a carbon sequestration project? How could this project help the Maya?

NOTES

1. Laura K. Snook, "Sustaining Harvests of Mahogany from Mexico's Yucatán Forests: Past, Present and Future," in *Timber, Tourists, and Temples: Conservation and Development in the Maya Forest of Belize, Guatemala and Mexico*, Richard Primack, David Barton Bray, Hugo A. Galletti, and Ismael Ponciano, 66–67 (Washington, D.C.: Island Press, 1998).

2. Robert Redfield and Alfonso Villa Rojas, *Chan Kom, a Maya Village*, Washington, D.C.: Carnegie Institution of Washington.

3. Instituto Nacional de Estadistica, Geografia e Informatica, *Quintana Roo: Resultados Definitivos, VII Censo Agricola-Ganadera* (Mexico City: Government of Mexico), 20–25.

4. Nelson Reed, *The Caste War of Yucatan* (Stanford, Calif · Stanford University Press, 1964), 183.

5. Arnold Stricken, "Hacienda and Plantation: An Historical-Ecological Consideration of the Folk-Urban Continuum in Yucatan," *America Indigena* 25 (1965): 35–63. Cited in Victoria Reifler Bricker, *The Indian Christ, the Indian King: The Historical Substrate of Maya Myth and Ritual* (Austin: University of Texas Press, 1981), 89.

6. David Barton Bray, Marcelo Carreón, Leticia Merino, and Victoria Santos, "On the Road to Sustainable Forestry," *Cultural Survival Quarterly* 17, no. 1 (1993): 40.

7. Leticia Merino, "El Aprovechamiento del Bosque por los Maya de Quintana Roo" (unpublished manuscript), p. 188, translated by David Barton Bray.

8. Allan F. Burns, "The Caste War in the 1970s: Present Day Accounts from Village Quintana Roo," in *Anthropology and History in Yucatan*, ed. Grant D. Jones, 270 (Austin: University of Texas Press, 1977).

9. Paul Sullivan, *Unfinished Conversations: Mayas and Foreigners Between Two Wars* (New York: Alfred A. Knopf, 1989), 6.

RESOURCE GUIDE

Published Literature

Bray, David Barton, Marcelo Carreón, Leticia Merino, and Victoria Santos. "On the Road to Sustainable Forestry." *Cultural Survival Quarterly* 17, no. 1 (1993): 38–41.

Bricker, Victoria Reifler. *The Indian Christ, the Indian King: The Historical Substrate of Maya Myth and Ritual*. Austin: University of Texas Press, 1981.

Reed, Nelson. *The Caste War of Yucatan*. Stanford, Calif.: Stanford University Press, 1964.

Snook, Laura K. "Sustaining Harvests of Mahogany (Swietenia macrophylla King) from Mexico's Yucatán Forests: Past, Present, and Future." In *Timber, Tourists and Temples: Conservation and Development in the Maya Forest of Belize, Guatemala, and Mexico*, edited by Richard Primack, David Barton Bray, Hugo A. Galletti, and Ismael Ponciano. Washington, D.C. Island Press, 1998.

Sullivan, Paul. *Unfinished Conversations: Mayas and Foreigners Between Two Wars*. New York: Alfred A. Knopf, 1989.

Videos and Films

The videos and films below are available through the Institute of Latin American Studies at the University of Texas-Austin.

ILAS Outreach
Sid Richardson Hall 1.310
The University of Texas at Austin
Austin, TX 78712
Telephone: 512–232–2404
Fax: 512–471–3090
e-mail: katebennett@mail.utexas.edu

Lost Kingdoms of the Maya, The National Geographic Society, 1993 (60 minutes).

Maya, the Blood of Kings, Time Life's Lost Civilizations Series, narrated by Sam Waterston, 1995 (48 minutes).

The Maya, Temples, Tombs and Time, Questar Video, Inc., Chicago, 1995 (53 minutes).

MayaQuest, the Mystery Trail, MECC, Minneapolis, Minn., 1995. (Based on the 1995 expedition, this CD-ROM (Windows or Macintosh) for ages 10 to 16 offers two educational interactive games and a multimedia resource tool with photographs, sound effects and text.)

Rain Forest, The National Geographic Society, 1993 (60 minutes). (Actually filmed in Costa Rica, this video is also recommended for those studying the Maya of the rain forest.)

The Ruta Maya Experience—Belize, Yucatan, Guatemala, Lonely Planet, IVN Communications, Inc., San Ramon, Calif., 1995 (47 minutes). (This Lonely Planet expedition may have special appeal for action-oriented, less academically inclined students.)

WWW Sites

For a good introduction to the ancient Maya, Mexico's University of Guadalajara maintains a good web site at *http://udgftp.cencar.udg.mx/ingles/Precolombina/ Maya/intromaya.html*.

To know more about tourism development on the "Riviera Maya" where the contemporary Maya mostly work only in building the hotels, you can consult *http://cancun.mayan-riviera.com/*.

For current news from the state of Quintana Roo you can consult *http://www.novenet.com.mx/*.

To learn how to go on a tour of the Sian Ka'n Biosphere Reserve, which adjoins the Mayan Zone, visit *http://www.cancun.com/siankaan/*.

For a good overview of issues of tropical forest management, see the following web page introduced by the Canadian International Development Agency, *http://www.rcfa-cfan.org/English/issues.8.html*.

Organizations

Amigos de Sian Ka'an is a Cancún-based conservation organization that works on conservation efforts in the Sian Ka'an Biosphere Reserve, and has worked with some of the communities in the Mayan Zone. Their web page is at *http://www.coa.edu/HEJourney/yucatan/SianKaan/directory.html*.

Conservation International works on conservation issues throughout southern Mexico and Guatemala, as well as in other places in the world, and can be reached at *http://www.conservation.org/*.

Chapter 2

The Rural People of Mexico's Northwest Coast

Maria L. Cruz-Torres

> There is unrest and discontent in the countryside. In many places this unrest has now become exasperation; in other places the discontent is often translated into acts of desperate violence. This is natural: industrialization and development have been paid for, in great part, by our rural population.
>
> Octavio Paz, Mexican poet, essayist, diplomat, and Nobel Prize winner[1]

CULTURAL OVERVIEW

The People

Various indigenous groups such as the Toteranos and the Nahoa inhabited the Mexican coast during pre-Columbian times. These groups were conquered in the late sixteenth century by Nuño de Guzmán, a particularly brutal conquistador (conqueror). In the early seventeenth century, Jesuit missionaries made their way through the coastal zone with evangelization campaigns targeted toward the native population. Currently, the majority of the rural people refer to themselves as mestizos, people of mixed indigenous and European ancestries; however, many other people in the region can claim some of their ancestry to be African, Greek, French, Chinese, Japanese, German, or North American.

Currently, 23 million people live in Mexico's rural areas, which accounts for about a quarter of the total population of the country. In Spanish, the term *campesino* (peasant) generally is used to refer to the mostly poor people who live in these rural areas. Throughout most of this century, life for Mexican campesinos has been characterized by a constant struggle for access to the basic resources needed to meet their daily requirements. During the past decade, the quality of life in rural areas has declined resulting in an increase in poverty and malnutrition.

The transformation and degradation of natural resources represent the biggest threat to the survival of the campesinos who inhabit Mexico's northwest coast. For a long time, campesinos in this region have struggled to maintain their access to land for farming and fishing grounds. Government policies, which favor the large-scale, commercial exploitation of these natural resources over the smaller-scale activities of campesino families, have resulted in many localized social and political conflicts.

The Setting

Mexico's northwest coast is mostly semiarid with a dry subhumid to a warm subhumid climate. There is a long, very marked dry season followed by a short rainy season. Since water is not always available, in many places irrigation systems have been built to guarantee a constant supply for the agricultural activities practiced in the region. One of the most important features of the west coast is the abundance of coastal lagoons, estuaries, seasonal floodplains, and mangrove forest ecosystems. These coastal ecosystems serve as nurseries and habitats to various species of fish, crustaceans, mollusks, and birds. Archaeologists have pointed out the importance of marine resources to pre-Columbian populations living along the coast. Indeed, the abundance of shell "middens" (piles of oyster shells) in many areas confirms this hypothesis. However, as a result of the development of the commercial, export-oriented agriculture, fishing, and aquaculture industries, as well as tourism, many of these coastal ecosystems have been transformed and negatively affected.

Traditional Subsistence Strategies

Mexico's northwest coast has a long history of depending on the commercial exploitation of its natural resources as a way to promote economic development. For the past three centuries, the mining of silver and other metals has been the pillar of the region's economy. Currently, large-scale commercial production of agricultural products, such as rice, cotton, tomatoes, mangos, sugarcane, and chili peppers, are produced in the region to be sold to the United States and other countries. Similarly, the large-scale development of the commercial fishing industry originated in the region with the tuna and shrimp fisheries comprising the two most important sectors of the fishing industry. Tourism is also an increasingly important industry in the region. The largest development for mass tourism has taken place in Mazatlán—a major seaport on the central northwestern coast of Sinaloa. Recently, the region's natural beauty has begun to be exploited commercially as part of a new trend in ecotourism development.

A family on their way out to visit relatives and friends in a nearby community. Courtesy of María Cruz-Torres.

Rural families in Mexico's northwest coast are able to survive through their participation in a wide array of economic activities, some aimed at producing crops or products for home consumption (subsistence activities) and others for sale in the local or national markets (commercial activities). Many also borrow money from relatives and friends, obtain remittances from migrant children, and exchange favors between households. For the great majority of the rural coastal population, fishing, farming, and wage labor constitute the three most important economic strategies. People fish for a variety of species including fish, shrimp, and crabs—mostly in the lagoons and estuaries that border their rural communities.

Fishing

People in rural coastal communities have a great deal of knowledge about the fishing resources they use and about the natural environment that surrounds them. Like most human populations who depend on the natural environment for daily survival, these campesinos can identify the taxonomies of various species according to their biological characteristics and behavioral patterns. Their knowledge systems are every bit as complex and sophisticated as those of professional agricultural and marine scientists. Campesinos use these "funds of knowledge" to plan what (and how) they farm and fish.

Fishing is generally a male activity, and most men engage in both the subsistence and commercial fishing sectors throughout the year. Coastal people take advantage of the various fish species and crabs abundant in the area's coastal ecosystems at different periods in the fishing cycle. The most commercially valued fishing resource is shrimp, for which the fishing season is three or four months, depending on the various environmental factors that influence the reproduction, growth, and migration of the species.

Groups of three to four men build fishing camps along the shores of the lagoons in which they reside during the entire fishing season. Since shrimp fishing takes place at night (using flashlights to attract and blind the shrimp), most men prefer to stay overnight at the shrimp camps, and they go home only when there is an emergency situation. The fishers either stand along the shore or use small motorboats known as *pangas* to catch the shrimp using a circular net known as an *atarraya* that is handled in an overhead sweeping motion not unlike that of a rodeo cowboy roping cattle. Both the small boats and nets are used for subsistence and more commercial fishing activities.

Organization of Production

Mexican law requires that those involved in the commercial exploitation of shrimp be organized into fishing cooperatives, which were first organized in the northwest coast in the 1930s. Since then, numerous fishing cooperatives have been organized in the region and throughout Mexico's coastal areas. Being a member of a fishing cooperative guarantees that a person has the legal right to capture wild shrimp. If someone is caught fishing illegally, his fishing gear is confiscated, he must pay a fine, and, in many cases, he is harassed or beaten by other fishermen. In return for being a member of a fishing cooperative, the member must sell his entire production to the cooperative at the price that it establishes.

Women also participate in the fishing activity in various ways. Many women process the fish or shrimp and sell it from their houses, on the streets, or in the town's market. Other women work in the packing plants in which the shrimp is processed for export. In recent years, as the economic conditions in the region have worsened, many more women have begun to fish both for subsistence and commercial purposes.

Farming

The type of farming practiced by rural households in the region is seasonal, rain-fed agriculture. People take advantage of the rainy season to prepare the land for cultivation and to plant the seeds. This type of farming, known in Mexico as milpa agriculture, originated thousands of years ago among the prehistoric indigenous population. The crops still cultivated are corn, beans, and chili peppers, which are part of the staple diet of rural households. "Intercropping" is a common farming technique used by most farmers in rural communities. In this system, different crops are planted closely together in the same field. Farming is an activity that involves all members of the household. Men usually work in the fields to prepare the land while women and children work during planting and harvesting. Usually groups of "extended" families work together depending on the nature of the task. For the most part, familial groups of ten or twelve adults and children work together as a cooperative group.

The reliance on wage labor by a large portion of the rural population of Mexico's northwest coast has increased during the last decade. Many landless households in rural communities depend on wage labor for their daily survival. In many other instances, family members who have land also seek employment as wage workers for a series of reasons. Soil erosion, desertification, and salinization are among those factors that no longer make the land unsuitable for cultivation. In many other instances, rural households lack the financial resources to buy seeds, fertilizer, or a water pump for irrigation.

Wage labor provides rural households with seasonal, short-term employment in agriculture. Campesinos sell their labor to landowners who grow cash crops for the national and international markets. The type of crop to be cultivated during a particular year depends on individual choices made by the landowners. These decisions, in turn, are influenced by the demands of national and international markets, as well as by existing climatological conditions. Coconuts, mangos, chili peppers, and lemons are the most commonly cultivated crops in coastal zones for the export market.

Normally, campesinos are hired at different stages of the agricultural cycle. Men usually are hired to help prepare the land before cultivation. Men, women, and children working together in labor gangs are employed during the planting and harvesting stages. Wages in 1998 for such work was approximately U.S. $6 for eight hours of work.

Aquaculture and Other Sources of Income

Recently, the development of the shrimp aquaculture industry or "industrial shrimp farming" in the region has provided wage labor for individual household members. Employment in shrimp aquaculture is generally short term and seasonal, and men are usually hired as guards or construction workers in the shrimp farms as well as to aid in the production of shrimp larvae in some of the hatcheries built in the region. Some women are hired as cooks in the shrimp farms and hatcheries; others are hired to process the shrimp for export in the packing plants. The salary paid to wage workers in shrimp aquaculture is the same paid to agricultural wage workers.

23

Many women in coastal rural communities engage in various income-generating activities in order to support their households. The majority of women seek employment as agricultural wage workers, but others sell food, groceries, clothes, and crafts made at home. Other women organize rotating credit associations, known as *cundinas*, in order to save money to meet the needs of their households as well as to invest in profit-making activities.

Social and Political Organization

The most basic local social unit comprises small households often related to each other by blood or marriage. "Clustered extended" households living within the same plot of land are very common. Residence after marriage is very flexible, but the couple is expected to establish their own separate households, usually close by. Only under special circumstances, such as the lack of money to build a house, are couples allowed to reside in either the husband's or the wife's parents' household. Women are expected to marry at a young age, but many women postpone marriage to pursue a professional career. On a daily basis, men and women interact throughout the communities often engaging in conversation and information sharing in small knots of relatives and friends. Given this arrangement, it is not surprising that the elderly are always treated with respect since they are considered a source of knowledge and experience and, more important, the connection between past and present to future relationships of *confianza*, or trust, and reciprocity.

At the level of community, people are organized into different types of committees with the goal of improving their quality of life. These include fiesta committees, community cleanup and improvement committees, church construction committees, and many others organized around cleaning the church and making sure that people attend Mass. Other committees organize fund-raising activities to support the community's school. All of these committees are based on the same central features of *confianza* and reciprocity and are often composed both of blood and marriage relatives as well as friends, neighbors, and even those with whom people are in conflict.

Rural communities in Mexico's northwest coast usually have a strong political leadership vested in *ejidos*. These are communities of common landholders in which, until very recently, people owned the land jointly but cultivated it individually. However, since 1992, individual households may own their plots of land privately. The political organization of the *ejidos* consists of a president, secretary, treasurer, commissary, and a president of vigilance elected by vote. Most of these posts usually are headed by adult men. Fishing cooperatives also are very important, and their political organization is similar to that of the *ejidos*. The various bonds of community life intertwine into a complex network of social relations.

Religion and World View

Everyone gets used to the place in which she or he lives. We don't lack anything because my husband is a fisherman. He helps to support the household. When he does not make enough money fishing, we all go to work to the mango or chili farms. Sometimes I find life here to be very sad, but other times I feel happy about it. This is a very quiet community. There are no bad people like in other places. We all have mutual trust in each other because we know each other. Here, both women and men work outside of their homes. Sometimes women have to play the double role of being mothers and fathers. After we come from the field, we must do household chores. Life is a struggle for the woman, but the man can no longer support the household by himself.

—Chabela, a campesina in Mexico's northwest coast, 1998.
Author's translation.

Rural communities in Mexico's northwest coast are by no means isolated from the wider society. In fact, these communities are also part of national and international markets through their participation in the commercial agriculture, aquaculture, and fishing industries. People are aware of the social and economic inequalities that exist between and among them, and between them and those who control the means of production in their region. They are also aware of the class differences between them and the Mexican elite. They see these differences constantly being played out in the *telenovelas* or soap operas, and in their interaction with the professional and wealthy elite of the region. People also are aware of the similarities that exist between them and other campesinos in the country and in other parts of the world.

Nevertheless, these great disparities between classes and groups of people are compensated for by belief systems that seem to cut across these cleavages. Among the most important of these are religion and distinct ways of looking at the world. Today, the majority of the rural population in Mexico's northwest coast are Roman Catholic, but other religions, including Jehovah Witnesses, Mormonism, and Pentecostalism, have expanded through many of the rural areas in the region. Nevertheless, since the sixteenth century, Catholic churches have dominated the rural landscape with Masses and other religious rituals celebrated throughout the year. Every community has an associated patron saint with festivals prepared every year in his or her honor. Thus, each town and rural community will have a particular festival and religious figure with which it is identified which cuts across class and other differences.

The most important religious celebration throughout the region, as well as throughout most of Mexico, is the Day of the Virgin of Guadalupe, the patron saint of Mexico. The celebration takes place every year on December 12, but rural communities begin to prepare a few weeks before then

25

when the women arrange altars at their homes. Usually the altar is placed on the porch or in the entrance way. A portrait or other representation of the Virgin is located centrally, and bright colored-paper flowers are arranged around it and usually flanked by an assortment of multicolored candles and ribbons.

Women also work together in the preparation of a special event to be held at their church to honor the Virgin of Guadalupe. They decorate the church with flowers and a *nacimiento* (manger) of Jesus that commemorates the Virgin's motherhood rather than Jesus' birth as is the case at Christmas. At midnight, the mariachis (Mexican troubadours) play and sing the *mañanitas* (a traditional Mexican birthday song) to the Virgin while hundreds of people offer bunches of freshly cut flowers and place them before her feet as an act of respect and obeisance.

Many other people from rural communities also attend *peregrinaciones* (pilgrimages) organized in the urban towns where they travel to a particular, naturally beautiful rural spot to make further offerings. They regard these *peregrinaciones* as an opportunity to pay back favors they have requested from the Virgin previously during the year. Interestingly, some of these sites originally were indigenous places of worship hundreds of years before Christianity arrived in the area.

Such important rituals are part of a much broader ritual and social cycle in most rural communities. Ritual is a type of "cultural glue." Embedded into this glue for daily interaction is the expectation of reciprocity and mutual trust or *confianza*. Reciprocity and mutual trust are systems of relationships and values that bind persons into a sense of community. People take turns in helping each other building houses, schools, and churches and working the land. Women also take turns caring for each other's children while they go to work, shop, or go to the medical clinic.

Such expectations of reciprocity and mutual trust are given meaning by other life cycle rituals. The institution of *compadrazgo*, or co-godparenthood, may be developed through various Catholic sacramental celebrations such as baptism. Through the ritual of baptism, godparents are expected to take care of the child in the event that something happens to the parents. These form part of a much broader "ritual cycle" in life cycle rituals, including baptism, confirmation, first communion, marriage, and *quinceañeras* (fifteenth-year debuts). This ritual commemorating the passage of a young woman from childhood to adulthood, is very elaborate, and rural households begin to plan and save money for a *quinceañera* two or three years ahead of time. Marriage and funerals form the adult and terminal parts of a circle of ritual participation. When daily interaction is added to this ritual cycle, the people in these communities have opportunities to develop very close social bonds of reciprocity and mutual trust.

THREATS TO SURVIVAL

Years ago this fishing cooperative produced a lot. During that time everything was going very well for us in here. Although the shrimp was sold very cheaply it was enough to support ourselves. There was no competition over the shrimp resources as there is now. Now we produce only enough to eat. The government has organized many fishing cooperatives because people can not make a living anymore by only working their land. These are not fertile anymore. Most people are entering into fishing. We cannot support ourselves anymore like we used to do.

—A fisherman, 1989. Author's translation

Fishing resources have supported the rural coastal population throughout different generations, and during the nineteenth century people from other parts of Mexico settled in the northwest coast and began to exploit the fishing resources. At this time, when fishing was done on a subsistence basis, there was a great diversity of species. Ocean, estuarine, and lagoon fishing were open access activities, and the fishing resources in many cases were held in common among all of the region's inhabitants. A more commercial fishing industry was developed around 1870 when the first Chinese immigrants arrived in the port of Mazatlán and began to export shrimp to California and China. A few years later, in 1917, the first processing plants were built in the northwest coast, and the tuna fishing industry developed.

Before the Mexican Revolution, which began in 1910, the fishing resources were exploited by small companies which settled in the area and by subsistence fishermen. The companies had been granted exclusive fishing rights to some of the best fishing grounds, but other productive fishing grounds were available as common property to the rural coastal population. After the Mexican Revolution, the companies ceased operation.

Subsistence fishing was declared free, and all fishing resources again became common property. By 1923 the Mexican government had implemented a plan to develop the fishing activity in the region by allocating the fishing resources to different sectors of the population. According to this plan, the rural population had the most privilege to exploit the fishing resources, but the state kept the ownership rights. Fishing for sale at national and international markets was also allowed. Although no restrictions were imposed, people dedicated to the commercial exploitation of the fishing resources had to pay for exploiting and exporting the product.

In 1928 the Mexican government granted specific fishing areas within the lagoons and estuaries to the rural population. This, however, was contingent upon the formation of fishing cooperatives in those areas in which rights to fishing grounds were granted. These cooperatives were to be formed only by people for whom fishing was the main occupation and who

wanted to improve their economic situation. In this way fishing cooperatives and the fishing industry became the focus of Mexico's economic development program.

Shrimp became the main export-oriented fishing resource due to its importance and value in the international market. In 1940 shrimp resources
were reserved for the exploitation of only those fishermen organized in
fishing cooperatives; these organizations operated with relative success for
several years. This success was the result of several factors, including the
abundance and diversity of fishing resources, the low density of the coastal
population, and the small number of fishing cooperatives organized in the
region.

Fishing cooperatives and their fishing resources have since become a
source of conflict in Mexico's northwest coast as the direct result of the
increase in population to the coastal rural areas. In the 1950s the increase
in population was attributed to the establishment of farming *ejidos* in the
region. Because in many instances the land was not productive, the majority
of people sought out other occupations, and fishing became an alternative
for those people whose *ejidos* were established near lagoons and estuaries.
The fishing cooperatives already organized in the region were reluctant to
accept new fishing cooperatives because of a concern that new cooperatives
would lead to the overexploitation of the shrimp resources. Nevertheless,
in 1972, *ejidos* were legally allowed to organize their own fishing cooperatives, a decision that may have contributed to some of the more extreme
pressures on the shrimp stocks in the present time. Currently the rural
population in Mexico's northwest coast continues to grow as people from
other parts of Mexico relocate to the area searching for work in the agriculture and fishing industries, which aggravates the conflicts over the access
to the exploitation of fishing resources.

Another source of aggravation is the development of an offshore commercial fishing sector. The fishing technology used by this sector is more
complex and less environmentally friendly than the technology used by the
fishing sector in estuaries and lagoons. The offshore sector uses bigger fishing boats and trawl nets which have been in part responsible for the overexploitation of the shrimp resources in the region and also responsible for
the virtual disappearance of some marine species, including the turtle and
small dolphin.

Mexican policies and regulations have not been effective in developing
the fishing industry in a sustainable manner. Even defining the appropriate
opening and closing of fishing seasons is often contradictory or nonen-
forceable. Although in theory access to shrimp resources is closed during
the off-season, in practice shrimp often are exploited much of the year.
Because of the worsening of Mexico's economic situation, rural people need
to diversify their economic activities, and shrimp fishing is seen as an at-

tractive opportunity for rural people because of the high monetary value of shrimp in countries such as the United States and Japan.

That the fishing resources in Mexico's northwest coast are being depleted as the result of these social, economic, and environmental factors is a reality. Studies conducted by various research institutes have shown that productivity has declined during the last ten years. Certainly people in rural coastal communities are aware of this depletion since they have been among the most affected by it.

During the 1980s, the Mexican government attempted to reduce the pressure on shrimp capture fishery by expanding shrimp farming; however, this strategy has had dire social and ecological effects. The stated goals used to justify the development of industrial shrimp farming included increasing shrimp production and profits generated through exports, creating jobs in rural communities to improve the quality of life of the population, and providing access to the exploitation of the shrimp resources to those people who lack it. Until 1990 the only people legally allowed to farm shrimp were campesinos organized in cooperatives. Since 1990, as the result of a series of political and economic changes promoted by the Mexican government, private entrepreneurs from Mexico and other countries have been given the means to participate in the industry legally.

Shrimp aquaculture has not fulfilled the government's goals. Instead, it has exacerbated the previously existing conflicts over access to the exploitation of the shrimp resources and has created new conflicts as well. Conflicts among cooperative members, the biologists in charge of the shrimp farms, and private companies have altered the social fabric of many rural communities. Recently, a series of environmental problems associated with the expansion of the industry have emerged. These are especially prominent in Mexico's northwest coast because the largest development of the industry has occurred in this region.

One of the main environmental problems has been the impact of the construction of shrimp farms upon the lagoon and estuarine ecosystems. In many cases, concessions have been granted to private entrepreneurs to build shrimp farms in coastal lagoons which are the fishing grounds that traditionally have been exploited by the fisher peoples in the region. As a result, serious conflicts between private investors and traditional fishing cooperatives have emerged.

The impact of shrimp farming on mangrove ecosystems have recently become a major concern in the region. An estimated 10,000 hectares (25,000 acres) of mangrove forests have been cleared to build shrimp farms. The water quality of coastal ecosystems including the lagoons and estuaries also has declined due to the construction of shrimp farms. The discharges of shrimp ponds, which in many cases contain large amounts of organic material, fertilizers, chemicals, and antibiotics, also are negatively affecting water quality.

The natural resources of Mexico's northwest coast have been degraded over time. The shrimp fishing and shrimp farming industries are partially blamed for this degradation. However, the large-scale, export-oriented, commercial agriculture prevalent in the region is also responsible for the environmental degradation of coastal ecosystems. Pesticides and fertilizers and other chemicals in agriculture drain into many of these coastal ecosystems. Fishermen in the area report that agricultural drainage is killing the fish and shrimp in lagoons and estuaries. Pesticides are also having harmful effects on the human residents of the coast.

The current situation of the rural poor in Mexico's northwest coast is very precarious. Most rural households struggle to survive in conditions of extreme poverty while the natural environment on which they depend continues to degrade. The serious economic crises faced by the Mexican nation over the last several decades have severely impacted the rural population. In recent years, the Mexican government has taken a variety of measures to privatize its major industries and services. This has further increased the inequalities among the Mexican people.

Current government policies continue to support the large-scale commercial exploitation of natural resources in order to promote the country's economic development. The pressure of a growing impoverished rural population upon the country's natural resources, together with the lack of sustainable management policies, is contributing to the degradation of those natural resources.

Tourism, often considered a socially and environmentally benign industry, is among the fastest growing industry in the region, with both national and foreign entrepreneurs investing in the sector. The largest development of the industry is concentrated in the coastal town of Mazatlán, in the state of Sinaloa. Numerous hotels, resorts, golf courses, discos, restaurants, and shops have been built in order to attract foreign tourism. Mazatlán is a popular destination for American and Canadian college students during spring break as well as for American retirees.

The industry is expanding and spreading to rural coastal communities. Tourists traveling to the region can now visit colonial churches, beaches, shrimp farms, mangroves, and the lagoon ecosystems found in small town and rural communities. Residential communities are being built for North Americans who are resettling in coastal areas in rural communities. As yet, tourism does not appear to have benefited the rural coastal population. The jobs created by the industry usually employ people who live in or close to Mazatlán, and many of these jobs require a university degree or some technical training and some competence in spoken English (the language of most of the tourists)—qualifications lacked by the poorer rural people. In addition, the tourism industry is competing with coastal residents for potable water and for access to traditional recreation areas.

Environmental and economic crises in Mexico are exacerbating the social crisis faced by people and rural communities. Recently, many rural communities in Mexico's northwest coast have witnessed an increase in malnutrition, alcohol consumption, and domestic violence. The lack of basic services, such as potable water, electricity, health care services, and educational and economic opportunities, is having a tremendous impact, especially upon the younger generations.

RESPONSE: STRUGGLES TO SURVIVE CULTURALLY

Household and Community Levels

As poverty continues to spread, households in rural areas have developed some survival strategies to guarantee their members a relatively secure supply of basic resources. One strategy has been for household members to engage in multiple occupations to generate more income. In most rural communities, adult males rotate through various economic activities throughout the year. The working cycle for most adult males includes fishing, farming, and wage labor. The cycle varies depending on a series of factors such as climatic conditions, availability of work, and the amount of income generated within the household. Those households with a large number of children usually have more people engaged in multiple occupations.

In recent years the participation of male adults in the trafficking of archaeological artifacts has been noticeable. People resort to the excavation and sale of indigenous archaeological artifacts out of desperation, need, and discontent. The existence of a black market in the region for these artifacts is an incentive for some households to engage in this illegal activity. These artifacts are often smuggled across the United States–Mexican border, especially through Tijuana.

Another household strategy has been to increase the number of wage earners. More women, adolescents, and children in rural households are participating in activities to earn cash. Many have been able to find seasonal jobs in the commercial agriculture sector, mostly during the planting and harvesting seasons. The need for more income in individual households has increased the workload of women and has transformed gender relations in rural communities. Traditionally, the men of the family were considered the breadwinners, and women were in charge of the social aspects and biological reproduction of their households. The need for multiple wage earners within the household, however, has changed this traditional pattern, posing new challenges for the household since women must divide their time between their families and their salaried work. One aspect that constrains women's involvement in income-generating activities is the lack of child-care facilities in rural areas. Most women solve this problem by asking relatives, friends, and neighbors to watch their children while they go to work. In other instances, women take their children with them to their workplace.

The organization and operation of rotating credit associations (RCA), known in Mexico as *cundinas* or *tandas*, have increased in rural areas recently. Generally, women administer these associations. They take turns rotating a sum of money among themselves. Thus, in a typical RCA, ten women in a ten-week period contribute 10 dollars each to a fund. In turn, a different woman will receive 100 dollars each week. These RCAs provide households with the opportunity to save cash in order to pay for items or services they need. Through these organizations, people have been able to save enough money to buy furniture and electric appliances for the house, to send their children to school, to go to the hospital, and to visit other parts of Mexico.

At the household level, another strategy has been to alter food consumption patterns. Consumption of certain products, such as meat and milk, has declined. Especially in times of financial difficulty, many households consume food that can be easily and freely obtained. There is a growing reliance on mangos, chilies, corn, beans, coconuts, cactus, fish, shellfish, and eggs, which are found or grown in the community. Tortillas are usually made at home instead of purchased at the store.

The current Mexican economic situation has affected the availability of health-care services for rural households. The costs associated with health care have increased, and households are faced with the uncertainty of what to do when someone gets ill. People often borrow money from relatives and friends to pay for a visit to the clinic or to purchase medicines. Sometimes people go to *curanderos* or healers in their own communities or to others nearby, since they charge less than physicians.

Migration as a household strategy to deal with growing poverty and economic uncertainty in rural areas has increased during the last decade. Members of individual households migrate to other northern border states such as Sonora or to border cities like Tijuana or Mexicali in search of employment. Usually one member of the household leaves first and later others follow. People often already have friends or families living in these places, so the transition from rural to urban settings is made easier by these networks. Once in the new setting, people seek employment in the factory assembling plants or *maquiladoras* and in the construction industry. However, many times, migration is part of an intermediate stage for eventual migration to the United States, where poor Mexicans from impoverished rural areas frequently work in low-wage jobs in the agricultural or service sector—as farmworkers, domestic servants, restaurant and hotel workers, and factory workers.

Environmental Awareness

There is growing awareness in the northwest coast, as well as in the rest of Mexico, about the serious effects posed by human activities on the natural environment. In this regard, the Mexican government has revised its National Development Plan to include an Environmental Plan. One of the main objectives of this plan is to encourage the sustainable use and development of the country's natural resources. The plan also stresses the importance of natural resources for economic development and for the benefit of the rural poor of the country. As part of this plan, the Environmental Sub-Program for the Coastal Zones was created when the country became a member of the Global Program of Action for the Protection of the Marine Environment against Land-Based Activities. The fishing and aquaculture industries have recently been the focus of new policies and regulations. New legislation requires the completion of an Environmental Impact Assessment Study before a shrimp farm can be constructed. The purpose of the environmental study is to determine the potential effects of a shrimp farm upon coastal ecosystems.

Coastal-urban communities also are taking an active role in dealing with the environmental issues that affect them. A group of academics and citizens in Mazatlán recently organized an environmental nongovernmental organization (NGO) that has been working with issues of pollution in coastal ecosystems. Currently, this NGO has several active projects including a nursery of native plants from the region and the rehabilitation and conservation of estuaries and lagoon ecosystems.

In coastal rural communities, fishing cooperatives have started to oppose the construction of shrimp farms near their fishing grounds. Cooperatives have openly denounced the harmful effects of shrimp aquaculture upon the mangrove ecosystems and the wild stocks of fish in their fishing areas. Some cooperatives and communities have joined efforts in protesting and stopping the construction of shrimp farms. For example, in southern Sinaloa, a group of twenty-one fishing cooperatives, including 2,000 fishermen, has gone to government agencies and asked them to stop the construction of a shrimp farm near their fishing area. The group also wrote a letter to the Mexican president, Ernesto Zedillo, asking him to stop the construction of the shrimp farm. This group of cooperatives previously was successful in halting the construction of a shrimp farm in another nearby community. In the northern region of the state of Nayarit, fishing cooperatives recently opposed the construction of another shrimp farm. In this case, the fishermen accused the private company in charge of the shrimp farm of destroying large tracts of mangrove forests in the region. A study was conducted and the company was held responsible for the destruction. The company is expected to start a reforestation program in the area at its own expense.

FOOD FOR THOUGHT

This chapter raises a number of issues about the relationship among economic development, environmental degradation, and rural poverty. Most Latin American countries are faced with the dilemma of pressure to exploit their natural resources commercially in order to generate profits while at the same time trying to conserve their precious resources. However, most government policies have favored the commercial, export-oriented exploitation of the most important natural resources. Usually the return on investments are used to pay external debts and loans provided by multinational lending corporations such as the World Bank and the Inter-American Development Bank. In other instances, profits go directly to the banking elite, transnational corporations, or government agencies. Given the recent pressure to promote "free enterprise," rarely do these profits reach the poor people in rural areas in the form of services such as health care or education. Latin American countries also face the challenge of trying to develop their natural resources in a sustainable way in order to ensure their availability for present and future generations. This has been a very difficult goal to achieve.

The Mexican nation has undergone a series of radical changes over the last two decades. The economic crisis during the 1980s had a severe impact upon the rural population that was measured in terms of increased poverty. More recently, in the 1990s, the country underwent a series of changes aimed at the expansion of the free market. This new model sought to attract economic investment to rural areas. As a result, article 27 of the Mexican constitution, which defines the land tenure system of *ejidos* and the fishing law, were modified. Under the "old" article 27, people could not sell or rent *ejido* lands. Under the "new" article 27, individuals are considered to be the sole owners of their plots of land and thus are entitled to sell it or rent it. The new fishing law allows for the investment of national and foreign private capital in the shrimp aquaculture industry. The new land tenure system has created difficulties in many *ejidos*, since there have been instances in which members sold their land under emergency situations, leaving entire families landless and without the means to buy new land. In some cases, coastal *ejidos* have rented or sold land to private investors who want to build shrimp farms. This has spurred the rapid expansion of the shrimp aquaculture industry on the northwest coast of Mexico and has contributed to the exacerbation of the social and environmental problems already existing in the region. Mexico is not unique in this sense; other Third World countries, including Ecuador, Honduras, Thailand, the Philippines, and Indonesia, where shrimp farming has expanded, face similar conditions.

Despite all of the changes taking place in Mexico, rural communities have been very active in devising ways to deal with the persistent economic uncertainty and natural resource degradation that characterize this region. Coastal rural communities are very dynamic entities with a strong sense of cultural identity. The various rituals and cultural practices performed in these communities act to ensure the continuity of communal and cultural identity through various generations. However, as Mexico's rural areas continue to change and become even more a part of a global economy, there is a risk that many of these cultural rituals and traditions may disappear.

Rural communities in Mexico's northwest coast are embedded in a daily struggle to ensure that people meet their basic needs. In doing so, rural households have developed a set of adaptive strategies to guarantee the survival of their members. Some of the strategies include an increase in the number of wage earners and household members engaged in multiple occupations. The contribution of women to the household economy has been enhanced by increased participation in income-generating activities. For many women, finding a balance between salaried work and housework is an extremely difficult task. Unfortunately, this is a common constraint for most rural women throughout Latin America. There is a finite line past which multiple employment and the contributions of women simply are not enough to cope with declining conditions. A growing number of rural Mexicans are compelled to leave their rural communities in order to survive. Migration—within Mexico, to Mexico City, to border towns, or to the United States—is an increasingly vital option when there are no other alternatives left.

Questions

1. Is it possible for Latin American countries to conserve their natural resources in a sustainable manner and at the same time promote economic development and increase the standard of living of their people?

2. What are the global, social, and environmental impacts of industrial shrimp farming?

3. What are the true costs of the shrimp on your dinner plate in the United States, Europe, and Japan—the countries to which most farmed shrimp is exported?

4. Can the people of Mexico's northwest coast maintain their cultural and social identity and become part of a globalized economy at the same time?

5. Given the recent events and laws in the United States aimed at curtailing immigration, do you think that the survival strategy of poor Mexicans to migrate to the United States may be short lived? If so, what options will be left to poor rural Mexicans?

NOTES

Information, data, and quotations in this chapter come from the author's unpublished Ph.D. dissertation, "Appropriate Technology and Shrimp Mariculture Development in Mexico," Rutgers the State University of New Jersey, New Brunswick, N.J. 1991, and from fieldnotes collected during subsequent field research through 1999.

1. Octavio Paz, *The Labyrinth of Solitude* (New York: Grove Press, 1985), 271.

RESOURCE GUIDE

Published Literature

Cruz-Torres, María L. "Shrimp Mariculture Development in Two Rural Mexican Communities." In *Aquacultural Development: Social Dimensions of an Emerging Industry*, edited by Bailey Conner et al., Boulder, Colo.: Westview Press, 1996.

Flores-Verdugo, Francisco et al. "The Teacapán-Agua Brava-Mearismas Nacionales Mangrove Ecosystems of the Pacific Coast of Mexico." In *Mangrove Ecosystem Studies in Latin America and Africa*, edited by Bjorn Kjerfve et al. Paris: UNESCO, 1997.

McGoodwin Russell. "Mexico's Conflictual Inshore Pacific Fisheries: Problems Analysis and Policy Recommendations." *Human Organization* 46, no. 3 (1987): 221–32.

Vélez-Ibáñez, Carlos. *Bonds of Mutual Trust: The Cultural Systems of Rotating Credit Associations Among Urban Mexicans and Chicanos*. New Brunswick, N.J.: Rutgers University Press, 1983.

Wright, Angus. *The Death of Ramón González: The Modern Agricultural Dilemma*. Austin: University of Texas Press, 1990.

Videos

Sweet 15. This video presents the ritual of Quinceañera. It can be purchased from Teacher's Video Company, P.O. Box WHG-4455, Scottsdale, AZ 85261. Tel. (800)262-8837.

Troubled Harvest. This video presents the life of Mexican and Central American farmworkers in California agriculture. It can be rented or purchased from Women Make Movies, Inc., 462 Broadway, Suite 500 D, New York, NY 10013. Tel. (212)925-0606.

Women and Work in Latin America. This video examines the various economic and subsistence activities of Latin American women from diverse economic and social backgrounds. It can be purchased from the Upper Midwest Women's History Center, 6300 Walker Street, St. Louis Park, MN 55416.

WWW Sites

The Mangrove Action Project
http://www.earthisland.org.

This site addresses various issues concerning the global degradation of mangrove forest ecosystems.

Mexico Online
http:///www.Mexonline.com/geogrphy.htm.

This site offers geographic and environmental information about Mexico. It also offers a list of the government and nongovernment environmental organizations in the country.

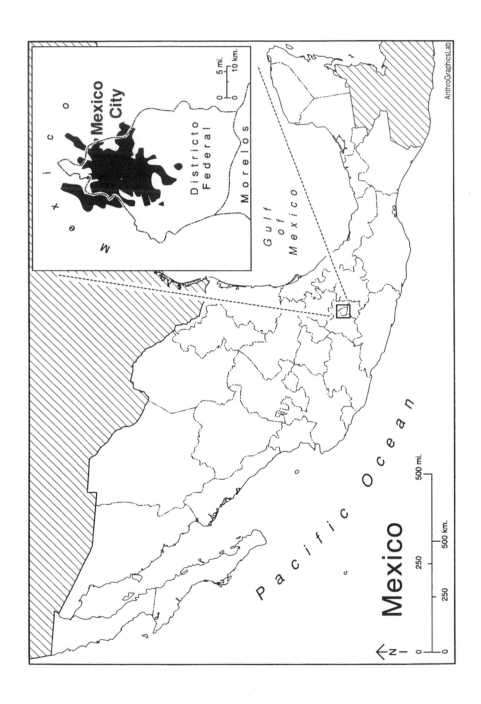

Mexico City
Districto Federal
Morelos

Mexico

Pacific Ocean

Gulf of Mexico

AnthroGraphicsLab

Chapter 3

Villagers at the Edge of Mexico City

Scott S. Robinson

CULTURAL OVERVIEW

The People

When the Spaniards arrived in the Valley of Mexico in 1521, they had no idea how many communities surrounding the lakeshore city of Tenochtitlán had been subdued only recently by the Aztecs. Today, from Iztapalapa on the eastern rim, around the volcanic cone hiding Milpa Alta and its eleven villages from the valley floor, westward through the highlands of Xochimilco, and then northward through Tlalpan and beyond, a network of seventy small villages still runs continuously around three sides (the east, south, and west) of the world's largest city, Mexico City. At the time of the conquest, this was not a homogenous set of villages; rather, it was an example of negotiated neighborliness among diverse peoples. At least three languages were spoken by the villagers: Mexica or Nahuatl, the language of the conquering Aztecs, whose speakers could distinguish local origins by special terms and shifts in certain sounds (what linguists call dialects); Tlalpanec (which gave its name to the district of Tlalpan, in the southwest corner); and Otomí (or Ñahñu, as they prefer) in the northwest quadrant. The shallow lake extended toward the distant hills in the northeast quadrant. No doubt there were many gods and named spirits that distinguished the groups of villages that spoke the same language. Neighbors speaking different languages tended not to share ceremonial obligations and exchanges. Different gods, different fiestas, was perhaps the rule. This band of contiguous yet diverse villages was a complex mosaic of cultures and communities that were well established before the Aztecs appeared and continued after the Spaniards arrived in search of gold and souls.

These villagers could monitor each other from their defensive promontories, as was the custom in the broken topography of the central highlands. Lakeside villagers were not fearful of the neighbors who lived above them because they shared a similar culture, language, beliefs, and ceremonies, as well as their sons and daughters in marriage. The territory of each culture on the lake was wedge shaped. The lowlanders at lakeside looked up, to the west, to the south, and to the east, to where their highlander cousins lived in the woods and protected the springs and sacred places, the flanks and backside of the territory. This vertically integrated ecosystem linked villages that shared the lake and the region's bounty at different elevations. These diverse cultures became consolidated only after the decline of the empire of Teotihuacán (A.D. 1100) which was governed from the city of pyramids in the northeastern corner of the valley. Every culture had its geographical boundaries, and surely, as now, there must have been some fence moving at night as well as poaching in a neighbor's territory. This was not an open space without rules of ownership; rather, it was communal property controlled by a hierarchy of civil and religious officials or by married couples. Every household was linked to others via kinship ties, much as can be found in the small towns on the North American prairie today. These were integrated cultures, only partially subservient to their conquerors. As often occurs, the most talented and brightest individuals probably joined the Aztec court where issues of state, faith, and history (time and space) were discussed and written down in a glyph language painted on bark parchment. No document attests to the personal friendships and alliances that may have mediated each dominated culture from harsh treatment. At the same time, these personal ties probably allowed some dialogue and negotiations between the conquered and the conquerors. There were, no doubt, a few major surprises (such as comets and asteroids) in the neighborhood, until the Aztecs physically conquered the lakeside cultures, extracted tribute, and began expanding their city on the mud islands in the middle of the lake. Then the Spaniards arrived and began a long period of colonization that continues to this day.

The Setting

With a population of around 20 million people (about 20% of the total population of Mexico), Mexico City (the Federal District) is one of the largest cities in the world. Today, the "rural" population of the Federal District is approximately 400,000 people, of whom only about 17,500 still farm their land. All together, these communities are caretakers of 79,400 hectares (196,000 acres) of land, which is subdivided as follows: 37,700 hectares (93,100 acres) of forest, 30,000 hectares (74,100 acres) of cultivated plots (29,000 hectares [71,600 acres] rain fed and 1,000 hectares [2,470 acres] of irrigated parcels), 7,700 hectares (19,000 acres) of grazing land, and 4,000 hectares (9,900 acres) of what is classified as "mixed uses."

This is a large territory composed of a complex network of continuously renegotiated neighborliness among natives and newcomers.

Until the 1970s, the inhabitants of the villages on the edge of the Federal District went "downtown" to market, to work, and to sightsee around the modernizing urban sprawl. The city only came "up" to the rim villages in order to deliver beer, soda pop, and junk food to the small mom-and-pop grocery stores on the corner of the village plaza. Most of the teachers and probably all of the young doctors and nurses who staffed the expanding network of schools and public clinics came from below. There were open spaces of cultivated land, orchards, and terraced hillsides between the villages and the city. The city continued to grow, fed by an economic boom that attracted many migrants from impoverished areas elsewhere in rural Mexico as well as by the expanding core of city folk or *chilangos*, as they are known in Mexican slang. Along the paved tentacles of urban boulevards, people moved "up the hill," purchased lots, and built their homes, rental apartments, repair shops, and small businesses. Today the geographical separation of the villages no longer exists.

Traditional Subsistence Strategies

At the time of the Spanish conquest, every household planted corn, beans, and squash on small, rain-fed parcels of land at the edge of each village. Many villages bordered the lake, with its winding shoreline full of reeds, migratory fowl, fish, and freshwater shrimp. Lush gardens (*chinampas*) were formed by dredging mud on top of human-made islands that were then framed by heavy stakes and woven reed mats. These *chinampas* still are used to grow vegetables, flowers, and medicinal plants. Staple crops were grown on the sloping floodplain or on plots, in Milpa Alta terraces, carved out of the hillsides. The nopal cactus (first cousin to a prickly pear) was cultivated as a vegetable, and its consumption remains important today. Food products and materials for tools and household utensils (such as reed sleeping mats) were traded "up the hill" to neighbors with access to dense forests of cedar, pine, oak, and other medicinal species. Fresh drinking water, firewood, corn, and the pitch or sap (copal) from certain species of pine came "down the hill" to the lakeside. Copal incense melted on hot coals housed in ceremonial dishes—some held in the hand, others in large bowls—smoked before shrines to gods and spirits. Its sweet, pungent aroma blowing around the neighborhood announced that the ceremony was under way.

Social and Political Organization

The *calpulli* is one of the intriguing mysteries linked to the changes taking place in this network of villages and, for that matter, throughout central

41

and southern Mexico after the Spaniards arrived and during the subsequent colonial period (1521–1810). *Calpulli* is a Mexica or Aztec term for a territorially based kin group, and many assume that today's barrios in every village are simply a renaming of this earlier form of organizing kinship, marriage, and rituals. The deaths of elderly grandparents who speak Nahuatl to each other may make it too late to research the social meaning of the *calpulli*. Nevertheless, let us assume each *calpulli* or barrio was a group of core families whose sons were required to marry the daughters of another *calpulli* or barrio on the other side of the village. Vice versa, their daughters were obliged to recruit their partners among the young men of the first barrio. In this fashion, one finds a system of barrios exchanging their daughters who go to live with their husbands and in-laws, thereby assuring the reproduction of that family. In some cases, the villages were too small to have more than one group of core families, but this village was linked to others in a network of kinship exchange. Smaller villages were thus combined into complete barrios. Where there is courtship and marriage, there is usually a calendar of fiestas or dances (*bailes*), as they are called by today's television-nurtured youth. In this culture, these moments of ritual license were and remain intense. Young people can touch each other in public while dancing, and the parents can see who is courting whom. Then, of course, there are weddings, baptisms, first communions, and the ceremonial coming of age of young women on their fifteenth birthday (quinceañeras). This cycle has been unending. The coming of mass education, especially beyond primary school, has transformed any prior barrio-based norms about a preference for partners from the other side of town or from the village that traditionally visits each year to honor the local saint with flowers on his or her birthday. Courtship in the schoolyard has overwhelmed the out-marrying tradition that was not actively promoted by the Church nor the local civil authorities whose insecurity required them to disdain things "Indian." As the gods became saints, marriage rules were relaxed, but the annual cycle of ritual obligations remained anchored in the barrios. Each barrio fiesta is coordinated by a group of married couples who agree to share the costs and labor involved in their corresponding ritual obligations. The cost of sponsoring a three-day party can be considerable since it usually includes paying and feeding the band, feeding all guests to the *mayordomo's* house, and buying fireworks, flowers, and new clothes for the religious saint being honored. This fiesta is called a *mayordomía*, and every barrio neighbor participates at least once in a lifetime. Everyone knows precisely their collective fiesta obligations as well as which street or lane is the barrio boundary. Nowadays, tradition still provides the norms for native families inside these villages and towns.

Feast of San Gerónimo. Courtesy of Scott Robinson.

Religion and World View

Around the lake and up in the hill villages, people in the days before the Spanish evangelization efforts worshipped gods carved from stone, awesome figures with feathered serpents, jaguars, fertility signs, and more. These were elevated shrines, or small pyramids in locations selected for reasons unknown to us now. These cultures were not monotheistic; they did not worship only one god. There was a hierarchy of gods, and one could pray to all and leave incense burning on every altar. Or one could invest personal energy and derive well-being by making offerings of food, flowers, and incense to the local gods and spirits, at the shrine down the path, beyond your uncles' houses, in the center of the village. Human faith takes many forms, and it is usually expressed by kin groups on their collective behalf. Today, the stone gods are gone, but the chapels and churches built atop the former shrines, with the same carved lava rock, are peopled with many saints and virgins. Sacred forms were substituted for others, and, perhaps, their functions and meanings remain the same. Food and flower offerings abound, as does the burning copal. The Spanish Inquisition, conducted downtown, was a form of symbolic warfare with satanic, pagan forces defined by those in authority at the time. Few villagers were

43

arrested and tortured by the Church; the names and intents of the deities simply changed during the religious conquest of Mexico.

Being practical people, however, and well adapted to their habitat, the villagers shared a general need to guarantee water and prevent crop failure, the continuity of life. During the rainy season (May to October), a major threat to the corn and beans growing in their fields were violent hailstorms. Young and old sometimes were struck down by lightning, as some still are today. Given these risks, those who could communicate with the rain god and control fickle weather spirits were the men and women who survived being hit by lightning. In this altered state of mind and body, these chosen people assumed their calling as communicators with the gods. Master shamans are those who can control these forces, assuring the arrival of the rains in time for a plentiful growing season, averting lightning and hailstorms. If one developed these awesome powers, then it was relatively easy to cure someone frightened by the dark or by a snake, or angry about a bad marriage, ungrateful children and the many other sources of ill-will and suffering among humans. These religious figures are called *graniceros* in Spanish, the hail people, and only a few elders practice this medicine today. In the old days, however, every village had an officiating shaman or *granicero*.

THREATS TO SURVIVAL

Today, this network of villages and small towns is being invaded by outsiders, or *avecindados* (those who come to be neighbors). The long process of negotiating neighborliness now is not about the "foreigners" (Aztecs and Spaniards) who live elsewhere and collect tribute from you. Today, the outsiders have purchased land (by hook or by crook), moved in, and wish to participate in local politics. These outsiders are a mix of poor families forcibly relocated by urban renewal downtown, others still frightened by the 1985 earthquakes and determined to reduce their anxiety, and still others who cannot afford to buy or rent in the central city neighborhoods. Wealthy land speculators, too, with good connections have cobbled together large, forested areas, often by purchasing illegally communal property that technically cannot be sold. These speculators find the local authorities who are responsible for communal properties (both cultivated and forest land) and who are willing to cut a deal. They then "legalize" title to these properties in a fast-track operation sanctioned by official government accomplices. As swiftly as possible, they build condominiums for the new, professional middle class who are only too happy to raise their children in a secure, walled, and forested compound only they can afford and with a lovely view of the city below to boot. Today this process, called real estate development, is a very lucrative business that the existing system of political impunity allows to operate.

How does this system work? On a national scale, Mexico is divided into a mosaic of 2,418 municipalities, or *municipios*. These vary in size from a few in the northern desert states that are larger than Rhode Island, to minuscule *municipios* no more than a small town and the surrounding lands in the southern mountains of the state of Oaxaca. In 1929 the federal government expropriated the *municipios* within the Federal District and transformed them into *delegaciones*, or delegations, akin to the boroughs of New York City. Until 1997 there was not a single elected official in the government of the Federal District, formerly the Department of the Federal District. Before this date, the president, as the post was called, appointed the regent. The regent, in turn, appointed the delegates (*delegados*) who are the highest authorities in each delegation. Without a professional civil service, all public officials in the Federal District served at the whim of either their delegation chief or someone on the regent's staff. This was a colonial system without any form of democratic representation (with the exception of federal deputies elected from districts within the capital city but without authority therein). When there is no system of checks and balances allowing for accountability of public officials' behavior, impunity is the rule. Yossarian, Joseph Heller's protagonist in the novel *Catch 22* would have coped well in Mexico City; he worked out the logic of the "catch": "They can do anything to you you can't stop them from doing."[1] This is a fair description of official conduct in Mexico City until the 1997 elections. The former delegation authorities, with administrative control over all public services (schools, clinics, markets, transport, and police) in the villages around the rim, could work their whims in conjunction with commercial interests who often were members of their own families.

How did the pattern of real estate speculation emerge? The colonial system in Mexico was consolidated over a lengthy period of time; in fact, it is still under way. In effect, it was and is a process of legalizing land taken from native communities who did not share the concepts of private property, a tradition of legal titles, or the legitimacy of their transfers from original "owners" to newcomer purchasers. Notaries were a special category of colonial official, sanctioned by the Spanish crown, to oversee this "legal process"; they were entrusted to "notarize," that is, by their royal (and nowadays, state) authority, approve transfers of land ownership. This meant the notaries were put in charge of the privatization of former native properties. Today notaries remain responsible for this process (with the addition of modern business law). While the expansion of the limits of private property is a cartographic history yet to be compiled in Mexico, the agrarian "victories" of the Mexican Revolution (1910–1917) add another element to contemporary land tenure rules: the creation of the *ejido* and the recognition of communal property. Native villages throughout Mexico had witnessed their land being grabbed and legalized by Spaniards and their descendants for over 400 years. The Constitution of 1917 per-

45

mitted the villagers to recover a great deal of land in the hands of the "white" (*catrin*) landlords; these are today's *ejidos* formed by dividing up the large, colonial estates (legally, the state retained title and granted use rights in perpetuity to a list of villagers).

The communal lands around each village were also surveyed, and the revolutionary government entrusted them to each village petitioning for recognition of their *bienes comunales* (communal goods). It may seem complicated, but every villager knows there are three kinds of property: private (urban lots and some cultivated land), communal, and *ejidal*. Because decisions about the disposal of communal and *ejidal* property remains among those villagers or their descendants who received the federal *ejido* land grant earlier in the century, it has been possible to convince some of these authorities to cede or "loan" parcels to kin or outsiders. Once land has been "loaned" (with cash payments for those responsible for the decision) and then farmed and structures built upon it, it tends to be very difficult for the local authorities to recover these parcels. As elsewhere, possession is nine-tenths of the law in Mexico. If the new "owner," a real estate developer, say, rushes to a notary for title transfer, and the procedure is actively endorsed by Federal District delegation authorities, the former *ejidal* or communal property becomes, in effect, privatized. Many variations on this theme of official chicanery can be found in the oral histories of the villages at the edge of the city. This irregular mosaic of de facto privatizations constitutes the largest block of disputed land tenure in all of Mexico.

Why is this happening now and not earlier? The answer has to do with the growth pattern of Mexico City and the surrounding metropolitan area (technically, this is the Federal District and adjacent municipalities of the state of Mexico). Previously, a shared culture and lack of outside pressure made it easier to maintain traditions.

The villages themselves have gotten larger over the past generation. With the expansion of the public health system into the rural areas of the country, including the semi-urban edges of the capital city, the rate of infant mortality has dropped dramatically, and longevity, or the average length of a person's life, has increased (from around fifty to more than seventy years). These facts translate into more mouths to feed. Kin groups need to negotiate access to rooms and housing for their members. In the villages, this has led to increased pressure to build houses on the garden plots next to existing homes and to gather more firewood in the upper woodlands to be used at home or sold to neighbors down the hill. As more schools were built, teachers from elsewhere came to work in the villages, and young people became better equipped for the jobs they sought down in the city.

The impact of a growing population of natives and outsiders has led to an average annual loss of 1,235 acres of forest. In addition, the remaining forest is being thinned by those who are too poor to install liquid propane gas tanks for their stoves and instead pick their kindling on a regular basis. Thousands of kindling pickers can thin a forest very quickly, and this has been occurring at an increasing rate over the past twenty years. Less forestland leads to a reduction in the flows of natural springs and less water to use for irrigating garden crops in the dry season. This results in reduced food production at the household level and consequently to a greater need to earn cash to purchase food. Those who continue to farm are using more agricultural chemicals which, in turn, are contaminating the water supply for those who live at lower elevations. This environmentally dangerous scenario can be summarized. As a result of real estate development, increased human population, and accelerated deforestation, previously cultivated lands have become either subdivisions for the rich or a chaotic mosaic of self-built housing for the poor.

RESPONSE: STRUGGLES TO SURVIVE CULTURALLY

The native inhabitants of this wide ring of neighboring villages have resisted the many pressures on their land and culture by simply doing what they know best: respecting their traditions. Nowadays, they are becoming more politically active. When the gods and spirits are on one's side, and one has enough to eat and is healthy, "foreigners" cannot cause too much damage. When foreigners begin taking the land and moving in, there is a real threat to one's integrity and well-being. If the foreigners speak the same language and share many symbols, as is the case here, intermarriage inevitably will occur. When marriages are made up of young couples who belong to different groups, natives and new neighbors, the traditions likely will be modified. Each spouse brings a distinct yet overlapping set of cultural rules about the nurturing of children. The next generation learns a "mixed" set of beliefs and norms about the proper way to behave and relate to neighbors and sacred places. If, in 2021, the villagers celebrate (which they probably will not do) 500 years of the Spanish presence in Mexico, a new generation will have grown up together, married, and had children who will be nearing adulthood. By this time, only the elderly will recall the *costumbres*, or customs, the fiestas with all the reciprocal obligations, processions, chants, floral designs, music, and paraphernalia. Traditions can change quickly, in a generation's time, as happened when the Nahuatl language was lost with the deaths of unschooled grandparents only twenty years ago.

Remember, however, that class and culture segregate newcomers to the villages. Social inequality is embedded within the spatial structure of the city as modern geographers remind us. These villages represent a process of cultural change and segregation taking place throughout Mexico. Herein, the rich, a minority with access to credit through the banking system, are the ones who can afford to purchase a lot and build a separate home. Without access to credit, most of the children of poorer residents are obliged to remain with their parents after marriage, often building more rooms in the back, on the roof, or behind the patio of their parents' homes.

It is important to recall that most of the village land was, and remains, communal and *ejidal* (technically, federal land ceded in perpetuity after the Mexican Revolution to a specific list of users who control its management). By the 1970s, a new middle class of professionals, doctors, lawyers, engineers, and top-level government employees began buying land in the wooded and tranquil villages above the urban din of Mexico City. Real estate developers acted quickly to meet this demand by pressuring local communal and *ejido* authorities to part with some of their parcels for a price. Technically, this was illegal, but given the volume of these deals as well as the political clout of those purchasing the land, only the federal agrarian authorities could have intervened, and unsurprisingly, they chose not to. In 1999 there was a special project within the Federal District to "legalize" the thousands of acres of parcels, small and large, that have been "transferred" to private hands over the past thirty years or more.

Can the villagers sustain their cultural integrity in the near future? This is a question germane to most of rural and semi-urban Mexico, where communities, large and small, maintain a system of barrios, rituals, and cosmology distinct from what is projected by the public media—especially television. Some call this the "Profound Mexico" as opposed to what is seen on television. Television has created and reproduces a culture of consumption and values (e.g., Disney World, Cancún holidays, new homes in the hills on the Upper West Side, sports utility vehicles, and many other things) very distinct, and perhaps incompatible, with the traditions described here. This is occurring throughout the world, and Mexico is no exception. How can one defend one's self while being physically invaded and bombarded with alien messages? It may be even more difficult if there are few democratic forms of representing local, village, and barrio interests in the larger political entity, in this case the government of the Federal District. It is not easy to be sure, and it is unclear which cultural forms will remain significant and collectively supported, practiced, and handed down to the next generations.

The villagers' struggle to defend their customs has become overtly political. This story is linked to a larger effort to wrest control of the Federal District's government from the hands of what used to be Mexico's monopolistic political party, the PRI (Partido Revolucionario Institucional). Opponents of the PRI succeeded in their quest only recently, in 1997. Since December 1997, a freely elected head of the Federal District replaced the colonial regent, appointed by the president. In 1995 there was a rehearsal of sorts for the 1997 campaign within the Federal District: "citizen councilors" were chosen in very small, local election districts. The vote among the rural villages on the rim of the Valley of Mexico was much larger and had less abstention than the vote in urbanized neighborhoods elsewhere in the city. This was probably due to the faith of the native villagers that the new councilor figure could represent their interests for the first time in city politics. This was not to be the case. The PRI-appointed regent ordered his delegation chiefs to ignore those councilors who were linked to the opposition (meaning all those who protested the top-down management of public affairs at the village level) and favor only those tied to the government party. The frustration of the villagers' expectations about recovering control of some local services fed the massive support for the opposition party that swept to power in the July 1997 elections.

Since taking office on December 1, 1997, the first elected government in the history of Mexico City is paying respectful attention to the social and environmental demands of the villages on the rim. Nevertheless, in 1998, the nineteen communities formed the Alliance of Native Villages, *Ejidos* and Communities of Anahuac (Alianza de Pueblos Indigenas, Ejidos, y Comunidades del Anahuac). (Anahuac is the Aztec word for the Valley of Mexico.) The precursor to this coalition was the CUALOCOTLA, a loose confederation of villagers who successfully opposed a scheduled 100-meter- (328-foot)-wide swath of highway right-of-way to be expropriated by the former Mexico City regent. This was clearly a clever real estate speculation scheme (or scam), whereby the toll road to be built with public funds would serve a ring of high-rise condominiums along the upper rim on the west side of the valley, affording a dramatic view for the upscale professionals who lived there. The new government of the Federal District promptly shelved the toll road proposal, but the villagers are justifiably wary. With the democratic opening in Mexican and Mexico City politics, villagers know that only solid community-based organizations can withstand the kind of legal and extralegal pressures they have been resisting from the colonial period until now. The integrity of their barrio-based system of *mayordomias*, including married couples' committed to sponsoring village saints' fiestas, has been an important tool until now.

FOOD FOR THOUGHT

This chapter raises a number of important questions regarding cultural continuity and change in the context of significant economic changes (i.e., real estate development) and human population growth.

Questions

1. How does one transform a local network of trust among neighbors who share religious traditions into a village organization capable of negotiating with ex-

49

ternal public agencies on behalf of the group? In other words, how does the religious organization become an effective civic group?

2. How can one respect the grandparents' traditions and still participate as citizens in a modern society? Young people in these small towns face this dilemma in the new millennium.

3. Does a culture "die" when its language is no longer spoken?

4. What happens to a traditional community when its forest resource base disappears?

5. Can "conquered" peoples retain their original religious beliefs?

NOTES

Information and data presented in this chapter are based on field research conducted by the author.

1. Joseph Heller, *Catch 22*, New York: Dell, 1961.

RESOURCE GUIDE

Published Literature

Gibson, Charles. *The Aztecs Under Spanish Rule*. Stanford, Calif.: Stanford University Press, 1964.

Ingham, John M. *Mary, Michael, and Lucifer: Folk Catholicism in Central Mexico*. Austin: University of Texas Press, 1986.

Lopez Austin, Alfredo. *El Pasado Indigena*. Mexico City: Fondo de Cultura Económica, 1998.

Pezzoli, Keith. *Human Settlements and Planning for Ecological Sustainability: The Case of Mexico City*. Cambridge: MIT Press, 1998.

Sanders, W., J. Parsons, and R. Santley. *The Basin of Mexico: Ecological Processes in the Evolution of a Civilization*. New York: Academic Press, 1979.

Ward, Peter M. *Mexico City: The Production and Reproduction of an Urban Environment*. London: Belhaven Press, 1990.

WWW Sites

A Spanish language WWW site dedicated to the sustainable development of the villages located on the rim above Mexico City can be found at http://servidor.rds.org.mx/sirds/surdf/ix.html. This site contains information on the history of the villages, maps, and current information on the area's environment and natural resources.

CENTRAL AMERICANS

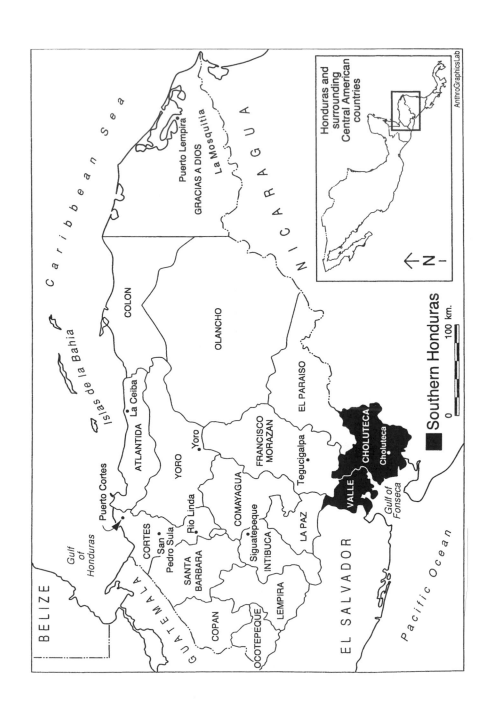

Southern Honduras

Chapter 4

Artisanal Fisherfolk of the Gulf of Fonseca

Jorge Varela Marquez, Kate Cissna, and Susan C. Stonich

> The principle that "the polluter pays" is transfigured by investors into "the polluter collects" . . . and the people pay. The social and ecological must be given equal weight with the economic consideration. To the degree that the [shrimp farming] industry continues to extend itself at our expense, we will complement their actions with our logical education of consumers, and our actions against financial institutions who patronize this activity.
>
> —CODDEFFAGOLF (Committee for the Defense and Development of the Flora and Fauna of the Gulf of Fonseca), 1996[1]

CULTURAL OVERVIEW

The People

The Gulf of Fonseca and adjacent areas of southern Honduras, Nicaragua, and El Salvador were among the first places that were exploited by the Spaniards in their search for wealth in the New World. When the Spaniards first arrived in the 1520s, this was a culturally diverse region that was home to a conflux of northern (Mexican), southern (lowland South American), and indigenous Central American peoples who spoke different languages and had discrete ways of life. The Spanish conquerors of the sixteenth century described a region that was home to "more people than hairs on all the deer." These peoples lived in fairly large settlements and farmed the rich volcanic soils along the Pacific Coast. Most groups practiced slash-and-burn agriculture to cultivate corns, beans, and squash. They supplemented their diets with domesticated chilies, peanuts, fruits, and turkeys.

Equally important to their survival was the *monte*, or uncultivated land, where they gathered nuts, roots, and grubs for food, and where they hunted and trapped deer, iguana, birds, and jaguars for meat and skins. The *monte* also was a source of brush, timber, and reeds that were used to construct houses and boats. In the mangroves and mudflats along the Gulf of Fonseca, the people collected shellfish and other aquatic species and fished from dugout canoes. Cacao and cotton were also grown, and the indigenous groups probably participated in local, coastal, and long-distance trading networks which involved these crops.

These conditions changed abruptly after the Spanish arrived; by the 1540s, the region's indigenous peoples had nearly been exterminated. Only in the early part of the twentieth century did the human population of this region reach pre-conquest levels. The rapid decline of the native peoples was not so much a result of the military operations but the more far-reaching consequences of malnutrition, from the disruption of indigenous food production and distribution systems, and deadly epidemics. Extremely high rates of mortality also occurred in association with forced labor in the newly opened mines and haciendas, or large landed estates. In addition, large numbers of native people were captured and sent in slave ships to Panama and Peru. By the third quarter of the sixteenth century, the coastal lowlands adjacent to the Gulf of Fonseca had been virtually depopulated. The various indigenous peoples had been reduced to remnant populations, most of whom were forcibly resettled in reservations in the southern Honduran highlands.

At the same time, Spanish land grants apportioned the fertile, lowland areas of the Gulf of Fonseca among Spanish conquistadors and Catholic religious orders. These large landowners quickly established ranching (cattle and mules) as the major economic activity in the region. The labor on these large haciendas was supplied by the few remaining indigenous peoples and later by poor peasants. The Spaniards also expropriated the indigenous salt-making operations for their own use. The growing number of silver and gold mines started by the Spaniards required a constant supply of meat, leather bags, tallow candles, and other goods. The cattle, mules, salt, and other agricultural commodities produced in the lowlands were transported to the mines in the highlands or exported by ships to other parts of the expanding Spanish empire. One result of the decimation of the indigenous peoples in a context of expanding mining and ranching was a labor shortage. To meet labor demands, hacienda and mine owners in southern Honduras, as well as in much of the rest of Spanish Central America, began importing labor to meet growing needs. The result of the combination of the rapid demise of the indigenous peoples and the need to bring in others to meet the labor needs of the mines and haciendas is evident today in the makeup of Central America's contemporary population. Central American ladinos, as they are called, are a genetic and ethnic mix of indigenous,

Spanish, African, Middle Eastern, and other ancestry. This diversity is apparent in the physical appearance of the ladino population of southern Honduras, as well as in most of the rest of Central America. Currently, approximately 600,000 people live in southern Honduras, about 10% of the total population of Honduras. At the time of the last population census (1988), 75% of the residents of the region lived in rural areas, and the remaining 25% lived in the major regional urban centers of Choluteca, San Lorenzo, and Nacaome. The vast majority of the region's rural and urban inhabitants are ladinos.

The Setting

The artisanal fisherfolk of the Gulf of Fonseca live in a region that is classified as southern Honduras. This region usually is delineated on the basis of a combination of geopolitical and environmental boundaries: on the north by a portion of the Central American Antilles chain of mountains, on the south by the Gulf of Fonseca, on the west by the Rio Goascoran which forms the national border with El Salvador, and on the east by the Rio Negro which constitutes part of the political departments (similar to states in the United States) of Choluteca and Valle. The two departments of Choluteca and Valle are divided into twenty-five smaller geopolitical units called municipalities (similar to counties in the United States). Each of these municipalities is divided into smaller towns and hamlets. All three of the region's largest urban centers are located in the lowlands near the coast.

Southern Honduras is a triangular-shaped region covering approximately 6,000 km² (2,300 miles²) in the southern part of the country along the Gulf of Fonseca. It is located primarily in tropical dry and subtropical moist forest zones in the Pacific watershed of Central America. The area that borders the Gulf of Fonseca is covered by a band of mangrove and marsh grass. Beyond the mangrove forests lies one of the few broad plains on the Pacific Coast of Central America. This savanna gives way to steep foothills which quickly become the jagged mountain ranges to the northeast that make up about 60% of the region. Few of these volcanic mountains reach altitudes of more than 1,600 meters (5,250 feet), but they are extremely rugged and fashion innumerable segregated valleys. The region is marked by a distinct dry and rainy season with unpredictable precipitation patterns and soils that are prone to erosion. Consequently, agriculture is very risky, and the area is highly vulnerable to environmental degradation.

Honduras shares political jurisdiction of the Gulf of Fonseca with Nicaragua and El Salvador where the shrimp farming industry is expanding rapidly. There has been little research on the physical and biological characteristics of the gulf, and the lack of reliable information has been a critical factor in resolving recent conflicts. Because it is a large shallow depression, it is vulnerable to both pollution and siltation. The coastline is dominated by approximately 50,000 hectares (123,500 acres) of mangrove wetlands that are fed by five major river systems. The biologically diverse mangrove ecosystems have many important ecological functions: they provide habitats, especially nursery areas for aquatic and terrestrial species; they protect coastlines from inundation and contain sediment to form new land; and they are an important stopover for an uncounted number of migratory birds. During the rainy season, the extensive mudflats form temporary shallow lakes which sustain large populations of fish and shellfish that are harvested by local inhabitants primarily for domestic consumption. The suitability of this region for industrial shrimp farming has led to a largely uncontrolled conversion of mudflats and mangroves, as well as some agricultural lands, into shrimp ponds in recent years.

Traditional Subsistence Strategies

Coastal communities vary considerably, with members of some communities more dependent on income from fishing than from agriculture. In other communities, fishing and agricultural activities are more in balance while in still others agriculture is more important. The economic livelihood strategies of households share a great deal with the survival strategies of peasants living in predominantly agricultural communities of southern Honduras: they are extremely diversified, flexible, dependent on cash remittances, and they can shift among economic resources in response to changing market conditions and resource availability. Most households integrate subsistence and wage activities by combining fishing, small-scale agriculture, gathering wild foods from coastal wetlands, and doing wage work (e.g., as hired laborers for their more affluent neighbors, as larva gatherers or laborers for the shrimp farms, or as workers in the shrimp processing plants). Although some shared labor occurs within communities, it generally takes place within extended families. Households also earn income by cutting mangrove for fuelwood and charcoal, producing salt, extracting bark for tannin, and collecting turtle eggs, mollusks, and crabs.

Social and Political Organization

Because the coastal areas of southern Honduras' mangroves, mudflats, estuaries, and seasonal lagoons were unsuitable for the large-scale cultivation of cotton, sugarcane, pasture, or other commercial crops, they were not valued highly by outsiders or violently contested until the shrimp industry began to boom. Until then, the Honduran state (the legal owner of the coastal wetlands) allowed local people access to much of the zone. Compared to agricultural areas, the coast remained less densely settled until poor families, dislocated first by the expansion of cotton in lowland areas and later by beef cattle (in lowland, foothill, and highland areas), began migrating to the coast in the late 1950s. Families settling in existing communities or starting new ones survived by exploiting the wetlands. They cleared adjacent areas to cultivate crops but depended as well on fish, shrimp, shellfish, animals, and wood gathered from the surrounding common resource areas. By 1990 about 110,000 people lived in the rural areas of the municipalities bordering the Gulf of Fonseca, including an estimated 2,000 artisanal fishers and an additional 5,000 individuals who apportioned their time between fishing and small-scale agriculture.[2]

The vast majority of artisanal fisherfolk are ladinos and share many social characteristics with ladinos and mestizos living elsewhere throughout Central America. They are intimately connected to Honduras and the wider world economically, socially, and politically. Diversification characterizes even the smallest communities. Families engage in a wide range of monetary and non-monetary income-generating activities as discussed above. There is a fair range in wealth as measured in terms of ownership of land, animals, boats, and other fishing equipment as well as in income and human well-being (nutrition and health). Extended families often share their labor in order to complete necessary work in agriculture, fishing, construction, child care, and other household tasks. Virtually all families have family members (men, women, and older children) who have migrated outside of their home communities in search of work. The remittances sent by these migrants are very important to the survival of the families remaining within the communities. Coastal residents belong to a number of clubs or voluntary associations including women's groups and religious organizations. The most important of these groups is the Committee for the Defense and Development of the Flora and Fauna of the Gulf of Fonseca (CODDEF-FAGOLF).

Religion and World View

Diversity in religion and religious views also characterizes the people of southern Honduras including those who live in coastal areas. Since the 1960s, southern Honduras has been the site of several efforts made by the liberal wing of the Roman Catholic Church within the rubric of "liberation theology." These efforts have included supporting peasant and workers organizations and maintaining a radio school that broadcasts information to the people of the south. Liberation theology asserts that the Church should maintain an activist political role, intervening to promote economic equity and social justice and to curb human rights abuses. Not surprisingly, southern Honduras has been the site of numerous peasant movements and protests. While many inhabitants continue to belong to the Roman Catholic Church, a growing number of coastal residents have joined a number of evangelical Protestant churches in recent years. The position taken by these

Jorge Varela Marquez (center) and CODDEFFAGOLF supporters. Courtesy of Jorge Varela Marquez.

more conservative movements is that religion should concentrate on spiritual aspects and not be politicized.

THREATS TO SURVIVAL

Recent Events and Conditions

The environment of southern Honduras and the Gulf of Fonseca have provided ample natural resources for large numbers of indigenous peoples. Yet today, the United Nations has designated southern Honduras a "critically endangered region," an area where basic life-support systems, including water and soils, are in jeopardy. Deforestation, erosion, deterioration of watersheds, the indiscriminate use of agricultural pesticides, and overgrazing have transformed the southern Honduran landscape. The region's ladino inhabitants, among the poorest in Latin America, also are at risk. Recent nutritional assessments conclude that 65% of the children under five years of age and 37% of first graders suffer from moderate to severe undernutrition. Recently, too, the region has been the site of significant, sometimes fierce, conflicts stemming from the explosive growth of the shrimp-farming industry in the coastal wetlands along the Gulf of Fonseca. On one side of the struggle are the powerful shrimp-farming interests who stress the economic benefits of the expanding industry. On the other

side of the controversy are artisanal fishers, fisher-farmers, other rural people, and environmentalists responding to the diminished access to natural
resources vital to rural livelihoods and the environmental destruction aris-
ing from the largely unregulated growth of the industry.

Central to the environmental and social transformation of southern Honduras has been the loss of common pool resources. Especially significant
has been the post–World War II period during which the Honduran government, with the assistance of international donor and lending institutions,
promoted a series of agricultural commodities for the global market—principally cotton, sugarcane, and beef cattle. By the 1960s, growing human
impoverishment and environmental destruction provoked extensive migration from the south to urban centers, to coastal zones within the region,
and to the tropical humid forests in the northeastern portion of the country.
Recently, economic development efforts have focused on the production of
nontraditional agricultural exports (especially melons and cultured shrimp).
By 1987 shrimp (most cultivated on farms along the Gulf of Fonseca) had
become Honduras' third highest source of foreign exchange after bananas
and coffee. Although the industry has provided an important source of
export earnings, created a limited (and highly contested) number of pre-
dominately temporary jobs, and stimulated the start-up of related businesses, the industry also has significantly restricted access to the south's
remaining common pool resources: coastal wetlands, fisheries, and water.

Expansion of the Honduran Shrimp Industry

Aquaculture, the cultivation or farming of aquatic species, includes both
plants, such as various seaweeds, and animals, including such species as
salmon, carp, mussels, tilapia, and many others. Recently, aquaculture has
been hailed as the Blue Revolution—a crucial means to meet the food needs
of the growing human population of the world. Globally, among the most
commercially important species farmed are several kinds of shrimp, carnivorous species that are cultivated using industrial methods in tropical coastal
zones of Asia, Latin America, and Africa. While almost all cultured shrimp
are raised in poor, Third World, or developing countries, virtually all these
shrimp are exported to rich industrial countries including the United States,
Western Europe, and Japan. Currently about one-third of global shrimp
production comes from farms (the rest are captured by boats), but it is
likely that within the next few years, most of the shrimp consumed in the
world will be farmed. The fact that most shrimp is farmed in poor countries
and then exported to rich countries has raised serious concerns about the
extent to which shrimp aquaculture (or shrimp farming) can improve the
diets and nutritional status of the world's poor. An additional nutritional
concern comes from the fact that most commercial shrimp feed pellets contain a large percentage of fishmeal. Most fishmeal is composed of cheap

(low-value), less commercially desirable species such as anchovies—precisely the less-expensive species of fish that are consumed by the poor. Using cheap fish to produce fishmeal that is fed to expensive (high-value) species such as shrimp, in effect, puts the poor in competition with shrimp for these low-value species.

Shrimp Farms Are Aquatic Feedlots

Industrial shrimp farms can be seen as aquatic feedlots—water-based equivalents of the industrial feedlots in which cattle, pigs, and chickens are raised. As in those kinds of operations, juvenile shrimp, collected from the wild or purchased from hatcheries, are placed in grow-out ponds where they are fattened with commercial feeds. When the shrimp reach the desired size and maturity they are harvested, processed, packaged, and exported. Shrimp farming has environmental problems parallel to those of other kinds of industrial livestock-feeding operations.

The basic pattern of shrimp pond development for the semi-intensive systems of production that predominate in Honduras requires the excavation of a shallow depression varying from 1.0 to 1.5 meters (3 to 4.5 feet) in depth. The excavated material is used to form a low earth dike around the pond. The pond is linked to the ocean or a brackish estuary by a shallow canal that leads to sluice gates in the dike that permit water to flow into and out of the pond at high tide. Diesel-powered pumps are frequently incorporated into the design when adjustments in the salinity levels in the pond are required. Construction is usually done with bulldozers, and some of the channel digging is done with dragline cranes.

Shrimp farms vary from extensive, through semi-intensive, to superintensive systems of production. In extensive systems, an enclosure is built close to the sea often by damming a seasonal lagoon. Tidal flows into and out of the enclosure provide stocking of shrimp, feed, and water exchange. The semi-intensive systems that predominate in Honduras and the intensive systems that prevail in much of Asia function more or less as forms of brackish water feedlots for shrimp. In the Honduran semi-intensive systems, shrimp postlarvae, produced in hatcheries or captured, are stocked in ponds where the water has been fertilized to create an algal bloom. The water in the ponds is aerated to maintain dissolved oxygen and replaced regularly to prevent the buildup of metabolic wastes. The shrimp are fed formulated diets made from imported commercial feed to produce rapid growth. In the tropics of Asia and Latin America, where most shrimp are farmed, two crops per year are possible in such ponds. The fattened shrimp are then cleaned, deheaded (for export to the United States), and packed for export either on the farms or in one of the regional packing plants.

Environmental and Social Problems Associated with Shrimp Farming

Currently, Honduras ranks after Ecuador and Mexico in the production and export of cultured shrimp from Latin America. All shrimp farming in Honduras is located in the southern region along the Gulf of Fonseca, one of the most environmentally degraded and most impoverished regions of the country. Although the first shrimp farm in southern Honduras was constructed in the early 1970s, it was only in the 1980s that the industry began to expand significantly. By 1998 approximately 14,000 hectares (34,600 acres) of primarily semi-intensive shrimp farms existed in southern Honduras; approximately 70% of them were located on government-leased concessions of national land rather than on private property. Although about ninety farms operate in the country, various factors have led to the exclusion of small farmers from the shrimp-farming industry and the domination of the industry by a few firms. Most of these large firms are part of vertically integrated international companies that include feed mills, hatcheries, processing plants, and worldwide marketing. The two largest firms in southern Honduras account for about half the total area in production in the country as well as the majority of exports. The largest enterprise, Grupo Granjas Marinas (Sea Farms Group), is an international company that ranks among the largest shrimp-farming operations in the world with production from 6,500 hectares (16,000 acres) that accounts for 60% of the cultivated shrimp exports from Honduras. The second largest integrated shrimp farm in Honduras is Grupo Deli with 700 hectares (1,700 acres) of ponds that average 20 hectares (50 acres) each.[3] According to the southern Honduras Chamber of Commerce, the shrimp industry provides employment to 11,900 people through commercial farms, six packing plants, and ice-making operations. These employment figures, however, are hotly disputed by local people and other critics of the industry.

Faced with chronic economic crises in the 1980s, the Honduran government began encouraging investment in the industry with the support of international development organizations, including the World Bank and the United States Agency for International Development (USAID). Through its concession process, the government began granting rights over state-owned coastal land to investors, thereby supplanting the previous claims of traditional, communal users. Renewable concessions are leased to individuals or corporations for twenty-five years at the ridiculously low cost of about U.S. $4–5 per year. Concessions cannot be legally transferred or sold, but entrepreneurs have circumvented the law by remaining minority investors in new farms, and they have established a black market for leaseholds which has stimulated land speculation. Despite the low cost of leases, their lack of political power to influence the award of concessions (along with the high costs of farm construction and maintenance, lack of technical assistance, insufficient credit opportunities, and high interest rates) has impeded the entry of small producers, agrarian reform cooperatives, and poor coastal communities into the industry. Although concessions confer only use rights, investors treat their holdings much like private property. Repeating past "enclosure movements" in which small farmers were evicted from good agricultural land, often violently and with the help of local authorities, concession holders exclude others by means of armed guards, barbed-wire fencing, and no-trespassing signs. Over 25,000 hectares (61,750 acres) have been leased through concessions, although more than half the area remains undeveloped. Estimates of mangrove loss due directly to the construction of shrimp farms range from about 2,000 to 4,000 hectares (5,000 to 10,000 acres), while the remainder of shrimp farms have been constructed on mudflats and lagoons. Since World War II, half the gulf's mangrove areas have been destroyed, and if conservation policies are not put in place, estimates are that all the mangroves will be gone within twenty years.

While areas in mangrove and mudflats have the most clearly designated property rights under the concession process, activities affecting estuaries take place under a largely unregulated open access system. Seed to stock shrimp ponds comes either from captured wild shrimp postlarvae or (increasingly) from hatchery-produced seed. From 1,500 to 3,000 larva gatherers trawl the coastal estuaries in boats or on foot collecting shrimp postlarvae in nets. They work individually or in teams under a variety of contractual arrangements. Some are paid on a piece rate while others receive a wage from labor contractors. Larva collecting does provide a source of employment, but it also entails environmental costs. Even though these costs are poorly understood, artisanal fishers assert that their catches have fallen since the larva gathering began. This may be due to the loss of by-catch: an estimated five other organisms die for each shrimp larva that is captured. Significant environmental costs in estuarine areas also include declining water quality from farm effluent that contains high organic loads. Several farms usually recycle water from the same estuary among themselves—the waste water pumped from one farm is the source of water repumped into adjacent ponds. Degraded water quality affects not only the sustainability of the shrimp farms and the livelihoods of artisanal estuarine fishers but also myriad other aquatic organisms.

All of these circumstances have contributed to reductions in the sources of food and income for gulf fisherfolk and, for many, the loss of an ancestral home and way of life. By privatizing former common pool resource areas, the industry's expansion has converted biodiverse, multiple-use habitats to mono-crop, single-user habitats. Artisanal people are forced to go elsewhere to seek other kinds of wage work or resource-extractive activities, or they are pushed into smaller fishing areas, increasing the competition among themselves. In some cases, the problem is that of access to fishing sites. The access problem is partly due to the fact that shrimp farmers have rarely left buffer zones around their operations, leaving shrimp ponds whose perimeters are immediately adjacent to estuaries, vulnerable to robbery. This situation has provided a basis for some shrimp farmers to consider all fisherfolk who pass near to their property as potential thieves. According to the executive committee of the CODDEFFAGOLF,

The artisanal fishermen cannot tranquilly move through the estuaries and mangroves where they once found their sustenance, because the shrimp farmers have not only appropriated the grounds of their concessions, but also the surroundings. With the complicity of all our governmental system, we have given the patrimony of our people over to a select few national citizens and foreigners, and we have taken away the very medium for subsistence for thousands of people.[4]

The insistence of artisanal fishers on their rights to use the estuaries, as well as the insistence of shrimp farmers to patrol those estuaries with security forces, has resulted in tragedy for some fishing families. On the evening of October 4, 1997, two fishermen, Israel Ortiz Avila, thirty years old, and Marín Zeledonio Alvarado, twenty-eight years old, were fishing in the Todo Mundo estuary, adjacent to CRISUR shrimp, which is established within the Las Iguanas wildlife refuge. According to a witness, the two men were trapped, tied up, and tortured by shrimp guards. In the early morning hours of the next day, the two men's bodies were deposited by the owner of the shrimp farm at the entrance to Guipo, the town where the men lived. They had been shot at gunpoint. Immediately after the incident, before any investigation had taken place, the National Aquaculture Association of Honduras (ANDAH) defended the killings, implying that the fishermen were thieves. Ortiz's widow pleaded, "If they were thieves, why were they killed? Why were their bodies dumped here in our town, rather than left at the scene for an investigation? What is the code of ethics of ANDAH?" In total, between 1988 and 1997, at least nine fishermen who were active in a regional fishermen's alliance have been murdered. Their cases have been reported to national and international human rights organizations. To date, there have been no prosecutions of any of those responsible for the fishermen's deaths, but the law has not been lenient in disciplining several individuals accused of stealing shrimp from farms. They received penalties of more than five years in jail.

RESPONSE: STRUGGLES TO SURVIVE CULTURALLY

The Evolution of Organized Resistance

Southern Honduras has been the site of several peasant movements that have resisted the loss of common pool resources associated with the earlier spread of the cotton, sugar, and beef cattle industries. In response to the current promotion of shrimp farming, poor people from coastal communities founded their own resistance movement, the grassroots Committee for the Defense and Development of the Flora and Fauna of the Gulf of Fonseca (CODDEFFAGOLF) in 1988. In contrast to past peasant movements, the members have successfully received the backing of an extensive global network including the public, the press, and international organizations of environmental and social activists. It remains to be seen whether this support will significantly enhance the ability of local people to have a voice in the development plans for the Gulf of Fonseca or amplify their access to crucial coastal resources in light of the influential groups actively opposing their goals.

The name of the ecological grassroots alliance formed by coastal fisherfolk and peasants is a mouthful, but it says something important. The participants do not believe it is possible to *defend* the environment without also *developing* the resources that allow people to survive. From a base of dozens of village-level informal associations, comprising over 5,000 fisherfolk and peasants, CODDEFFAGOLF has become one of the strongest environmental organizations in Central America today. It has instituted a variety of programs in training and technical assistance, institutional development, environmental education, and improved production projects for artisanal communities. However, the shrimp industry is of paramount concern because it is considered the greatest single factor affecting the marine waters and coastal zone, as well as the human and environmental rights of the gulf's artisanal fishers. In addressing the shrimp industry, the gulf's artisanal movement draws on a long history of peasant organizing in Honduras, in which landless peasants have occupied large landholdings and, as a people, have demanded some redistribution of land ownership to procure the basic human rights of livelihood and physical survival. Like the environmental movements of the poor in various regions of the world, CODDEFFAGOLF's goals are equal parts justice and ecology.

The organization began by providing workshops by, and for, fisherfolk about the ecological principles of their marine environment. The workshops were conducted jointly by university-trained marine biologists and artisanal fisherfolk who had long-term experience fishing in the gulf and intimate knowledge of local flora and fauna. Aimed at helping artisanal people improve sustainable practices in a heavily pressured gulf environment, the workshops also became an important place for people to discuss how to understand and respond to social justice and environmental concerns about the expansion of industrial shrimp farming. From this beginning, the role of CODDEFFAGOLF has evolved into a complex mixture of direct, nonviolent action, negotiation, dialogue, and participation in governmental efforts to resolve resource problems and conflicts in the Gulf of Fonseca.

In 1991 CODDEFFAGOLF took its complaints and proposals to the

National Congress in Tegucigalpa, the Honduran capital, and hundreds of artisanal people marched in front of the Presidential Palace. Other direct actions began to take place locally, including blocking access to shrimp farms, destroying fences and surveillance stations, blocking major highways, and burning the nets used to collect juvenile shrimp. Major efforts being made by CODDEFFAGOLF are to educate its members about national laws and regulations and to provide information that may affect artisanal people through meetings and its newsletter. Up and down the coast, CODDEFFAGOLF has created an active network of local residents who report illegal mangrove clearing and harassment and assassinations of fisherfolk to local and national authorities. They also bring these incidents to light to a growing international and transnational network of supporters.

The Global Context

Despite their conflicts with shrimp farmers, CODDEFFAGOLF does not lay all the blame at their feet or just blame the Honduran government. Rather, CODDEFFAGOLF has targeted international financial institutions and development agencies, foreign investors, and consumers in its efforts to alter the wider processes that bear upon local people in the Gulf of Fonseca. Such processes include structural adjustment policies promoted by the International Monetary Fund. In addition, shrimp farmers are often faced with difficult decisions because, in order to satisfy investors and compete successfully in international markets, long-term environmental considerations are sacrificed. CODDEFFAGOLF's response has been to increase the awareness of international financial institutions and consumers about the serious social and ecological costs of producing and eating shrimp, costs that are being paid by local people, some with their lives.

In addition, CODDEFFAGOLF has tried to influence multilateral agreements and institutions such as the United Nations Convention on Biological Diversity (UNCBD), the UN Commission for Sustainable Development (UNCSD), and the UN Food and Agriculture Organization (UNFAO) to exert pressure on the government and industry of Honduras. For example, the UNFAO Code of Conduct for Responsible Fisheries states in article 6, clause 18,

Recognizing the important contributions of artisanal and small-scale fisheries to employment, income and food security, States should appropriately protect the rights of fishers and fishworkers, particularly those engaged in subsistence, small-scale and artisanal fisheries, to a secure and just livelihood, as well as preferential access, where appropriate, to traditional fishing grounds and resources in the waters under their national jurisdiction.[5]

In order to better accomplish these goals, CODDEFFAGOLF has acquired international partners, including environmental and development organizations in the United States, Canada, and Europe. Moreover, Honduran activists also have reached across political, cultural, language, and geographical barriers to link with other grassroots organizations in other tropical countries in Asia, Africa, and elsewhere in Latin America where shrimp farming also is expanding. In fact, CODDEFFAGOLF has played an important role in facilitating the development of a global network, the Industrial Shrimp Action Network (ISA-Net), which formally emerged in 1997 to link people and organizations in over sixty nations. Organizations in many countries have seen a critical need for international solidarity for two reasons: to strengthen one another's local or national struggles and to cooperate in addressing the global aspects of industrial aquaculture. In 1997 CODDEFFAGOLF called for a worldwide moratorium on the expansion of industrial shrimp farming:

With much respect, we suggest a moment of reflection and more time to investigate and develop mitigation measurements that could convert this industry into an activity more appreciated by the local communities.[6]

The Bioregional Context

CODDEFFAGOLF has participated actively in international efforts to create coordination and cooperation among the national governments and resource users of all three countries that border the Gulf of Fonseca. One important focus has been the Tri-Partite Commission, an advisory body of government officials from Nicaragua, El Salvador, and Honduras, along with representatives of development institutions, shrimp farmers, and organizations such as CODDEFFAGOLF. Some positive changes have resulted from the bioregional approach, mainly in ecological matters. One example is the research on water quality which is financed by USAID. CODDEFFAGOLF participated in the PROARCA-COSTAS project in Central America, an ecosystem management effort that includes the Gulf of Fonseca, which is being funded and developed by USAID, the World Wildlife Fund, the Nature Conservancy, and the University of Rhode Island.

The National Context

The Honduran artisanal movement in the gulf represents neither a local withdrawal from the Honduran nation nor an effort merely to bypass or replace the national arena with that of the international or global arena. In many ways, the struggles of artisanal people may be seen as an effort to increase their voices and rights as national citizens. CODDEFFAGOLF has claimed a place at the national "table" as a protagonist in the sustainable national development of the country and frequently explains its activities in terms of national interests. In the struggle for equal footing, CODDEFFAGOLF has sought a dialogue with shrimp farmers individually and through the national shrimp aquaculture association, ANDAH. Subsequent to a 1996 ISA-Net meeting held in Choluteca, Honduras, and a mass protest staged in Tegucigalpa in 1997, the government of Honduras has twice decreed an annual moratorium on the expansion of shrimp farming, which was supported by many shrimp farmers, though not all.

In 1998 a precedent was set when CODDEFFAGOLF and ANDAH cooperated in producing feasibility studies for a series of protected areas in the Gulf of Fonseca. In October 1998, the Honduran government approved a plan to implement the protected areas, placing more than 75,000 hectares of wetlands in the Gulf of Fonseca under different categories of management, according to the nomenclature developed by an international scientific nongovernmental organization (NGO), the International Union for the Conservation of Nature (IUCN). The Declaration for the Protected Areas aimed to increase the control of all gulf-based industries including shrimp farms, fisheries, and others. As one member of CODDEFFAGOLF stated recently, "An important issue for all of us is having sincerity in the dialogue, and concerted efforts by CODDEFFAGOLF and ANDAH. . . . This isn't the end of the problem but it might be the beginning of the end."

FOOD FOR THOUGHT

The shrimp aquaculture industry has brought with it economic growth for a relatively small sector of the Honduran national society. It has also made a very important contribution to the financial needs of the debt-ridden Honduran government. It has benefited foreign investors. Consumers have benefited from the increasingly cheaper prices of shrimp that have been created by international growth and competition in the shrimp aquaculture industry. However, CODDEFFAGOLF argues that the shrimp aquaculture industry has not created real development in the coastal communities because of the excessive stimuli to production and commercialization at the expense of local livelihoods and the environment. While shrimp aquaculture is the most important industry that affects the marine waters and coastal zone, other traditional activities have negative impacts: salt production, the collection of firewood, artisanal fishing, urban pollution, and the production of other agricultural commodities such as cotton, melons, and cattle. As shrimp farmers have rightfully pointed out, everyone affects the environment to some degree.

One response to try to reduce the environmental and social harms taking place through initiatives to certify products that are produced with agreed standards for ecological and sometimes also social practices. This way, consumers have the opportunity to use their buying power to discourage destructively produced products and to encourage those that have a more positive impact on people and environment. Ranging across a broad array of goods and institutions around the world, such efforts include the organic food movement in the United States and tropical timber certification by such organizations as the Forest Stewardship Council. One difficulty encountered in applying the certification concept to shrimp products is that the place of origin and method of the production of shrimp are rarely identified in grocery stores or restaurants, although this is changing in some stores. Still, a variety of institutions are now rushing in to acquire the right to "green" shrimp aquaculture, including the Marine Stewardship Council (a partnership of the World Wildlife Fund and Unilever, the world's largest seafood company). The Global Aquaculture Alliance, an international association of shrimp producers, also is considering a program to identify "responsibly" produced shrimp for consumers. Other corporations have simply placed their shrimp products in "green" packaging, packaging that claims that their products are produced in an environmentally friendly way. However, to date, none of these efforts have included an independent (noncorporate) review that takes into account local people, such as the Gulf of Fonseca fisherfolk, who are directly impacted by shrimp aquaculture operations.

This chapter points to the complexity of causes and local responses to the life and death problems that are faced by local fisherfolk in southern Honduras. Some might argue that artisanal fisherpeople have become an anachronism in the modern world—they persist in a way of life that is antiquated, inefficient, strenuous, and rapidly vanishing. On the other hand, the prehistory of the Gulf of Fonseca suggests that the natural resources of the region are sufficient to sustain a large number of human inhabitants using relatively simple agricultural and fishing technologies that do not permanently degrade the environment or natural resource base. Shrimp farming is just the most recent example of the kind of export-oriented production that has degraded the environment of southern Honduras while also impoverishing local people.

Questions

1. Do you think there is a place in the modern world and the global economic system for artisanal fisherfolk such as those of the Gulf of Fonseca?
2. Do you think it is possible for shrimp farmers and other artisanal fisherfolk to solve jointly the environmental and social problems discussed in this chapter?
3. What are the social and environmental consequences of your last shrimp dinner? What can you do to ensure that your decision to eat shrimp does not destroy

the environment or the lives and livelihoods of local people in Honduras and elsewhere?

4. Consider the role that CODDEFFAGOLF has played in attempting to solve the environmental and social problems associated with industrial shrimp farming. Can you think of any similar examples of this kind of involvement by environmental organizations in your community, or state, or country?

5. Do you think that shrimp farmers should be allowed to "self-police" their industry and even to certify that the shrimp they produce is environmentally friendly and socially sound?

NOTES

Unless otherwise noted, the data and statistics included in this chapter are based on information in the following published materials: Susan C. Stonich, "*I Am Destroying the Land!*" *The Political Ecology of Poverty and Environmental Destruction in Honduras* (Boulder, Colo.: Westview Press, 1993); Susan C. Stonich, "Reclaiming the Commons: Grassroots Resistance and Retaliation in Honduras," *Cultural Survival Quarterly* 20, no. 1 (1996): 31–35.

1. Statement by the executive committee of CODDEFFAGOLF, 1996.

2. Denise Stanley, "Explaining Persistent Conflict Among Resource Users: The Case of Honduran Mariculture," *Society and Natural Resources* 11, no. 3 (1998): 267–78.

3. Bob Rosenberry, *World Shrimp Farming 1998* (San Diego, Calif.: Shrimp News International, 1998).

4. Statement by the executive committee of CODDEFFAGOLF, 1997.

5. Food and Agriculture Organization of the United Nations, *Code of Conduct for Responsible Fisheries* Rome: FAO, 1995.

6. CODDEFFAGOLF, *Bulletin Informativo #36* (San Lorenzo: CODDEFFAGOLF, 1997).

RESOURCE GUIDE

Published Literature

Bailey, Conner, Svein Jentoft, and Peter Sinclair. *Aquacultural Development: Social Dimensions of an Emerging Industry.* Boulder, Colo.: Westview Press, 1996.

Bardach, John E., (ed.) *Sustainable Aquaculture.* New York: John Wiley & Sons, 1997.

Stanley, Denise. "David and Goliath: Fishermen Conflicts with Maricultralists in Honduras." In *Green Guerillas: Environmental Conflicts and Initiatives in Latin America and the Caribbean,* edited by Helen Collinson. Montreal and New York: Black Rose Books, 1997.

Stonich, Susan C. "*I Am Destroying the Land!*" *The Political Ecology of Poverty and Environmental Destruction in Honduras.* Boulder, Colo.: Westview Press, 1993.

———. "Reclaiming the Commons: Grassroots Resistance and Retaliation in Honduras." *Cultural Survival Quarterly* 20, no. 1 (1996): 31–35.

Stonich, Susan C., John Bort, and Luis Ovares. "Globalization of Shrimp Mariculture: The Impact on Social Justice and Environmental Quality in Central America." *Society and Natural Resources* 10, no. 2 (1997): 161–79.

WWW Sites

Many of the groups involved in the debate over industrial shrimp farming maintain WWW sites. The following list includes the most important (but certainly not all of these sites). Most of the following sites include links to hundreds of other sites on shrimp farming and related topics.

Aquaculture Magazine Online
http://www.aquaculturemag.com/

CODDEFFAGOLF
http://coddeffagolf.org

Earth Summit Watch: The Shrimp Sentinel
http://www.earthsummitwatch.org/shrimp/index.html

Global Aquaculture Alliance
http://www.gaalliance.org

The Industrial Shrimp Action Network (ISA-Net)
http://www.shrimpaction.org
email: *isanet@shrimpaction.org*

International Center of Aquaculture and Aquatic Environments, Auburn University, Auburn, See Pond Dynamics Honduras
http://www.ag.auburn.edu/dept/faa/pdhond.html

Mangrove Action Project—see projects list, Earth Island Institute
http://www.earthisland.org/

Mangrove Web Sites—a selection of useful web sites dealing with mangrove ecosystems and other tropical wetlands
http://www.ncl.ac.uk/tcmweb/tcm/mglinks.htm

The National Fisheries Institute (USA)
http://www.nfi.org/

NGO Statement Concerning Unsustainable Aquaculture to the United Nations Commission on Sustainable Development, May 1996
http://darwin.bio.uci.edu/~sustain/shrimpecos/declare2.html

Third World Network
http://www.twnside.org.sg/

Chapter 5

The English-Speaking Bay Islanders
Susan C. Stonich

Our children are our most important resource.
—Statement by the Native Bay Islanders Professionals
and Labourers Association, 1995[1]

CULTURAL OVERVIEW

The People

Although politically part of Hispanic, Spanish-speaking Honduras, the Bay Islands, with their predominantly Afro-Caribbean population, are one of the English-speaking enclaves in the western Caribbean region. Over the last several centuries, the Bay Islanders have attempted to maintain cultural, social, and economic ties with other English-speaking enclaves, especially British Honduras (now Belize), the Cayman Islands, and the United States. They also have successfully retained their use of the English language and have adhered to their Protestant religions. Through these means, the Bay Islanders isolated themselves fairly successfully from Honduran influences even after Great Britain returned sovereignty of the islands to Honduras through the Wykes-Cruz treaty in 1859. Following four centuries of Anglo-Hispanic conflict in the western Caribbean region, the current efforts of the Honduran government to promote international tourism on the islands is the most recent attempt to integrate the islands into the Honduran nation's economy, society, and culture.

Several distinct groups have occupied the Bay Islands at one time or another: pre-Columbian indigenous peoples—most likely the Paya, a group that also lived on the Honduran mainland; Spanish soldiers, pirates, and agriculturalists; English buccaneers, sailors, and farmers; Garifuna (Black

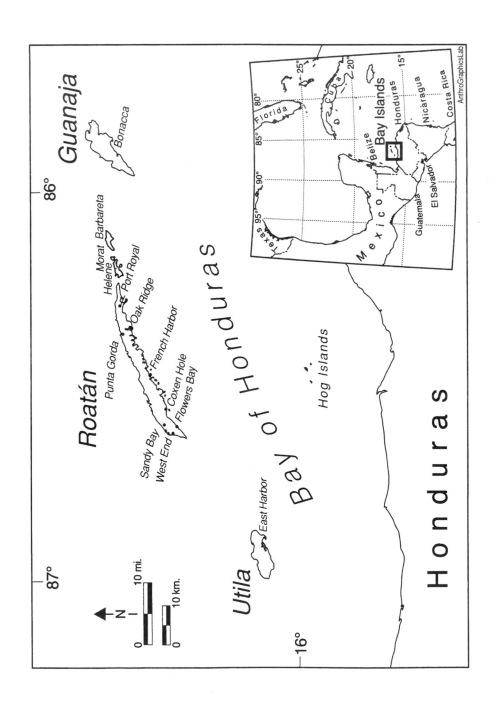

Guanaja

Bonacca

Roatán

Punta Gorda
Sandy Bay
West End
Morat Barbareta
Helene
Port Royal
Oak Ridge
French Harbor
Coxen Hole
Flowers Bay

86°

87°

16°

Utila
East Harbor

Bay of Honduras

Hog Islands

Honduras

N

10 mi.
0
10 km.
0

Bay Islands

Florida
Cuba
Belize
Honduras
Nicaragua
Costa Rica
Mexico
Guatemala
El Salvador
Texas

80°
85°
90°
95°
25°
20°
15°

AnthroGraphicsLab

Caribs) from the island of Saint Vincent in the eastern Caribbean who were marooned on Roatán by the British in 1797; Anglo-Caribbeans and Afro-Caribbeans from the Caymans and Belize who migrated to the islands starting in the 1830s; North American adventurers, fugitives, tourists, and retirees who began arriving around the turn of the twentieth century; Spanish-speaking ladinos (individuals with mixed ethnic and racial ancestry) from the mainland of Honduras whose migration from the mainland has accelerated over the last two decades; and various European adventurers, castaways, travelers, tourists, and investors.

Although the Bay Islands currently are characterized by an ethnically diverse population, until recently the majority of the residents of the islands were descendants of freed black slaves, an Afro-Caribbean people who immigrated to the Bay Islands from the Cayman Islands after slavery was outlawed in British colonies in 1837. Lighter-skinned Creole (persons of mixed African and European ancestry) plantation owners from the Caymans were the first to settle on the islands in anticipation of the repeal of slavery. Their former slaves followed, especially during the period between 1844 and 1858 when many existing towns on the islands were established. This dark-skinned Afro-Caribbean, English (and Creole) speaking population settled in strings of hamlets and small villages that hugged the western shoreline of Roatán, Morat, and Helene; their far less numerous, lighter-skinned former masters predominated in the larger towns of Coxen Hole and French Harbour. From that time to the present, considerable disparity in wealth, along with considerable racial prejudice, has persisted between the "white" Bay Islanders (who became the elite) and the majority of black Bay Islanders, who now refer to themselves as the English-speaking Bay Islanders.

The Setting

The Bay Islands are located about 50 kilometers (31 miles) off the northern coast of Honduras and are easily accessible from the mainland by plane or boat. Made up of eight islands and sixty-five cays, they have a total land area of approximately 258 square kilometers (about 92 square miles). The largest island is Roatán, which covers 127 square kilometers (49 square miles) and is the site of most of the tourism business, although tourism has grown significantly on the other islands in the last few years. A mountainous ridge, which runs the length of Roatán, abruptly ends at the coastline with steep slopes. Although Roatán boasts only a few palm-tree-skirted beaches, these beaches are spectacularly beautiful and provide ideal sites for swimming, snorkeling, and sunbathing. The islands' main international tourism attraction, however, is a coral reef that scuba divers place in the same class as the Great Barrier Reef of Australia. The reef provides critical habitats for numerous marine species and protects the shorelines from

Bay Islander children. Courtesy of Susan C. Stonich.

flooding. Although rainfall averages at least 200 centimeters (79 inches) per year on all the islands, most precipitation occurs during the rainy season, the fall and early winter of the Northern Hemisphere, especially October and November. The primary tourist season is during the dry season, from January through June, during which less than 10 centimeters (4 inches) of precipitation falls.

In addition to the captivating tropical beaches and spectacular coral reefs, reminders of the islands' exciting history are evident in ruins of pre-historic archaeological sites, pirate strongholds, English fortresses, under-water shipwrecks, and an ethnically diverse population. Together these attractions make the Bay Islands ideal for the most important types of international tourism currently promoted throughout Central America—sun, sea, and beach tourism; adventure and ecotourism; and cultural heri-tage tourism.

Traditional Subsistence Activities

It makes little sense to designate any set of economic activities of the Bay Islanders as traditional (unchanging since some bygone days) or as purely subsistence (produced only for consumption within the home or family). The Bay Islanders emerged during recent history and have always engaged in economic activities that provided cash income and goods for home consumption as well as for sale in the marketplace. At the time of the initial, modern settlement around the mid-1800s, when the Bay Islands were a colony of Great Britain, the economy of the islands has flourished. In addition to subsistence activities—farming, fishing, and turtling—the Bay Islanders have produced a growing quantity of commodities for sale and export including coconuts, coconut oil, bananas, fish, and yams. Most of these goods were shipped to the United States and Belize. After Great Britain relinquished control of the islands to Honduras in 1859, the export-oriented economy of the islands declined and was replaced by a greater overall economic dependence on the sea. The Bay Islanders became renowned for their prominence as merchant sailors and fishers. During the last thirty years, the Bay Islanders' economic survival has depended on their employment in the shrimping and lobster industries, on cruise ships, and most recently on the tourism industry.

Social and Political Organization

Until recently, social and political organization among the English-speaking Bay Islanders was confined for the most part to the level of the family. In general, the islands do not have a history of concerted efforts to organize and to establish local institutions, with the exception of the Protestant churches which continue to play an important part in community concerns. In part, this pattern is explained by the economic independence of families and the long absences of male family members because of their employment in various seafaring enterprises. Relying on incomes earned at sea demanded that men be away from home for long periods of time from a fairly early age. This, in turn, required that women assume most of the responsibilities connected with family and household, including child care, cleaning, cooking, washing, and making decisions regarding the day-to-day maintenance of the household. Lack of widespread, well-integrated organization beyond the level of the community may help explain the lack of organized response to recent efforts by the Honduran government to Hispanicize the islands and to promote tourism in ways that many Bay Islanders judge to be detrimental to their cultural and material survival.

Religion and World View

In addition to their devotion to the English language (rather than Spanish), the Bay Islanders' vigorous adherence to their Protestant faiths distinguishes them from their Spanish-speaking, predominantly Catholic counterparts on the Honduran mainland. Currently, Bay Islanders belong to a number of Protestant sects including Methodist, Baptist, Seventh Day Adventist, and Church of God. Their religions are very important to the Bay Islanders who view the influx of tourists as formidable threats to their basic values and beliefs. For example, most Bay Islanders abhor the sight of scantily clad tourists and have erected signs banning topless and nude bathing throughout the islands. They also fear that the increased accessibility and growing violence associated with the drug trade on the islands is negatively affecting their young people.

THREATS TO SURVIVAL

In late October 1998, Hurricane Mitch grew into a devastating hurricane with wind speeds in excess of 200 miles per hour and took deadly aim at Honduras. Described as the most destructive Atlantic hurricane in the last 200 years, it stalled with its eye over the Honduran Bay Islands for thirty-nine hours before it made landfall along the northern coast of Honduras. On the Bay Island of Guanaja, over which Hurricane Mitch directly hovered for almost two days, the destruction was overwhelming. Although the loss of human life was miraculously low, all the island's buildings were badly damaged or destroyed, and virtually all the island's vegetation was stripped away by the high winds and rain. Although Hurricane Mitch posed a serious threat to the Bay Islands, it is only one of the many dangers that have recently threatened the survival of the Bay Islands' people and natural environment. Most of these recent threats are linked to the explosive and largely unregulated growth of international tourism on the islands. Since the early 1980s, the number of international tourists who visit the islands has grown from a few thousand to 100,000 every year, making the Bay Islands the most important tourist destination within Honduras.

Honduras is one of the poorest countries in Latin America with more than 75% of its population living on less than U.S.$2 a day.[2] It also is among the Latin American countries with the greatest gap between rich and poor, the most unequal distribution of income and consumption, and the lowest levels of education and health. In order to try to improve the standard of living of its population, the government of Honduras has been promoting various economic development schemes over the last several decades. Since the early 1980s, one of the most important of these economic strategies has been the expansion of the international tourism industry. The particular focus of this strategy has been the pristine coral reefs, scenic beaches, and historical ruins of the Bay Islands. In the aftermath of Hurricane Mitch, the Honduran government has singled out the tourism industry as the major means of economic recovery and reconstruction and is accelerating its efforts to expand the industry.

We don't know where you came from . . . We don't know who you are . . . You have no history. (Honduran minister of culture, during a meeting with Bay Islanders in 1996)

This statement, made by the Honduran minister of culture, reflects the prevailing views held by Spanish-speaking Hondurans regarding Bay Islanders—that they are neither "Honduran" nor "indigenous." Although the government of Honduras is mandated by its constitution to protect the cultures of Honduras' indigenous peoples, the minister's statement implies that the government does not recognize that responsibility in the case of the Bay Islanders. If the minister is alluding to the non-Hispanic and non–Central American origin of the Bay Islanders, he is accurate, although it is quite incorrect to say that Bay Islanders have "no history." Like many peoples of the Caribbean, they are a mix of relocated peoples—in this case, with roots in the Cayman Islands, Belize, Jamaica, and elsewhere.

The Bay Islands are among the diminishing number of English-speaking enclaves in the western Caribbean that lie on the periphery of Spanish-speaking Latin America. (The English-speaking western Caribbean generally is defined to include Belize (formerly British Honduras), the Mosquito coast of Nicaragua and Honduras, the Isle of Pines, the Cayman Islands, Jamaica, the Corn Islands, and the Islands of Providence and San Andres.) They are part of the *Spanish Main*, that region of the Caribbean that was the nucleus of the Spanish empire, the site of the first tragic confrontations between Europeans and native Americans, and the locus of centuries of violent conflicts among various European powers. The Bay Islanders' identity has emerged in this marginality, shaped, in part, in terms of their relations to more powerful Spanish and subsequent Honduran mainland forces. Throughout the nineteenth century, well after they were formally incorporated into the Honduran national territory, the Bay Islands effectively persisted as a relatively autonomous economic and cultural entity. Despite the efforts of the government to extend its control throughout this century, the native people of the islands continue to regard themselves as having an ethnic and cultural identity that is quite distinct from the Spanish-speaking majority. Their separate identity, however, is now threatened because of the enhanced efforts of the government of Honduras to integrate the islands into Honduras.

Until recently, the Bay Islands' relatively low population density, comparative isolation, and poor communications protected them from many of the adverse social and environmental effects of tourism that have characterized much of the eastern Caribbean region. Beginning in the 1960s, a small number of tourists made up mostly of recreational sailors and divers "discovered" the islands' splendid reef, clear waters, secluded harbors, and tranquil beaches. At the same time, according to most social, economic, and health measures, the Bay Islanders enjoyed a quality of life that significantly surpassed that of Honduran ladinos living on the mainland. Unfortunately, these conditions changed radically in the 1980s in the context of the largely uncontrolled growth of the tourism industry, which included the migration of thousands of desperately poor ladinos from the mainland seeking employment in the expanding tourism sector. By the late 1990s, approximately 100,000 tourists visited the islands annually—about twice the resident population; and by the end of the decade, ladinos constituted more than 50% of the islands' 50,000 residents—an increase from 16% a decade earlier.

By the mid-1990s, the combined effects of the escalating numbers of international tourists and ladino immigrants from the mainland elevated the human population to a level at which the islands' freshwater supply, food supply, and other natural resources were threatened, and the ability of many communities to maintain health services and other vital services was overwhelmed. The environmental health effects of this degradation are considerable and include high rates of respiratory and diarrheal infections, malaria, dengue fever, and other waterborne diseases, particularly among the poorer segments of the islands' population. These conditions raise the serious question of whether population growth per se is the root cause of the environmental degradation occurring on the islands. An essentially demographic explanation is an oversimplification of reality, however, since the majority of population growth is due to the escalating numbers of tourists and ladino immigrants, which is directly associated with the expansion of the tourism industry. The root cause of environmental degradation on the Bay Islands is the rapid, largely unregulated expansion of the tourism industry. Part of this growth has included significant infrastructure development in certain domains, especially airport improvement and road construction, and a simultaneous lack of infrastructure development in other critical domains, especially drinking water, sewage, and solid waste disposal systems. Although it is clear that escalating numbers of tourists put more pressure on the islands' environment and natural resources, the major effort of development efforts has been to increase the number of tourists— regardless of the environmental and human costs.

The expansion of tourism has had considerable social, cultural, and economic costs as well as environmental ones. The price of tourism has included a growing gap between rich people and poor people; and less affluent residents feel that their standard of living has fallen along with the growth of tourism. Although tourism has provided an increasing number of jobs, the majority of Afro-Caribbean Bay Islanders and ladinos have access only to the lowest status, lowest paying, temporary jobs. A growing number of environmental regulations designed to protect coral reefs for use by tourists have also reduced access for local people to the natural resources on which they depend for their livelihoods. This is particularly serious for poorer members of island society who rely on the fish and shellfish collected from reef areas. Compounding the problems associated with a diminished access to reef species for food and sale, demand from a growing number of tourists has escalated prices for commercial food as well as for manufactured goods and housing. These price increases again are most serious for the poor and middle class. Tourism also has prompted great land speculation and spiraling land costs, what many call a "land grab." This too has had the most negative effect on poor and middle class islanders, many of whom have lost title to land that has been in their families for generations. Land speculation also has resulted in increased outside ownership of land and other local resources by foreigners and by Honduran nationals from the mainland. In the aftermath of Hurricane Mitch, the government of Honduras enacted several measures, including changing the Honduran constitution to make it easier for foreigners to buy property on the Bay Islands and in other tourism zones, in the hope of encouraging foreign investment. While this strategy may indeed stimulate foreign investment in the tourism industry, it will also likely increase local-level conflicts over land on the islands.

The establishment of marine reserves as part of the environmental conservation effort (such as the Sandy Bay–West End Marine Reserve on Roatán) has diminished the economic options of the English-speaking Bay Islanders, most of whom make up the poorer and middle class segments of Bay Island society, as well as the poorer ladino families, by enforcing rules that prohibit or limit the taking of reef and inshore species. There is little question about why residents are suspicious of the recent designation of the Bay Islands as a national marine park. In addition, poorer island residents (both Afro-Caribbean Islanders and ladinos) are angry at being told to curtail their fishing and hunting activities by the wealthier inhabitants who own commercial fishing fleets, hotels, resorts, and other businesses. It is these island "elites" and foreigners who are responsible for overfishing shrimp and lobster and are absorbed in a hotel building spree (despite a shortage of fresh water and the absence of sewage and other waste disposal systems). It is these wealthy residents and investors who are engaged in unsound road building, mangrove destruction, extensive dredging of the reef, and other environmentally destructive activities in connection with the construction of new tourism businesses. Although poorer local users admit that the reef and other aspects of the environment have suffered, they believe that their own restraint will be of no benefit unless everyone can be made to cut back on fishing and other environmentally destructive activities. The discrepancy in wealth between resort owners, whose guests make the most use of the reef, and local users only reinforces the attitude of poorer users that they should not bear the burden of environmental conservation alone. It is not surprising that the one marine reserve, long supported by the owner of a prominent diving resort, is having difficulty limiting subsistence use by local people and has prompted escalating conflict and sometimes deadly violence among resort owners, tourists, islanders, and ladinos.

At present, Afro-Caribbean Bay Islanders face dangerous threats to their cultural and ethnic survival as well as to their economic and physical well-being. These threats all are linked directly or indirectly to the recent, unregulated expansion of the tourism industry. Threats to cultural and ethnic survival stem from enhanced efforts being made by the government of Honduras to integrate the islands and the islanders into Honduran culture and society through the imposition of laws requiring Spanish-only instruction in schools, the replacement of islander civil servants with ladinos from the mainland, and the intimidating presence of the Honduran military. The islanders also face considerable threats to their economic well-being from loss of land as a result of widespread land speculation which often results in the islanders' loss of title to land holdings, loss of access to fishing and hunting grounds crucial to their livelihoods, and increased dependence on low-paying jobs in the tourism sector. These economic costs are tied to cultural loss as well because they diminish the high degree of economic independence that has traditionally characterized Bay Islander society. Dangers to the Bay Islanders' physical well-being also are considerable as environmental health risks associated with enhanced environmental degradation have increased as well.

RESPONSE: STRUGGLES TO SURVIVE CULTURALLY

> Is it fair to say that we are becoming strangers in our own land, while a wave of non-islanders are drowning our culture and threatening our identity? We must rise above the wave and claim the rights as a people with dignity and pride in our society.
>
> —Native Bay Islanders Professionals and Labourers
> Association, 1995

The history of the Bay Islands reveals a lack of widespread or well-integrated efforts made by Bay Islanders to protect their cultural and ethnic identity. These factors help explain the lack of organized response to efforts being made to Hispanicize the islands and to promote tourism in ways that many islanders judge to be detrimental to their ethnic and material survival. The islanders' staunch defense of their British ancestry, increasingly militant efforts to maintain the English language, and recent attempts to raise cultural consciousness are significant expressions of their perceptions of their own distinct ethnic identity. So too is the islanders' preference for U.S. baseball rather than soccer, including naming one of the islands' baseball teams the Pirates. In the present context, long-used derogatory, ethnic slang terms have taken on new significance. Native Bay Islanders continue to refer to themselves as "British" or "English" and to mainlanders as "Spaniards," "*indios*" (Indians), or "natives." Mainlanders in turn refer to all Bay Islanders as "pirates," to white islanders as "*caracoles*" (conch or snails), and to black Islanders as "*negritos*" (Negroes).

The founding of the Native Bay Islanders Professionals and Labourers Association (NABIPLA) in 1991 is evidence of current accelerated efforts to protect islander ethnicity and culture from several perceived threats. Two young men from the Afro-Caribbean communities of Flowers Bay and Gravel Bay (located on the southwestern shore of Roatán) started NABIPLA in response to "the people from the mainland who were coming in and controlling everything" (president of NABIPLA, 1997). The attitude of the organization toward mainland efforts to assimilate the islands was expressed quite simply by a member of NABIPLA in 1997: "The government used to leave us alone. . . . It was the Islands for the Islanders. . . . If we didn't have the pressure from the government these islands would be much improved" (author's field notes). By 1997 membership in NABIPLA had grown to several thousand and consisted primarily of poor and middle-class black islanders. According to NABIPLA's president, the grassroots organization now has a committee in virtually every community on all the islands. Fifteen women and men make up the board of directors—one for each major program area of the organization. Many of the leaders are pastors from the different Bay Islands' Protestant churches (e.g., Baptist, Church of God, and Adventist).

NABIPLA has a broad agenda that includes promoting social justice, maintaining black Bay Islanders' cultural and ethnic identity, protecting islanders' rights over land and other natural resources, enhancing human health, and conserving the islands' environment and natural resources. Its major efforts, however, have been promoting bilingual education throughout the islands, which it feels is key to achieving its other objectives. The organization wishes to collaborate with an educational institution, such as the University of the West Indies, to establish a Center for Bilingual Education for the Bay Islands that would provide secondary school education for Bay Islander youth. NABIPLA also is putting pressure on the government of Honduras to implement its recently enacted legislation allowing and facilitating bilingual education among Honduras' diverse indigenous peoples.

It was largely through the efforts of NABIPLA that the English-speaking Bay Islanders were officially recognized as an indigenous ethnic group in 1996. Since its membership in the major organization of indigenous peoples of Honduras, the Confederation of Autochthonous Peoples of Honduras

(CONPAH), NABIPLA has taken an increasingly activist position as indicated by the numerous human rights complaints it has brought to national and international bodies since 1998. In their words, "We have somewhat lost control of the islands. We are looking forward to taking it back" (member of NABIPLA, author's field notes, 1997).

NABIPLA is quite interested in improving the day-to-day lives of Bay Islanders. In 1997 NABIPLA started a food cooperative in one Afro-Caribbean community as a way to help poor islanders deal with the escalating cost of food on the islands. NABIPLA began dealing directly with wholesalers on the mainland, thus bypassing the supermarkets and food-distribution channels controlled by the island elite. Members get a 20% discount on all merchandise in the store: meat, chicken, vegetables, canned goods, paper products, and other manufactured items such as soap. Thought of as a pilot project, NABIPLA hopes to establish a network of such cooperatives in other communities.

NABIPLA also is thinking of ways for Bay Islanders to benefit more directly from the growth of tourism. They have started a Board of Tourism to control buses and taxis. The idea is to train islanders as tour guides for the passengers of the Norwegian Cruise Line who now stop on Roatán every week. Currently most cruise passengers visit West Bay Beach where they snorkel and picnic at a new resort owned by the brother of the owner of the largest resort located within the Sandy Bay–West End Marine Reserve. The Board of Tourism also plans to set requirements for dive masters—most important from the perspective of NABIPLA is that they be Honduran citizens rather than foreigners, who currently make up most of the islands' dive masters.

One of the major objectives of NABIPLA is to preserve islander ethnicity and culture. To this end, one of their proposed projects is to build a cultural village in the community of Gravel Bay. They are attempting to raise U.S.$40,000 to purchase a site for the project. The village will demonstrate to tourists how Bay Islanders used to live—their traditional foods (plantains, corn, dried plantain, and salted fish), ways of making a living, stories, songs, boats, and buildings.

The attitude of NABIPLA toward environmental conservation initiatives on the islands was conveyed quite forcefully in their first newsletter published in May 1995:

We know that in every society laws and prohibitions are important but are we implementing them correctly? How can we stop a poor man from selling the sand on his beach; and allow a rich man to dredge, fill up our sea and terminate our mangrove? Is it fair to prohibit a poverty stricken family from cutting down a tree in their back yard? When the wealthy are destroying our flora by the thousands daily? Is it right to construct roads that benefit the elite only and neglect the underprivileged while they are stuck to [their] knees in mud? They want us to clean and dispose of our litter. Where are the garbage collecting trucks? . . . NABIPLA believes that for our islands to go forward successfully, biasness, corruption, political propaganda, unequal education, and partiality on the whole must be eliminated. We must conserve our children, our environment, our good customs, traditions and belief that all men are created equally. (Native Bay Islanders Professionals and Labourers Association, 1995).

Despite the efforts of NABIPLA, major risks to Bay Islander ethnicity and culture remain. These stem from government attempts to further integrate the islands into the Honduran polity; a national agenda that emphasizes the significant expansion of tourism as a primary economic development strategy; the massive migration of Spanish-speaking mainlanders who now constitute a slight majority on the islands; the loss of critically important land and marine resources; and the influx of large numbers of foreign investors, residents, and tourists.

Bay Islanders are attempting to sustain their culture, lives, and livelihoods in many ways. They are trying to maintain their knowledge of the English language, Protestant religions, and other cultural practices. They are attempting to conserve the natural resources on which they depend for their livelihoods. They are encouraging young people to marry within their own group of Bay Islanders rather than marry outsiders. They have founded NABIPLA, which is coordinating action among Bay Islanders and promoting a unified political and economic agenda. They are enhancing power among the islanders by building strategic alliances with national and international groups. These diverse efforts, however, are not attempts to inhibit change, including the growth of the tourism industry, but rather efforts to give the islanders greater power and a greater say in determining their own futures.

FOOD FOR THOUGHT

The decision by the government of Honduras to make tourism one of the pillars of economic recovery in the aftermath of Hurricane Mitch is understandable given the growing importance of tourism to the economies of many countries throughout the world. This is especially true of poorer countries located in the developing or Third World where foreign tourists provide national governments with substantial income and provide a crucial source of employment and income for local people. However, a number of the negative consequences of tourism have attracted criticism and have led to heated debates about the extent to which international tourism actually can sustain rural livelihoods, communities, cultures, and environments. In addition, tourism often has provoked significant local-level conflicts in the areas in which it has expanded. Hostility often stems from the loss of critical natural resources on which local people depend for their

83

living as well as the loss of local cultures. The Bay Islands of Honduras are one of the clearest examples of the uneven distribution of the costs and benefits of tourism and of community-level discord associated with the spread of tourism. On the Bay Islands, conflicts surrounding the cultural, social, economic, and environmental impacts of tourism have been substantial as the English-speaking Bay Islanders continue to strive for their cultural, ethnic, and economic survival. More positively, tourism has stimulated a much higher degree of cultural unity and political action among Afro-Caribbean islanders than ever before. This unity has resulted in the English-speaking Bay Islanders being recognized as one of Honduras' indigenous peoples, and they are thus able to claim the rights that go along with that recognition.

Questions

1. Is the government of Honduras justified in promoting tourism on the Bay Islands in the name of economic growth, national unity, and national reconstruction?

2. How best might the government reconcile national economic goals with the needs and aspirations of the English-speaking Bay Islanders and other poorer residents of the Bay Islands?

3. In regard to the role of local residents, how might English-speaking Bay Islanders and recent ladino immigrants from the Honduran mainland overcome several hundred years of ethnic animosity and at times violent conflict in order to collaborate in their efforts to increase the benefits of tourism for themselves?

4. "Indigenous" or "native" people often are thought of as having lived in a specific place for hundreds or even thousands of years where they have practiced "traditional" culture. Yet, the English-speaking Bay Islanders first came to the islands in the 1830s, and their emergence and recognition as an indigenous group are quite recent. What does this imply about our concept of "indigenous" or "native" peoples?

5. Finally, how does the example of the Bay Islands affect the choice of your next vacation or diving trip? How does your choice of a vacation destination affect the local people who live there? How can you make sure that your travel dollars help rather than hurt local residents?

NOTES

Unless otherwise noted, all information, data, and quotations included in this chapter were taken from Susan C. Stonich, *The Other Side of Paradise: Tourism, Conservation, and Development in the Bay Islands* (New York: Cognizant Communication, 1999).

1. *Bay Islanders' Echo: The Way We See Things* (Newsletter of the Native Bay Islander Professionals and Labourers Association [NABIPLA]), vol. 1, May 1995.

2. World Bank, *World Development Indicators 1998*, Poverty Table 2.7 (Washington, D.C.: World Bank, 1998). http://www.worldbank.org/data/

RESOURCE GUIDE

Published Literature

Davidson, William. *Historical Geography of the Bay Islands*. Birmingham, Ala.: Southern University Press, 1974. This gives an informative historical background on the Bay Islands.

Gollin, James D., and Ron Mader. *Honduras: Adventures in Nature*. John Muir Santa Fe, N.M.: John Muir Publications. 1998. This travel book presents the costs as well as benefits of tourism in Honduras including the Bay Islands.

Houlson, Jane Harvey. *Blue Blaze: Danger and Delight in Strange Islands of Honduras*. London: Duckworth, 1934. This is an entertaining tale of Houlson's travels with Mitchell Hedges in the Bay Islands.

Mitchell Hedges, F. *Battles with Giant Fish*. London: Duckworth, 1923. This colorful book recounts the travels of Mitchell Hedges, adventurer, amateur anthropologist, and fisherman in the Bay Islands and elsewhere in Central America and the Caribbean.

Stonich, Susan C. *The Other Side of Paradise: Tourism, Conservation, and Development in the Bay Islands*. New York: Cognizant Communication, 1999.

WWW Sites

Honduras This Week Online, a weekly newspaper about Honduras in English often has articles about the Bay Islands and about tourism in general. http://www.marrder.com/htw/

Planeta.com-Eco-travels in Latin America, the best WWW site on tourism and the environment in Latin America with links to many other related sites, can be found at http://www.planeta.com.

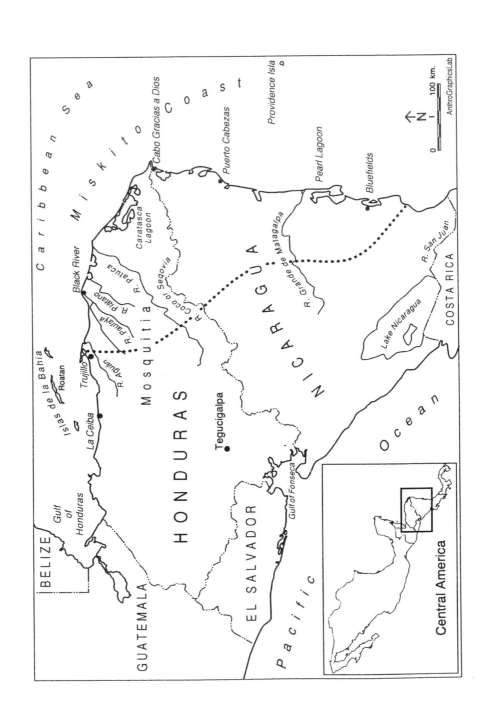

GUATEMALA

BELIZE

Gulf of Honduras

Islas de la Bahía

Roatan

La Ceiba

Trujillo

R. Aguan

R. Paulaya

R. Plátano

Black River

R. Patuca

Caratasca Lagoon

M o s q u i t i a

HONDURAS

Tegucigalpa

EL SALVADOR

Gulf of Fonseca

P a c i f i c

O c e a n

C a r i b b e a n   S e a

M i s k i t o   C o a s t

Cabo Gracias a Dios

R. Coco or Segovia

Puerto Cabezas

Providence Isla

Pearl Lagoon

Bluefields

N I C A R A G U A

R. Grande de Matagalpa

R. San Juan

Lake Nicaragua

COSTA RICA

AnthroGraphicsLab

N

0   100 km.

Central America

Chapter 6

The Miskito of Honduras and Nicaragua

David J. Dodds

CULTURAL OVERVIEW

The People

The Miskito are one of the largest groups of indigenous peoples in lower Central America. Altogether there are about 200,000 Miskito: about 40,000 to 50,000 in Honduras, and as many as 150,000 in Nicaragua.[1] They have lived for over 300 years along the coasts and rivers of eastern Nicaragua and Honduras, a region historically called the Mosquito Coast, the Miskito Coast, or the Mosquitia. The Miskito are an interesting people because their ancestry is strongly rooted in an indigenous New World culture and people—yet Africans and Europeans have influenced Miskito physical appearance, language, subsistence system, and cosmology (religion). Miskito culture is a "contact" culture created by the mixture of indigenous Americans with African and European peoples. The Miskito, in contrast to many other indigenous peoples of the Americas, have thrived since contact with Europeans, expanding in both population and territory since the mid-1600s. During the last four centuries, the Miskito have made their living from slash-and-burn farming, fishing, and hunting. They have also worked in many boom-and-bust industries, such as mahogany cutting, gum tapping, gold mining, turtle fishing, and, since the 1970s, lobster diving. Work in these industries provided much of the contact between the pre-Miskito indigenous peoples and shaped what is now the modern Miskito culture.

The first contact known between the Miskito (or pre-Miskito indigenous peoples) and Europeans occurred in 1611 when three Spanish priests ascended the Rio Coco, baptized 130 Indians, but were then killed. The first sustained contact came about with the establishment in 1633 of a trading post at Cabo Gracias a Dios by a company of Puritans from Providence Island. The trading station operated until 1641 when the Spanish captured Providence Island. The wreck of a slave ship at Cabo Gracias a Dios some time between 1641 and 1652 instigated the admixture of pre-Miskito peoples with Africans.

In contrast to most of Central America, the history of the Miskito Coast was more influenced by the British than the Spanish, up until the mid nineteenth-century. The lowland Caribbean region of Central America, from Belize to southern Nicaragua, was the scene of constant struggle between the British and Spanish. In this history, the Miskito played an important role by participating in trade and military exploits with the British. In addition to these activities, the turtle-fishing skills of Miskito men were highly valued by European ship crews, who often hired them as provisioners on their voyages. Miskito men also worked with buccaneers on their sea raids throughout the Caribbean.

The present day Miskito face a variety of challenges to their cultural survival: political representation within the republics of Honduras and Nicaragua that will allow them to have a national voice, defense of their traditional lands as land-needy farmers and ranchers migrate into their traditional territories and as nature reserves are created to save the rain forest, defense of traditional sea territories against commercial fisheries, defense of their labor rights as workers in industries such as lobster diving, and acquiring adequate health and education services in this relatively isolated region.

The Setting

The Miskito Coast, or the Caribbean coast from the Rio Tinto Negro of Honduras to the Pearl Lagoon area of Nicaragua, includes the lowland and hill countries extending toward the interiors of the two countries. Because of its latitude (between 12 and 16 degrees north of the equator), the climate is tropical and hot. There are two seasons: a dry season from February to May, and a wet, rainy season from June through January.

Ecologically, the Mosquitia is most famous for its rain forests and pine savannas. In addition to providing the indigenous peoples with many resources, the rain forests of the Mosquitia have provided export materials such as mahogany for furniture and tunu sap for chewing gum for export to the United States and Europe, especially during the nineteenth-century. During the seventeenth century, pirates visited the Mosquitia to cut pine trees for ship masts. Animal and plant species of the Mosquitia are mostly neotropical (belonging to the New World tropics), similar to much of lowland South America, like the Amazon. Because of its location in Central America, the Mosquitia is important as a cross-over zone for North and South American species, especially mammals. Many endangered animal species inhabit the Mosquitia, including such mammals as tapir, white and collared peccary (similar to a wild pig), paca (a rodent), white-tailed deer, red brocket deer, puma or mountain lion, jaguar, ocelot, howler monkey, spider monkey, and manatee. The harpy eagle, red macaw, and green military macaw are endangered bird species native to the region. The Mosquito Coast is also an important habitat for migrating birds who fly through its forests and savannas to the Yucatán Peninsula, and then across the Gulf of Mexico to the southern United States.

Because of its isolation and important biodiversity, the governments of Honduras and Nicaragua have created several reserves to protect the region's natural resources. In Honduras, the largest reserve is the Río Plátano Biosphere Reserve, covering 5,000 square kilometers (1,900 square miles); in Nicaragua, the largest is Bosawas Reserve, covering 8,000 square kilometers (3,000 square miles). A series of linked reserves, which will link the protected areas of Honduras and Nicaragua into one large conservation area in the Plapawans reserve system, is almost complete.[2] Much of the area being declared as "reserves" in the name of nature conservation is the traditional territory of the Miskito and related peoples including the Sumu Indians.

Traditional Subsistence Strategies

The Miskito have traditionally made their living from swidden farming, care of domestic animals, fishing, and hunting. However, this has usually been complemented by money or trade goods obtained by working in the extractive industries mentioned previously.

Swidden farming, also called slash-and-burn farming, is practiced in many parts of the world. Swidden agriculture follows a cyclical pattern of cutting a plot from forest, then burning to further prepare the soil for the planting, weeding, and harvesting of crops. Typically, Miskito households maintain two types of agricultural plots: house gardens, which are planted around dwellings within the village and may contain fruit trees and condiments, and outlying fields along natural waterways, in which are planted the bulk of the major subsistence crops. The five major crops planted by the Miskito are swidden plots banana/plantain varieties, manioc, rice, beans, and maize. These crops, especially manioc and banana/plantain varieties, provide the majority of the carbohydrate intake in the Miskito diet.

Important domestic animals, raised by the Miskito for food, include chickens, cattle, and pigs. Most meat and dietary protein comes from these domesticated animals. Fishing in lagoons or streams is also important, especially when there is not enough money for a household to buy meat. Hunting is practiced less now in some coastal communities, probably because of the influence of cash which allows households to buy meat from

89

domesticated sources. The Miskito gather some materials from the forest, but not for food; gathering is done mostly for construction materials for building houses (wood for boards, leaves for thatch) and for traditional herbal medicine.

However, most Miskito consider themselves poor if they have no money or jobs to acquire money. Wage work, like lobster diving, and the money it provides are important to the Miskito. Money is used to buy many food-stuffs now considered traditional—coffee, sugar, salt, and lard—to complement the foods grown in gardens and swidden fields. Money is also important for buying clothes, medicines, and many other useful items like cooking utensils, radios, watches, and outboard motors for canoes.

Social and Political Organization

In everyday life, kinship is very important to the way in which Miskito work, worship, and travel. Most Miskito villages comprise a number of household clusters of people who are related as an extended family. A typical settlement pattern is to find from two to six houses located around the house of a senior couple, usually the parents of the wives in the surrounding houses (thus the children are the grandchildren of the senior couple). When people marry out of their village, it is usually the men who move to the other village; women usually stay in their own village. This matrilocal marriage pattern is important for the Miskito because most family household clusters are related through women who are sisters, daughters, and aunts. These women then share household chores and raise their children to be Miskito while men are away engaged in wage labor. The Miskito have a Hawaiian kinship system: the main feature is that a person's siblings and cousins are called by the same term (e.g., in American kinship terms, one would call one's cousins "brother" and "sister"). Because kinship is so important, people know their extended relatives, and a traveling Miskito can almost always find some relative to stay with in another village.

Above the level of the family household cluster, political organization is not strong, but it is considered egalitarian. Traditionally, a local older man, or *wita*, was considered to be influential in village affairs, but he was not a "chief" with authority. Moravian lay pastors (*sasmalkra*) and school-teachers have been important leaders within villages. In Honduras, the governor of the department (state) appoints local men to represent the villages to the department government. Until the 1990s, the Miskito of Honduras did not participate much in state politics, and they still pay very few taxes. In Nicaragua, after the Sandinista-Contra war in the 1980s, which had split Miskito communities and families by political ideology and violence, the Miskito became very politically active and negotiated with the Nicaraguan national government to create their own semiautonomous governments in eastern Nicaragua: in the northern half, the RAAN (Región Autónoma del Atlántico Norte) and in the southern half, the RAAS (Región Autónoma del Atlántico Sur).

Religion and World View

Most Miskito consider themselves to be Christians. Moravian missionaries arrived in Nicaragua in 1849 and in Honduras in 1930 to proselytize among the Miskito, who accepted Christianity readily. Christian groups represented among the Miskito, other than the Moravian church, include Roman Catholic, Assembly of God, and Pentecostal churches. In Honduras, a few Miskito follow the Bahai faith after the establishment of a Bahai hospital. However, the Moravian church is by far the most important. Almost every Miskito village has a Moravian church, if not a lay pastor. Church meetings are held every Sunday morning, with other meetings during the week. Many Miskito learn to read so that they can read Miskito translations of the Bible and the Moravian hymnal. In the 1970s, the Moravian church of Honduras and Nicaragua became independent of support from the United States. Some Miskito view the Moravian church as restrictive and too obligating of their time and money and so avoid it.

Despite their general acceptance of Christianity, the Miskito also believe in many spirit-beings derived from an indigenous cosmology that includes a variety of types of spirit-beings. Some are evil and are associated with the Christian Satan. These evil spirits can cause people to become sick, kill children, and make people crazy by possessing them. Other types of beings are those which live in nature. Contact with these beings is dangerous because they are powerful and can also make people sick. For example, *liwa* live in streams, rivers, lagoons, or the sea. There are male and female *liwa*, and the *liwa* of the opposite sex are dangerous to a person. When Miskito lobster divers suffer from decompression sickness, caused by diving too long and surfacing too fast, they often blame this on the *liwa mairin*, or the woman water being, who has seen them and caused them to be ill. Other spirits, like the *unta dukia* (forest thing) live in the forest; other spirit beings inhabit the pine savanna, swamps, and rain forest; yet others live in whirlwinds and waterspouts. In addition to these nature beings, many plants have spirit owners. If an herbal healer wants to harvest a particular plant for making medicine, the healer must first speak to the plant's spirit owner and leave a coin at the foot of the plant before uprooting it; otherwise, the spirit owner will be displeased and the plant will lose its medicinal value.

Since many sicknesses have spiritual causes (e.g., by being seen by a *liwa* or by having a spell placed on one), cures involve a spiritual dimension. There are various kinds of Miskito healers. First are the herbalists who know about plants and the medicines that can be made from them. Second are the spiritual healers who may use plants, the power of plant spirit owners, or prayers to the Christian God to heal people. Some herbalists and spiritual healers say they learn their knowledge in dreams by angels sent from the Christian God. Third, are *sukias*, or shamans, who are religious leaders and healers. *Sukias*, who may be men or women, are considered powerful people who can directly contact the spirit world, either to cure or cause harm by invoking various kinds of spirits and casting spells. Consultations with *sukias* are serious events and usually cost significant sums of money to the person requesting service.

THREATS TO SURVIVAL

The Miskito have successfully survived at least three centuries of contact with "outside" people such as Europeans and various other ethnic groups. Yet, the Miskito face difficulties as they become even more linked to the international economy and integrated with the nation-states of Honduras and Nicaragua. Three of the most important difficulties are the dangers of lobster work for Miskito males; the need to protect natural resources legally; and population growth, land need, and nature conservation.

Dangers of Lobster Work

One of the most serious threats to the Miskito is the work of men and boys in the lobster export industry: many have been injured or killed in diving accidents. In Honduras, as many as 4,000 Miskito males may work in the lobster industry and, in Nicaragua, from 2,000 to 2,500.[3] A medical study conducted in Honduras found that, from 1976 to 1989, at least fifty-six Miskito divers died, and 157 were paralyzed or injured.[4] Despite the risks of lobster work, many Miskito choose to do the work because there are few other well-paying jobs in this region. In one two-week trip, a lobster diver can earn as much as he would in a year working hard in the fields farming and growing a crop like rice for sale.

Miskito males generally work at two kinds of lobster jobs: as divers (*buzos*) or canoemen (*cayuceros*). Divers and canoemen work in pairs: the canoeman accompanies the diver to the lobster bed and maintains the position of the canoe (*cayuco*) above the diver—in the canoe are deposited the lobsters and extra diving tanks. Lobster boats based in the Bay Islands of Honduras hire the Miskito as divers, and canoemen then go out to 'lobster banks' throughout the Caribbean, from the Bahamas to Colombia. After spending usually ten to fourteen days at sea, the boats drop off the Miskito crew at their coastal villages and return to the Bay Islands where the lobster tails are frozen and exported to the United States. One of the

Miskito men constructing dugout canoe. Courtesy of David J. Dodds.

largest buyers of Honduran lobster is the company Red Lobster USA which owns the Red Lobster restaurants.

During the 1970s, lobsters were so plentiful along the banks (continental shelf) of Honduras and Nicaragua that lobsters were found in relatively shallow waters and lung diving with no tanks was possible. However, by the early 1980s, lobster populations became depleted in the shallow waters, and divers began using pressurized diving tanks to pursue the lobsters ever deeper. As depths have increased so have injuries and deaths to divers. Diving demands great physical strength since divers may descend to depths of ninety feet or more and may spend up to four or five hours a day underwater. The great depth and length of diving has led to the injury and death of many Miskito divers as a result of decompression sickness, or "the bends." In addition to the risk of decompression sickness, divers are exposed to sun, wind, heat, cold, strong underwater currents, and the risk of bites by sharks and barracudas. In Honduras, a diving school was created at the impetus of the Moravian church in the coastal village of Cocobila. During 1994 the schools' graduates had experienced no diving deaths and a reduced rate of injury. However, during a visit to the Río Plátano Biosphere Reserve in 1997, coastal residents told me about numerous cases of paralysis and death which had occurred to divers in their villages since then. The plight of the Miskito lobster divers has received increasing press attention in both Honduras and Nicaragua but continues to be a serious problem.

Natural Resource Needs and Legal Protection

Like many other indigenous peoples elsewhere, the Miskito face the threat of loss of land to outsiders. The threat of land loss comes from a variety of sources. First, in Honduras and Nicaragua, an agricultural frontier of ladino farmers and ranchers has steadily been advancing from the west to the east into traditional Miskito territories. Second, various international companies have tried to obtain access to the natural resources of the Miskito Coast. For example, in Honduras, the Stone Container Corporation, based in Chicago, Illinois, signed an agreement with then President Rafael Callejas to clear-cut most of eastern Honduras to obtain trees for pulp to be processed into paper. When word of the deal leaked out, international protest by environmentalists, the indigenous inhabitants, and others led to the abandonment of the project in 1992. In Nicaragua, in 1991, a Korean firm almost obtained rights to extract timber from 90% of the Miskito Nation territory, but protest by environmentalists and Miskito activists stopped the project. In 1996 a U.S. engineering company began plans to build one of the largest dams in Central America in the Honduran Mosquitia, but the project was stopped in 1999 after a series of events, such as Hurricane Mitch (1998) and protests by indigenous people and environmentalists, made the project difficult to complete.

In Honduras, the 1982 constitution guarantees the right of indigenous peoples to have land, but in reality not much law has been created to protect the land of indigenous peoples, and many competing government agencies can claim "control" over the land (e.g., the National Agrarian Institute versus the Honduran Corporation for Forest Development). In Nicaragua, the situation is more complex historically because the British recognized a "Mosquito Reservation" (i.e., Miskito Reservation) in eastern Nicaragua. In 1894 the Nicaraguan government took control of the territory but did not respect the reservation. However, the Mosquito Reservation became the basis for the 1987 Autonomy Law by which the government of Nicaragua created the RAAN and RAAS as semiautonomous territories. The government of Nicaragua, however, retains the right to manage the natural resources within the RAAN and RAAS.

But not only land resources are threatened. Because the Miskito are a coastal people, much of their traditional territory extends into the waters of the Caribbean Sea. A geographer at the University of California-Berkeley calls the lobster boats of Honduras "pirates" for taking lobsters from the coastal shelf of Nicaragua.[5] Shrimp boats also came from many countries to the coast of Nicaragua after the 1980s war had ended.

Population Growth, Traditional Agriculture, and Conservation

Like many other peoples in the tropics, the Miskito practice slash-and-burn, or swidden, agriculture. Under conditions of low population density, such as the Miskito before the twentieth century, slash-and-burn agriculture was very efficient because it allowed farmers to use fire to help them prepare their fields making it unnecessary to use draft animals like oxen for dragging a plow.

The swidden system is cyclical. Miskito farmers identify the crop they want to plant and the type of forest they want to clear. They can clear virgin forest or secondary (regrowth) forest. Virgin forest areas have the advantage of good dark soils with few weeds, but secondary forest areas are easier to clear by ax or machete because the trees are not as big as they are in the tall rain forest. After a field is used for one or two years, it is abandoned and allowed to regrow into forest again. After five or more years, the farmer may come back to the same plot to clear it, burn it, and plant it again.

The future impact of Miskito swidden agriculture on the environment may become more negative with time. First, there are more and more Miskito. In the twentieth century, the Miskito populations of Honduras and Nicaragua have been growing at over 3% per year, which means that population doubles in twenty-three or fewer years.[6] Second, the Miskito have adopted new crops which change the amount of fields they clear each year from virgin forest. Dry rice is a very useful crop because it can be stored all year and can be sold at a good price, but in one Honduran village it is responsible for 45% of the new clearing of virgin forest.[7] Third, the area of land to which populations can expand is becoming more limited because of rain forest reserves like the Río Plátano and Bosawas. These reserves define core zones, where no people are supposed to live, and "cultural" zones, where people can live. This kind of zoning is good for nature conservation, but it forces us to ask how the Miskito will be able to practice traditional agriculture in the future if they run out of forest areas in their cultural zones to clear for fields.

Many Miskito realize that the best lands are already cleared for agriculture and that it is harder and harder to find accessible lands near a river with good soils (usually rain forest) to plant their fields. Can anything be done to reduce the pressure on local forests? One idea promoted by MO-PAWI (Mosquitia Pawisa), a nongovernmental organization (NGO) funded by the World Wildlife Fund and other agencies, is to use the velvet bean as a "green manure" in old fallowed fields. "Green manures" are crops that put nitrogen back into the soil. The idea is that if Miskito farmers planted velvet beans after harvesting their last crop (instead of letting it grow back into secondary forest), the soil would retain its fertility, and the farmer could come back to the same plot to clear, burn, and plant, rather than clear a new field from virgin forest. An added benefit is that if a farmer has planted an abandoned field in velvet beans, it is less work to clear the vines of the bean than to clear the saplings and vines of the secondary forest. The velvet bean has been adopted by many ladino (Hispanic) farmers in the highlands of Olancho in Honduras because it raises crop yields and reduces re-clearing work. So far only a handful of Miskito farmers have chosen to use velvet beans.

Another possibility is that population pressure could be reduced by helping Miskito families reduce the number of children they have. A study with 200 indigenous women in the Río Plátano Biosphere Reserve showed that women on the average had eight children but preferred to have only four or five children.[8] Many women are interested in using modern contraception to limit the number of children they have, but there are many difficulties. Government clinics often run out of birth control pills. Also, some men want to have as many children as possible and do not want their wives to use contraception. An added complication is that the Miskito are a minority population. If the Miskito adopt family planning and have fewer children and a lower growth rate than the rest of Honduras, they will become even more of a minority through time.

However, it is important to keep in mind several ideas while thinking about the problem of Miskito population growth, their need for future agricultural lands, and local deforestation rates. First, the Miskito are long-time occupants to the region who have successfully managed to live with their environment for hundreds, and maybe thousands, of years (if you count the pre-Miskito people from which they descended). The Miskito plant small plots for subsistence agriculture (food eaten by the same household), rarely plant huge areas for commercial production, and have cleared relatively small amounts of forest to make cattle pastures (in contrast to local ladino ranchers).

RESPONSE: STRUGGLES TO SURVIVE CULTURALLY

How have the Miskito responded to the difficulties they face? As for many indigenous peoples, struggles to sustain their cultural survival often mean political organization and action.

The most important response of the Miskito to threats to their well-being, lands, and way of life has been the creation of indigenous federations which work with each other, NGOs, and governments. In Honduras, before the 1990s, the most important federation was MASTA (Moskitia Asla Takanka), which was formed by a group of Miskito schoolteachers. However, many Miskito believed that MASTA did not adequately represent their interests. In the late 1990s, MASTA reorganized so that each village was represented by a local chapter, and each region of the Mosquitia had its own chapter. This kind of democratic organization has been more successful in representing the needs of local communities to government officials regarding health, education, and other needs.

Organizations like MASTA often coordinate their interests with local NGOs. A recent example is the mapping project led by a geographer at Kansas University, who helped train local men from twenty-one regions of the Honduran Mosquitia to draw maps and identify key features of the landscape. After performing a series of field surveys and conducting workshops, a map was produced and printed by the Honduran National Geographic Institute, which depicted, for the first time on a map, all of the native communities of eastern Honduras as well as their natural resource use areas (see chapter 7). This kind of participatory research and involvement of indigenous people in documenting their own knowledge and history will be critical for the future success of indigenous peoples as they seek to represent themselves and their interests to others.

FOOD FOR THOUGHT

This chapter raises several important questions regarding the specific dangers of lobster work as well as more general concerns about human population growth, traditional agriculture, environmental conservation, and the implications of religious changes on indigenous cultures.

Questions

1. What should be done about the injuries and deaths of Miskito lobster divers? Should North Americans stop eating lobsters or support bans of lobsters imported from Honduras?
2. Should the Miskito stop traditional slash-and-burn agriculture to help save the rain forest?
3. Should the Miskito have fewer children to lessen population pressure on the rain forest?
4. Do outsiders like Honduran government officials or North American conservationists have the right to tell the Miskito they should have fewer children?
5. Do you think it was right of missionaries to teach the Miskito new (Christian) religious ideas as well as ideas about modern medicine and how to read and write in Miskito or Spanish?

NOTES

1. Population estimates for Honduras are based on the author's estimates: David J. Dodds, "The Ecological and Social Sustainability of Miskito Subsistence in the Río Plátano Biosphere Reserve, Honduras: The Cultural Ecology of Swidden Hor-

ticulturalists in a Protected Area" (Ph.D. diss., University of California, Los Angeles, 1994), 368–400. (Available from University Microfilms International, Ann Arbor, MI). Population estimates for Nicaragua come from Peter H. Herlihy, "Central American Indian Lands and Peoples Today," in *Central America: A Natural and Cultural History*, ed. Anthony G. Coates, 215–240. (New Haven, Conn.: Yale University Press, 1997).

2. Peter H. Herlihy, "Indigenous Peoples and Biosphere Conservation in the Mosquitia Rain Forest Corridor, Honduras," in *Conservation Through Cultural Survival: Indigenous Peoples and Protected Areas*, ed. Stan Stevens, 99–133. (Washington, D.C.: Island Press, 1997).

3. David J. Dodds, "Lobster in the Rain Forest: The Political Ecology of Miskito. Wage Labor and Agricultural Deforestation," *Journal of Political Ecology* 5 (1998): 83–108.

4. Proyecto Nautilo, *Proyecto Nautilo Para el Buceo Seguro y Desarrollo de la Moskitia: Estudio Socioeconómico, Laboral y de Salud de los Buzos: Informe de Primeros Resultados con Conclusiones y Recomendaciones*. (Tegucigalpa: Ministerio de Salud Pública, Programa de Salud de los Trabajadores, Fuerza Naval (Escuela de Buceo), IHRM, PROMEBUZ, 1993).

5. Bernard Nietschmann, "Protecting Indigenous Coral Reefs and Sea Territories, Miskito Coast, Raan, Nicaragua," *Conservation Through Cultural Survival: Indigenous Peoples and Protected Areas*, ed. Stan Stevens, 193–224. (Washington, D.C.: Island Press, 1997).

6. Dodds, "Ecological and Social Sustainability of Miskito Subsistence."

7. Dodds, "Lobster in the Rain Forest."

8. Dodds, *Informe Preliminar sobre Demografía de Tres Pueblos Indígenas en la Reserva Biósfera del Río Plátano*. (Preliminary Report on the Demography of Three Indigenous Peoples in the Río Plátano Biosphere Reserve.) Working paper no. 98–1. (Bloomington: Population Institute for Research and Training, Indiana University, 1997. Internet: http://www.indiana.edu/~pirt/wp98 1.html.

RESOURCE GUIDE

Published Literature

Bell, Charles Napier. *Tangweera: Life and Adventures Among Gentle Savages*. Austin: University of Texas Press, 1989. Facsimile of 1899 Edition; Edward Arnold.

Dozier, Craig L. *Nicaragua's Mosquito Shore: The Years of British and American Presence*. Tuscaloosa: University of Alabama Press, 1985.

Floyd, Troy S. *The Anglo-Spanish Struggle for Mosquitia*. Albuquerque: University of New Mexico Press, 1967.

Helms, Mary W. *Asang: Adaptations to Culture Contact in a Miskito Community*. Gainesville: University of Florida Press, 1971.

———. "Miskito." In *Middle America and the Caribbean, Encyclopedia of World Cultures*. Volume 8, 170–72. James W. Dow, volume editor. Boston: G. K. Hall, 1991.

Nietschmann, Bernard. *Between Land and Water: The Subsistence Ecology of the Miskito Indians, Eastern Nicaragua.* New York: Seminar Press, 1973.

Videos and Films

The Turtle People. Bernard Nietschmann, narrator. Prod. B and C Films, 16 mm, 27 minutes (1973).

WWW Sites

Mosquito Coast Ethnohistory, by Professor Michael Olien, Department of Anthropology, University of Georgia. http://quat.dac.uga.edu/research/miskito/

Journal of Political Ecology, "Lobster in the Rain Forest: The Political Ecology of Miskito Wage Labor and Agricultural Deforestation," by David Dodds, 1998. Describes the Honduran lobster industry with color photographs of Miskito divers and slash-and-burn fields. Available on internet at http://www.library.arizona.edu/cj/jpe/volume_5/4dodd.pdf (Adobe Acrobat reader is required to view this file.)

Honduras This Week Online. Weekly newspaper in English about Honduras often has articles about the Miskito and nature conservation. http://www.marrder.com/htw/

Smithsonian Institution, National Museum of Natural History, Department of Botany. Information about the Río Plátano Biosphere Reserve in Honduras where many Miskito live. http://nmnhwww.si.edu/botany/projects/centres/platano.html

Patuca River Campaign. Describes a proposed dam project in the Mosquitia region of Honduras. http://www.ben2.ucla.edu/~alexagui/patuca/index.html

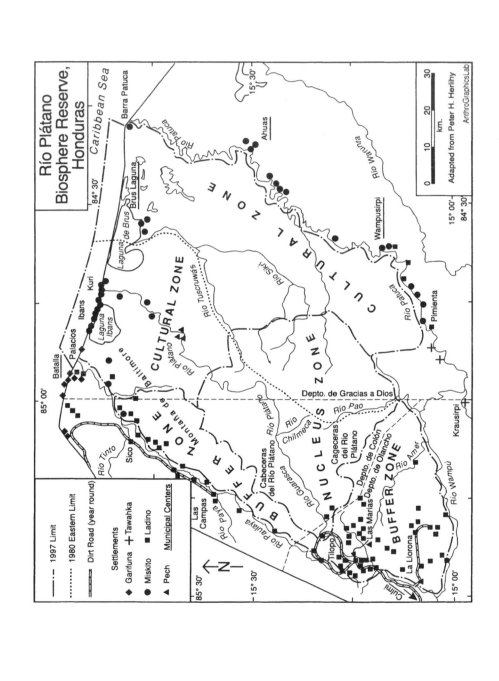

Río Plátano
Biosphere Reserve,
Honduras

Caribbean Sea

Adapted from Peter H. Herlihy
AnthroGraphicsLab

km.
0 10 20 30

84° 30'
15° 30'
15° 00'
84° 30'

Barra Patuca

Ahuas

Río Patuca

Wampusirpi

Río Wans

Pimienta

Río Patuca

Brus Laguna
Laguna de Brus

Laguna de Brus

Kuri
Ibans
Palacios
Batalla
Laguna Ibans

Balimore

CULTURAL ZONE

CULTURAL ZONE

Río Tuscruwás

Río Siksi

Río Plátano

Depto. de Gracias a Dios

NUCLEUS ZONE

Río Pao
Río Chilmeca

Cabeceras
del Río Plátano

Cageceras
del Río
Plátano

Depto. de Colón
Depto. de Olancho

Río Amer

Krausirpi

85° 00'

Río Tinto
Sico

BUFFER ZONE

Montaña de Balimore

Río Guaraska

Las Marías

Río Guaraska

Río Paulaya

Las Campas

Río Plátano

Tilopo

BUFFER ZONE

La Llorona

Río Wampú

Cuilmi

85° 30'
15° 30'
15° 00'

N

1997 Limit
1980 Eastern Limit
Dirt Road (year round)

Settlements
◆ Garífuna + Tawahka
● Miskito ■ Ladino
▲ Pech   Municipal Centers

Chapter 7

Indigenous and Ladino Peoples of the Río Plátano Biosphere Reserve, Honduras

Peter H. Herlihy

CULTURAL OVERVIEW

The People

The Río Plátano Biosphere Reserve in Honduras is one of Central America's most important protected areas. The reserve is also home to indigenous populations who have maintained the forest cover through centuries of settlement and use, but who have been uninformed and little involved in conservation and development initiatives affecting their lands and life.

The lands of the Río Plátano Biosphere have been the cultural intersection of different Amerindian groups for centuries. Little is certain about the pre-Hispanic past, but when Christopher Columbus sailed along this coast in 1502, he probably saw native Pech (called Paya) who lived up the Plátano, Paulaya, Wampu, and possibly Patuca rivers in those days. Their populations once occupied the lands between the Aguán and Patuca rivers, but they were reduced by slavery, missionization, and exploitation by the Spaniards.

The biosphere's well-known Miskito people are a hybrid population with origins going back to the mixing of natives (probably Sumu) with black Africans during the mid-seventeenth century. They expanded out from a hearth around Cabo Gracias a Dios to settle up and down the Caribbean coast incorporating blacks, natives, and even Europeans into their population. The Miskito developed their strongest alliances with the British at Black River (present-day Palacios) where 300 whites, 600 slaves, and 3,000 well-armed Indians, Zambos, and Miskitos occupied the nearby area in 1759. Cattle thrived on the savannas, while sugarcane, bananas, and tropical fruits were grown on the river margins. Sea resources were plentiful.

The aggressive Miskito raiders gradually displaced the Pech settlements on the Plátano, Paulaya, and Wampu rivers.

British presence on the Spanish Main was always contested. In 1787, after a series of conflicts and accords, the British yielded control of Mosquitia to the Spaniards and evacuated their settlement. The Spaniards reoccupied Black River, but the Miskito destroyed it soon after. During the late eighteenth century, the Miskito formed new communities on the north coast on the Brus and Ibans lagoons. They followed a loose political system begun by the British well into the nineteenth century—a Miskito General controlled the lands between the Aguán and Patuca rivers stationed near the mouth of the Plátano. By the 1840s, however, the Miskito population had been reduced by smallpox epidemics, and only five or six small hamlets in the biosphere area existed between the Black River and the Patuca River.

Garifuna populations came to Mosquitia in the early 1800s from the Caribbean Island of Saint Vincent where African slaves mixed with Island Caribs to become the hybrid black-Indian culture once called the Black Caribs. When they became rebellious, the British banished them to the Bay Island of Roatán in 1797. From there, they crossed to the mainland at Trujillo and spread along the coast. They reached the Patuca River in 1804, but retreated shortly after to the Black River area. Plaplaya, the only Garifuna community in the Plátano Biosphere, formed at the end of the century as the easternmost Garifuna settlement in Honduras.

Miskito

The Miskito are the dominant indigenous group in the Río Plátano Biosphere today with a population of 17,874, accounting for 44% of the reserve's population (see also chapter 6). They live along the northern coast and up the Patuca, Plátano, and Tinto rivers. The two largest settlements in the biosphere, Barra Patuca with 2,237 inhabitants and Brus Laguna with 1,811, are both Miskito communities. Other Miskito towns, including Ahuas, Paptalaya, Wawina, and Wampusirpi, each have over 1,000. Most villages have several hundred people, and some families still live dispersed along the river margin.

The Miskito language, which belongs to the South American Chibchan group, contains a large number of English and Spanish loan words. Most Miskito in the biosphere are bilingual: they speak their native dialect at home and in the village, and they learn Spanish in schools. Men, who travel and have more contact with outsiders, are more skilled in Spanish than women. With the absence of working men from the coast, strong ties develop among mother, daughters, and sisters who play powerful roles in maintaining the social fabric of the community. It is the women who maintain the Miskito language dominance and pass down traditions in the family.

The Miskito have a diverse economy that exploits both the sea and rain forests for food and cash. They use slash-and-burn cultivation to grow yucca, bananas, plantains, rice, beans, and corn, and they hunt and fish and raise chickens and Muscovy ducks for fresh meat. Some families raise cattle on the savannas, along the river margins, or even in the settlement area.

The Miskito live in the breezy coastal villages during the May to November wet season, but spend considerable time on the family's riverine agricultural lands, called *kiamps* (from English "camp"), during the December to April dry season. The coast is the hub of Miskito life with the stores, churches, graveyards, schools, health services, transportation, and communication networks. The coastal villages are located on the easily traversed sandy strip of land, but are backed by lagoons, swamps, and savannas to the south. Therefore little agricultural production occurs along the coast aside from occasional yucca fields or fruit tree cultivation. Up river on the family's *kiamp* the Miskito grow most of their produce and family members hunt, fish, and collect from the rain forests, savannas, rivers, and lagoons.

Miskito men worked for foreign companies during the eighteenth and nineteenth centuries cutting mahogany, harvesting sea turtles, and extracting sarsaparilla, rubber, and animal skins from the forest. Traditional Miskito subsistence economy was based on reciprocity, gift-giving, and sharing among related households. Now store-bought foods and manufactured goods are deeply integrated into daily life. Since the 1960s, Miskito men have worked as divers in a lucrative lobster industry run mostly by businessmen from the Bay Islands. The divers partake in the conspicuous consumption of beer, rum, cigarettes, or buy radios or flashy clothing. Their dangerous work and lifestyle have caused many young Miskito men the loss of life or crippling injury (chapter 6).

The Miskito seem to have a special ability to adapt easily to changing social, economic, and environmental conditions. Miskito men changed their cash-earning focus to exploiting different coastal and rain-forest resources while working for foreign companies in different boom and bust economies. They have also expanded their populations by mixing and absorbing native Pech, Tawahka Sumu, and Garifuna, but also outside Europeans, black Creoles, ladinos, North Americans, and even Chinese. The Miskito were indoctrinated into the beliefs of the Moravian church during the early 1900s. Evangelical missionaries preached a strict work ethic, communal cooperation, and Puritan ideology against vices. Today, however, Moravian dominance is losing ground as many Miskito convert to Catholicism or other Protestant churches.

Pech

The Pech, more than Miskito, have characteristic Amerindian features with their small stature, straight dark hair, reddish skin, and flat noses.

Only 479 Pech live in two separate parts of the biosphere today. The Las Marias area along the middle Río Plátano continues to be a Pech stronghold. Despite long-standing animosities, many Pech there have intermarried with Miskito and have lost much of their distinctiveness as a result. About 153 inhabitants in the Las Marias area (total population of 501) consider themselves to be Pech. The other Pech settlements are located in the reserve's southwest corner where three out of every four residents of Jocomico (pop. 110) and Culuco (pop. 152) identify themselves as Pech. These villagers struggle to maintain their lands and identity when confronted with the massive colonization front that has circumscribed and reduced their historic lands.

The Pech language also comes from the South American Chibchan group. Many Pech lost their native language as a result of living in sustained contact with the dominant coastal Miskito economy to the north or the national ladino society to the south. Today only 77 villagers in the north and 112 in the southwest can speak it. Most Pech children learn Spanish in school and speak Miskito (north) or Spanish (southwest) in the village, but they cannot speak their grandparents' tongue. Many parents and leaders now sense the urgency to speak and teach Pech at home while promoting bilingual education initiatives. The Pech were historically indoctrinated to the Catholic faith, but today Moravian and other Protestant missionaries work among them.

The Las Marias Pech depend largely on slash-and-burn agriculture, hunting, and fishing for their livelihood. They grow the same crops as the Miskito but, unlike them, place greater emphasis on yucca and corn. They also raise chickens, Muscovy ducks, and some cattle, but much of their fresh fish and meat still comes from the rain forest around them. They have a less-developed cash economy than the Miskito and are less involved in the lobster industry. Their subsistence relies on sharing labor and resources among related families. They sell surplus crops, fish, or game and buy household needs in Barra Plátano and other villages on the north coast. Many families continue gold panning along upriver streams during the dry season, and families can now earn cash by providing room, board, transport, or guide services to national and international tourists.

Although the Plátano Pech have undergone a significant culture change from their contact with the more dominant Miskito and ladino societies, they have not abandoned their culture and work to maintain their language and identity.

Garifuna

The Río Plátano Biosphere contains the historic buffer zone between the Garifuna and Miskito cultures. Historic animosities are attested to, even today, by an unpopulated stretch of several kilometers that separates the settlements of the two groups. Strictly speaking, Plaplaya is the only Garifuna settlement in the Plátano Biosphere, but others line the coast to the west and use lands within its boundaries. Plaplaya's houses, school, stores, and churches are stretched out along the main east-west water route to Palacios. It has 421 inhabitants, of which 71% are Garifuna, 22% are ladinos, and 6% Miskito. The number of ladinos has risen in recent years due to intermarriages with colonists. The Miskito minority reflects a few families segregated in the historic neighborhood of Sambal.

More than the Miskito, the Garifuna are fisherfolk, and their seagoing dugouts (called dories), nets, and other fishing gear are visible as one walks through the community. They plant coconut groves and cultivate patches of yucca mixed with xanthosoma (an important food crop, whose roots, leaves, and stems are eaten), sweet potatoes, yams, and pineapples in the sandy coastal soils nearby their settlements. Fields for beans, rice, bananas, plantains, and more are prepared along the natural levees of rivers and streams behind the communities. Men also hunt and fish, in some cases sharing forests with their Miskito neighbors. Some earn cash working as fishermen aboard commercial fishing boats from the Bay Islands, but most also sell crops.

The Garifuna have both recognizable African and Amerindian heritage. Their native language, Garifuna, comes from the Arawakan group, and women still prepare cassava bread from bitter yucca using a technique learned in the Lesser Antilles. African influences are visible in their folklore, music, and dance. Most are Catholics, but Protestants are more and more common. The Garifuna are characteristically outgoing and vivacious when visitors pass through their communities, which is increasingly common with new eco- and ethno-tourism in the reserve. Like the Miskito, there are a large number of female-headed households because men are often away working in the Bay Islands or even in the United States.

Ladinos

Ladinos settled the remote and isolated area that would become the Plátano Biosphere in the first two decades of the twentieth century. As part of the national majority mestizo population, they came to work on commercial banana plantations set up by the United Fruit Company along the Tinto, Sico, and Paulaya rivers. Despite an enormous infrastructure development, productions failed due to banana diseases. Nevertheless, many families decided to stay. The descendants of these *bananeros* formed the base of the so-called native ladino (*ladino nativo*) population, principally in eight settlements. Their slash-and-burn agriculture, cash cropping of staple foods, hunting, fishing, and small-scale cattle-rearing practices were more akin to those of the indigenous villagers than those of ladinos elsewhere who are heavily involved in market economy and cattle production. Nevertheless, they remained culturally ladinos with their Spanish language and Catholic religion.

Today, these communities are growing rapidly because of the arrival of new ladino colonists from other parts of the country. The Paulaya Valley has experienced accelerated colonization in the last fifteen years. Thirty-five settlements in the valley with 5,019 inhabitants use lands within the limits of the Plátano Biosphere. Government plans for additional colonization have been met by opposition by conservationists and cattlemen alike. The Sico-Paulaya ladinos, who formed their own cooperative to represent local interests, point out that most lands already have owners.

A much larger ladino population lives in the southwestern part of the reserve. This area, drained by the headwaters of the Wampu and Paulaya rivers, part of the historic Pech area, remained isolated from the national economy until the 1950s when the pine and mahogany forests began to attract commercial lumber operations. Lumber barons cut roads from Culmi to Las Marias during the 1970s before the establishment of the reserve. During the 1980s, they extended the roads to the headwaters of the Paulaya and Plátano rivers, and east to the middle drainage of the Wampu to extract mahogany from lands in the newly established biosphere. Along these routes, land-hungry colonists established new homesteads after cutting fields from forests. Cattle ranchers then consolidated large holdings by buying up homesteaders' lands, planting exotic grasses, and introducing the grazing economy as the cattle front extends eastward into the Mosquitia Corridor. Today this southwestern corner of the biosphere includes lands used by more than eighty communities with nearly 15,000 inhabitants.

The ladinos of the colonization front participate fully in the cash economy of the national society. The cultivate corn, beans, rice, and coffee for cash sale and local consumption. Most families raise a number of cows or pigs for local sale and consumption, but some now have sizable cattle herds for sale to outside markets. Ladino men often work as wage laborers for the larger cattle ranchers. In general, the population has a vaquero lifestyle, riding horses, wearing cowboy hats, and carrying pistols. It can be a violent and lawless place, like other colonization frontiers, but it is also a place of families trying to carve a living out of the wilderness.

The Setting

The Río Plátano Biosphere Reserve was established in 1980 in the northern reaches of the Mosquitia Corridor located in the northeastern section of Honduras. The United Nations Man and the Biosphere (MAB) Program sets aside priority conservation areas into an international network of biospheres that accommodate protection, conservation, and human use through a conceptual model of a core or nucleus surrounded by buffer areas. The Río Plátano was an ideal choice for a biosphere with its expansive rain-forest ecosystems and limited outside influence. The resident indigenous population and rich archaeological remains also conformed nicely to MAB guidelines. A management plan was written, and the Río Plátano Biosphere became the first such reserve in Central America. Designated a World Heritage Site in 1982, it remains one of the region's most significant conservation units.[1]

The largest part of the reserve is made up of tropical rain forests, but there are significant areas of pine savannas, as well as swamps, marshes, mangroves, and other freshwater and saltwater habitats along the coast. The reserve covers 815,000 hectares (2,013,050 acres) of the northern end of the Mosquitia Rain Forest Corridor, which extends from the Caribbean south across the Bosawás borderlands into Nicaragua, and is the largest contiguous tract of rain forest in Central America today. The Plátano Biosphere is one of the most significant conservation areas in the greater Mesoamerican Biological Corridor—an idealized system of interconnected protected areas connecting the lands, flora, and fauna of Central America.

THREATS TO SURVIVAL

The Honduran Department of Renewable Natural Resources (RENARE) was initially responsible for the management and protection of the Plátano Biosphere. Even during peak RENARE involvement, shortly after the reserve was established, financial support for reserve management was limited and park personnel included only a resident director and a few rangers. International donors financed the building of an administration building, a visitor center, and two ranger stations, but residents were basically unaware of the reserve's existence. No concerted efforts to manage the reserve occurred during the 1980s as the western limits became part of the country's most active colonization front.

Indigenous leaders became alarmed over the encroachment of colonists onto their lands in the Plátano Biosphere during the early 1990s. Miskito leaders opened dialogue with the Honduran government to gain legal control of their lands over twenty years ago, and some now question the reserve's establishment on historic indigenous lands. Over recent years, however, indigenous leaders have come to view biosphere status for their lands as a beneficial thing. In the early 1990s, Miskito leaders in the biosphere formed the Land Vigilance Committee, now called *Rayaka* or "life" in Miskito, to protect both their lands and the reserve. Other indigenous federations formed in recent years at Ahuas (BAMIASTA) and Wampusirpi (BAKINASTA) express similar concerns for the protection of their lands and the conservation of natural resources.

The Plátano Biosphere sadly was just another "paper" park (that is, a park that exists only on paper). Only two ill-equipped park rangers worked in the reserve when management responsibility was transferred to the State Forestry Agency (AFE/COHDEFOR) in 1991. At the time, the Palacios office was abandoned, the Kuri visitor center was destroyed, and the Las Marias station was barely functioning. Development or conservation organizations were little involved in reserve management issues. As a result, lumbermen and agricultural colonists continued cutting forests into the heart of the reserve breaching the original nucleus zone. With the changing demographic and resource use patterns, only a little more than a decade after its establishment, the original biosphere boundaries needed redefinition.

The Río Plátano Biosphere fortuitously became a regional conservation priority as part of a 1992 biodiversity agreement signed by the Central American presidents. Along with other, more recent Honduran decrees, it calls for the development of a binational protected area system for the Mosquitia Corridor linking the Plátano Biosphere and the proposed Tawahka Biosphere Reserve with the Nicaraguan Bosawás Reserve.

Aware of the lack of financial and technical resources needed for management, the Honduran government, through the State Forestry Agency, solicited help from the German government to manage the Plátano Biosphere. The German Bank (KfW) hired a German consulting firm, Gesellschaft für Agrarprojekte (GFA), to do a feasibility study for a conservation project.[2] None was implemented, however, owing to the Honduran government's failure to meet two preconditions: the amplification of the biosphere limit and the relocation of the colonists from within the nucleus. When GFA updated the feasibility study in 1995, virtually no state presence was found in the reserve and very little nongovernment organization (NGO) involvement. The local population was without knowledge of the area or had little interest in it. The study proposed expanding the reserve's limits to include additional areas of rain forest, pine savanna, and wetlands with indigenous settlements and the relocation of the colonists from the nucleus. To facilitate the project's start, it was designed in two phases, the one-year preparatory phase and the five-year principal phase, to allow the Honduran government sufficient time during the preparatory phase to approve the new biosphere law.[3]

The project began in April 1997. Honduras approved the new law (Decreto 170–97) amplifying the biosphere limits later that year, according to the recommendations by the German consultants. A related decision was made by AFE-COHDEFOR to establish a new Río Plátano Forestry Region exclusively for the protection and management of the biosphere. The National Agrarian Institute (INA) then passed legal title to the Plátano Biosphere directly to AFE-COHDEFOR. These actions were apparently aimed at stabilizing the land tenure situation and facilitating reserve management.

The enlargement of the Plátano Biosphere eastward to include the lands and peoples along the Patuca River, coupled with the natural population increase and continual immigration of colonists, has changed the demographic image of the reserve. The biosphere population that was once primarily indigenous is now half ladino. The new limits include 815,000 hectares (2,013,050 acres) of lands used by 180 communities with over 40,000 inhabitants. About 53% of the population is ladino, 44% is Miskito, 3% is Garifuna, and 1% is Pech. The distribution of the ethnic groups is similar to the past with indigenous villages in the north, east, and southeast, and with ladino settlements to the west and southwest.

The new design of the Plátano Biosphere divides it into three macrozones. The Nucleus Zone, covering 215,000 hectares (531,000 acres) of the reserve's center, is for nature and ecosystem protection and will be free of human settlement. The existing ladino population of about 100 homes and 650 people living in the Tilopo area are being relocated by the Honduran government in fulfillment of a condition tied to continued German support. The Cultural Zone, which covers 400,000 hectares (988,000 acres) of lands used by about 60 communities with 20,000 inhabitants, still contains predominantly natural ecosystems. It is designed to maintain biological diversity over the long term, permitting the sustainable use of resources while proportioning rights to ethnic groups. The Cultural Zone is mostly the historic patrimony of the Miskito (with 84% of the population), but there are also Garifuna (5%), Pech (1%), and ladinos (10%). Land use has been primarily for subsistence. Finally, the Buffer Zone covering 200,000 hectares (494,000 acres) along the west and southwest of the reserve is managed to guarantee the protection of the biological diversity over the long term while meeting the needs of resident communities. It is almost exclusively the domain of ladinos including lands of 100 communities with about 20,000 individuals; only two Pech communities remain in the zone today. Land use in the Buffer Zone is mostly for subsistence but farmers are involved in commercial coffee cultivation, cattle raising, and timber extraction.[4]

RESPONSE: STRUGGLES TO SUSTAIN CULTURAL SURVIVAL

Participatory Mapping and Zoning

The participatory resource zoning (PRZ) aimed at empowering residents of the Río Plátano Biosphere in the management of their lands while aiding state regional development and natural resource conservation efforts. The primary objective was to define a community-approved land use zoning system for inclusion in the new management plan that reflects existing practices and is defined in consensus with the resident population. This would be done through using a participatory approach that helps local peoples articulate their own cognitive understanding of natural resource use into standardized forms. The indigenous and ladino societies of the reserve are fundamentally non text-based (not written down or dependent on written documents) and their traditions and knowledge even today are mostly passed down orally. Three related specific objectives were: 1) to incorporate reserve residents into research to increase their participation in the management and protection of the biosphere; 2) to produce large-scale maps of community land use in the reserve; and 3) to design a consensual zoning system that recognizes state-established regulations while respecting existing land-use practices and proposals defined by the resident populations.

A technical team was formed to direct the process. The author initiated activities working with fellow Rio Plátano Biosphere Reserve Project (BRP) staffer and GFA Consultant Lic. Luis Corrales. Moskitia Powisa (MO-PAWI), the most active NGO working on the development and conservation of the Mosquitia region, was contracted to handle the administrative and logistical aspects of the work, and a development expert was added to the team. The final member of the team was a university-trained Miskito leader. The PRZ process was directed primarily by this technical team, but other BRP project and AFE-COHDEFOR staff were involved in decision making and added valuable expertise during many events. The director of the new forestry region, Rosman Marquez, and his assistant, José Varela, were particularly valuable participants. Technical assistants from the National Geographic Institute (IGN), as well as graduate students from the Department of Geography at the University of Kansas, provided valuable support.

To begin the participatory process, the technical team met with organizations interested in the future of the reserve, explained the zoning proposal, and requested support. They also met with community leaders, indigenous and grassroots organizations, and municipal governments in the reserve. From the onset, it was always emphasized that the PRZ activity would respect the rights of the resident populations while bringing them into reserve management.

Next came the selection of the coordinators. The biosphere was divided into seven work zones: Batalla, La Costa, Brus Laguna, Ahuas, Wampusirpi, Tawahka, and Sico-Paulaya. Each would have its own coordinator and small number of surveyors. The technical team met with community leaders in each zone to explain the PRZ, look for their collaboration, and ask them to elect their own coordinator for the activity. While some people were suspicious or cautious, communities responded favorably and elected a respected group of three teachers, a nurse, a pastor, a businessman, and a mechanic. The coordinator comprised Garifuna, one Tawahka, one ladino, and four Miskito.

A two-day seminar provided the seven coordinators with training about the BRP project and PRZ activity. The coordinators would serve administrative functions, remain apolitical and nonsectarian, and act as conciliators. They would supervise and assist the work of the surveyors. The responsibilities, salary, and benefits of both the coordinators and surveyors

Participating mapmakers. Courtesy of Peter H. Herlihy.

were defined by consensus. Specific training focused on how coordinators would hold community meetings to explain the PRZ activity and to elect surveyors. The communities again responded by carefully electing twenty-four well-qualified representatives, of which fourteen were Miskito; six, ladino; two, Tawahka; one, Garifuna; and one, Pech. Alternate surveyors were also selected at this time.

Everyone came together for the first workshop (June 14–23, 1997) held in the coastal Garifuna community and municipal capital of Batalla. Given the enormity of the reserve, it was decided that each successive workshop should be held in a different part of the biosphere to bring as many actors as possible into the process. About seventy individuals participated in the event, including the participatory team of coordinators, surveyors, and the technical team, but also representatives from the State Forestry Agency, municipal governments, indigenous federations, NGOs, and cooperatives. A variety of educational and training activities provided participants with background about the conservation of natural resources and the concept of a protected area. Specific focus was placed on the objectives, limits, and population of the Río Plátano Biosphere. The technical team explained the PRZ activity to the assembly. The roles and functions of the surveyors were discussed, and the precise geographic area covered by each was defined. Exercises were developed to identify, describe, and analyze land-use activities in each zone of the reserve. Here, the surveyors used their own cognitive knowledge to explain how they farm, hunt, fish, pan for gold, and use the forest. Finally, draft land-use questionnaires and household census forms were critiqued and rewritten. Role playing, mock meetings, and interviews with Batalla residents were used to train surveyors how to administer the questionnaires.

Mapping was the keystone activity of the PRZ activity. The content, objective, and importance of maps were discussed in this first workshop, and the surveyors learned how to draw simple pencil-and-paper sketch maps of their rivers, settlements, and resource-use areas. They considered different ways to develop a collaborative mapping exercise during community meetings for recording toponyms, or place-names, and drawing cognitive sketch maps of village lands. The workshop concluded like the subsequent one with the coordinators and surveyors developing work plans and budgeting expenses for fieldwork.

The surveyors returned to their respective work areas and went from village to village administering the land-use questionnaires and drawing sketch maps in village meetings. They went from house to house administering the census. At times, this first field work was particularly difficult because it required repeated village meetings to gain confidence, complete questionnaires, and draw sketch maps. The surveyors stimulated participation and interest among families and community leaders more often than not, but some villagers remained suspicious. Coordinators helped by traveling to villages to meet with leaders to clarify the system and answer questions.

The second workshop (August 17–September 5, 1997) was held in the historic *bananero* community of Sico, now better known for its ranchers. Some indigenous surveyors, fearing reprisal given historic animosities, were apprehensive about meeting in this ladino community, but the event actually helped strengthen interethnic relations and cooperation.

Cartographic analysis of the community land-use questionnaire information was a central focus of the second workshop. Village resource-use locations for agriculture, hunting, fishing, forest use, and more were recorded as toponyms on the questionnaires. The surveyors' sketch maps provided firsthand accounts of locations. Participatory mapping combines the mental faculties of the surveyors, coordinators, and geographer for fixing location. The plotting of each toponym, settlement, and resource-use location involves relating the surveyor's knowledge to that of the sketch maps and standard cartographic procedures. Fixing location often involved "virtual trips," traveling up and down rivers, streams, and hillslopes in the mind's eye to determine distance and location. Thousands of resource-use sites were meticulously plotted onto large-scale base maps (1:50,000 scale) of each of the communities in each of the seven work zones.

The results of the household census were analyzed and organized by community and zone. Additional presentations and discussions about natural resource conservation, the PRZ process, and the roles of the participatory team occurred during this second assembly. Emphasis was placed on the objectives and geographical limits of the nucleus, cultural, and buffer zones of the reserve. The surveyors were then prepared for the next round of fieldwork, and an approach for validating the zonal maps was developed.

After the workshop, the technical team returned to BRP project headquarters in Tegucigalpa to redraft the cartographic information. New zonal maps, some exceeding 2 by 1½ meters (6 feet by 4.5 feet) in size, were drawn in black ink including rivers, settlements, and resource-use zones, and the boundaries of the BRP. Copies were sent to all the coordinators and surveyors. The logistical realities of working in the country's most inaccessible zone were daunting at times.

During their second fieldwork phase, the surveyors held community meetings to review advances in the work, to correct and validate the zonal maps, and to discuss the need for a zoning system. Taking the work seriously, many communities spontaneously formed their own "biosphere committees" to review the information produced. Members of the technical team also visited each zone to hold informative town hall-type meetings and to work with the coordinators and surveyors to begin a definition of a land zoning system.

The surveyors and technical team studied resource-use characteristics displayed on the zonal maps and tried to define appropriate land-use categories. Discussions led to the notion of a multiple-use zone where agriculture was present with other uses. The forests had more extensive use. The surveyors explained repeatedly that their communities had pretty clear understandings of where they did not want to see deforestation or the extension of agricultural lands. This clear criterion led to the simple proposal of a multiple-use (with agriculture and ranching) and extensive-use (without agriculture and ranching) zones. A special-use zone was added by consensus to accommodate the changing needs for the establishment of areas for watershed protection, forestry, protection, ecotourism, archaeological sites, and more. The technical team also used these field visits to train the coordinators and surveyors in the use of Global Positioning System (GPS) technology to collect map information.

The third workshop (November 11–24, 1997) was held in Brus Laguna, the municipal seat and historic center for education, the Moravian church, and Miskito activism. The event strengthened understandings of the zoning process, and its protagonists helped convince indigenous leaders and government authorities of the need to define a zoning system for the management plan. The assembly opened with a progress report and a more specific look at the validation of the zonal maps. The assembly divided into zonal groups to analyze existing land-use and tenure practices. The notion of establishing community regulations for conservation and protection was explained.

This workshop focused on defining the zoning system for the buffer and cultural zones of the Plátano Biosphere. The rationale for establishing land-use zones and boundaries was hotly debated. The assembly finally agreed on the simple zoning design of multiple-use, extensive-use, and special-use zones. The coordinators and surveyors worked together in their zonal groups to define potential land-use regulations by listing activities permitted, not permitted, and permitted with restrictions for each type of land use in the multiple- and extensive-use zones. Each group presented its results for debate in the assembly. Most proposals were logical and met assembly approval, but some were hotly contested. Much deliberation occurred, for example, over the size of a "protection strip" to guard water edges, decided to be 100 meters (328 feet) along rivers and 50 meters (164 feet) along streams and lagoons. Equally conflictive were the dimensions of the multiple-use zone put at a kilometer inland from the protection strip along rivers and half that for streams. Regulations concerning the transfer and sale of lands were unknown in the region. Differences in opinion also existed over the extent cattle ranching would be permitted. Reaching consensus often meant long and heated debates. Nevertheless, the assembly reached preliminary agreements over most matters concerning the proposed zoning system.

During the workshop, the technical team and surveyors plotted the proposed limits of the multiple-use zone onto the zonal maps while incorporating corrections and new GPS points from fieldwork. Surveyors were given additional training in GPS use. The workshop concluded with the development of a methodology to review and validate the proposed zoning scheme with the communities, emphasizing the need to attain the widest participation possible.

Copies of the proposed land-use regulations and revised zonal maps were forwarded to the coordinators and surveyors who held village meetings for their analysis. The surveyors discussed the content of the land-use activities permitted, not permitted, and permitted with restrictions with villagers. While the review process varied between one village and another, community participation was significant, and the villagers understood the importance of the work. More communities formed committees to conduct in-depth analysis. The increasing community involvement brought increasing support.

The fourth workshop (February 1–13, 1998) was held deep within the Mosquitia Corridor along the reserve's southeastern margin in the Miskito community and municipal seat of Wampusirpi. The technical team outlined the principal features of the new Plátano Biosphere law and an archaeologist from the Honduran Institute of Anthropology and History provided technical orientations about the documentation and protection of archaeological sites.

This workshop focused on the review of the land-use regulations following the observations and recommendations obtained from the communities. It took a week to discuss and revise the proposed land-use regulations of activities permitted, not permitted, or permitted with restrictions for the multiple-use and extensive-use zones. Long debates continued concerning some land-use practices, but a final draft was agreed upon. The limits of the multiple-use zone on each zonal map were revised to incorporate community recommendations, and new observations and GPS points were added.

The notion of comanagement (management of the reserve shared by the national government and local indigenous and ladino peoples) was debated for the first time in this fourth workshop. Discussion focused on the structure of the National System of Protected Areas which calls for establishing "orientation committees" at the zonal, regional, and national levels. Many communities had already formed similar committees, as mentioned above. The assembly discussed the composition and functions of the orientation committee that would supervise the implementation of zoning and land-use regulations in collaboration with AFE-COHDEFOR, the municipal governments, and other governmental organizations and NGOs. At the close of the workshop, the director of the forestry region worked with the assembly to identify sites for AFE-COHDEFOR control posts and initiated a selection process for employing the surveyors as park rangers, with community approval.

The technical team sent copies of the newly revised zonal maps and land-use regulations document to the surveyors who again reviewed the zoning system, maps, and land-use regulations in village meetings. Copies were also presented for analysis by government authorities, indigenous leaders, and representatives from cooperatives and other concerned organizations.

The final workshop was held in the ladino community of Palacios in an attempt to incorporate it more completely into the PRZ activity. Municipal and indigenous authorities, as well as high-level representatives from AFE-COHDEFOR, other conservation projects, and organizations participated in the event. The focus was on the final revision of the land-use regulations. In open assembly, the final contents of each of the more than 200 land-use regulations were discussed, sometimes hotly debated or eliminated, but usually slightly corrected or changed before approval by a consensus vote from each zonal group. Some broader dispositions concerning biosphere management were also added at this time. Additions and corrections were added to the zonal maps, and the limits of the multiple-use and extensive-use zones were reviewed one final time.

The development of the comanagement structure with the new AFE-COHDEFOR Forestry Region was a topic of speculation. Advances made in the formation of the orientation committees were impressive, and there was broad acknowledgement that these could help AFE-COHDEFOR apply the new zoning system and land-use regulations. This was also the occasion for the forestry region director to make final arrangements for contracting a number of the surveyors to work as park guards.

The workshop ended with the assembly questioning how to provide follow-up to the process. Now that the participatory zoning was ending, there was concern that the BRP project, state, and NGOs should continue related activities to maintain levels of interest and awareness and to develop the comanagement structure.

The participatory zoning of the Río Plátano Biosphere Reserve provides a powerful example of how maps and mapmaking can be used to enhance cultural survival and conserve biophysical environments. The participatory mapping process used here allowed the biosphere's indigenous and ladino populations to articulate their own knowledge of resource use into a community-approved zoning proposal, involving them in reserve management for the first time. Through the process, communities formulated their own land-use regulations, many of which were previously unthinkable.

The PRZ brought unprecedented levels of interest and participation in the management and protection of the reserve. Congressmen and conservationists, municipal authorities and leaders from indigenous and nongovernmental organizations, as well as from churches and other community-based groups, joined in some level of involvement. Most important, for the first time, reserve residents were brought into the conservation formula.

Indigenous and ladino community-elected representatives were integrated into a participatory team through 500 hours of instruction and training concerning the management and protection of the BRP. They worked with the technical team to develop the workshops, design the questionnaires, collect and analyze field information, draw sketch maps, draft standard maps, design the zoning system, formulate the land-use regulations, and create new comanagement strategies. Each in concert held dozens of community meetings for the collection, analysis, critical review, and validation of the information produced. Today they have emerged as vocal conservation experts, and about a dozen now work as park guards for the new Río Plátano Forestry Region.

The participatory mapping produced accurate standard maps of settlement and resource use at 1:50,000 scale for the entire biosphere. The process helped residents understand how their land uses relate to the biosphere limits and macro-zones. The maps and mapmaking process helped provide the spatial understandings needed for defining the new zoning system. Additional baseline information produced for reserve management included a census of every family in and around the reserve and a community-level questionnaire on socioeconomic conditions.

The PRZ activity developed a zoning system with land-use regulations as the central component proposed for the reserve's new management plan.

The system, which reflects existing practices, was defined together with the resident population. It has four land use zones: protection strip (along water edges), multiple use (agricultural and other uses), extensive use (hunting, fishing, collecting, and forest use), and special use (archaeological, tourism, water supply, and so on). It is regulated by the elaborate set of more than 200 community-approved land-use regulations which define the activities permitted, not permitted, and permitted with restrictions in each zone.

Another important outcome was the understanding and even empathy that developed between the different ethnic groups of the reserve who found themselves confronted by many of the same problems and opportunities. Broad consensus now exists to help manage and protect the Plátano Biosphere, and indigenous and ladino communities alike embrace the notion of comanagement committees for implementing the new management plan. At the same time, the process facilitated the entrance of the State Forestry Agency into reserve management. Past indifference and corruption by forestry personnel have been excused by biosphere residents who now embrace the possibility that AFE-COHDEFOR is opening a new era of cooperation and collaboration, and that their rights to lands and resources will be respected. Critics are not so optimistic.

The consensual zoning system is a powerful instrument for managing and protecting the biosphere. Significantly, indigenous federations, local governments, grassroots organizations, and NGOs openly endorse the design. Its implementation as part of a new management plan, however, will probably depend on the state's ability to accommodate community guidelines. Most should not be a problem, including the prohibition of new colonization, the absolute protection of the nucleus, and the ban on hunting endangered fauna; all these fit nicely with state policy. At issue are some homespun land-use regulations that do not conform exactly with state laws. Villagers want a protected strip along waterways (rivers, 100 meters [328 feet]; streams and lagoons, 50 meters [164 feet]), for example, but their dimensions do not conform with larger ones set in forestry law. Nevertheless, these restrictions are applied nowhere in Honduras, and the biosphere residents are serious about enforcing the limits they approved. Similarly, a regulation that limits landholding to about 35 hectares (86 acres) may seem excessive to some authorities who lament that farmers in other parts of the country have much less land; others think it too small eliminating the possibility for large landholdings. Dozens of these types of issues related to the community-approved zoning and management guidelines must be reviewed by state agencies. If viewed objectively, state authorities will find most of the community proposals reasonable. Then, even after state approval, administrators working on biosphere management will need to understand the values of the consensual zoning system and respect the fact that it reflects an enormous level of community involvement and decision making.

Additional dangers lie in the fact that AFE-COHDEFOR now holds legal title to the land in the reserve. Under enlightened stewardship, this can help protect the area from outside invasions. It is also possible, however, that given the corrupt history of the state forestry institution, this might open possibilities for granting concessions to business interests without considering the rights or desires of the local population.

FOOD FOR THOUGHT

The participatory zoning of the Río Plátano Biosphere confirms that diverse, local peoples can, and must, be involved in the comanagement of their lands and resources within protected areas. However, while the collaboration and community involvement needed for the success of such an undertaking are easily understood conceptually, practically speaking they are complex, expensive, and difficult objectives to attain. Community-based, participatory mapping initiatives in Central America, like the example discussed in this chapter, have enabled indigenous and rural mestizo populations to produce standard maps and descriptive information about their lands and livelihoods that are intelligible to both themselves and to outsiders—and can contribute to cultural survival. Similar approaches have gained wide acceptance in conservation and development projects affecting indigenous lands and protected areas around the globe. The PRZ demonstrates that participatory mapping can provide a keystone activity around which other greater concerns can revolve. The process shows that local peoples can be empowered in the management and control of their lands and resources while promoting natural resource protection, land tenure security, and improved indigenous-state relations.

Questions

1. What is participatory mapping? How is it different from other kinds of mapping?
2. How did this participatory mapping project demonstrate the political power of maps to sustain culture?
3. What do you suppose were the major conflicts between the various peoples living within the Río Plátano Biosphere Reserve (ladinos, Miskito, Garifuna, Pech)?
4. Given the past history of corruption within the Honduran forestry department, what are the likely constraints to successful implementation of the consensual comanagement plan for the Río Plátano Biosphere Reserve?
5. Advanced information technologies, including geographic information systems (GIS) and GPS, have been criticized because of their potential to increase the control of the poor or ethnic minorities in the Third World by the rich, powerful, and military. How does this project address this serious criticism?

NOTES

Unless otherwise indicated, information and data included in this chapter come from Peter H. Herlihy and Laura Hobson Herlihy, *La herencia cultural de las Reserva de la Biosfera del Río Plátano: Una area de confluencias étnicas en La mosquitia," Herencia de nuestro pasad: La Reserva de la Biosfera Río Plátano*, ed. Vicente Murphy, 1–15. (Tegucigalpa, Honduras: ROCAP (USAID), WWF, and COHDEFOR, 1991).

1. Denis Glick and Jorge Betancourt, "The Río Plátano Biosphere Reserve: Unique Resource, Unique Alternative," *Ambio* 12, no. 3–4 (1983): 168–73.

2. Gesellschaft für Agrarprojeke *Proyecto Manejo y Protección de la Reserva de la Biosfera del Río Plátano* (Tegucigalpa, Honduras: COHDEFOR and KFW-Kreditanstalt Für Wiederaufbau, 1992).

3. GFA, *Proyecto Manejo y Protección de la Reserva de la Biosfera del Río Plátano: Mision de Actualizacion del Estudio de Factibilidad* (Hamburg, Germany: Gesellschaft für Agrarprojekte, 1996).

4. GFA, *Censo Poblacional 1997/98 Resultados, Proyecto de Manejo y Protección de la Biosfera del Río Plátano*, (Hamburg, Germany: Gesellschaft für Agrarprojekte, 1998).

RESOURCE GUIDE

Published Literature

Denniston, Derek. "Defending the Land with Maps." *World Watch* 7, no. 1 (1994): 27–31.

Herlihy, Peter H. "Participatory Research Mapping of Indigenous Lands in the Honduran Mosquitia." In *Demographic Diversity and Change in Central America*, edited by Anne Pebley and Luis Rosero-Bixby. Santa Monica, CA: Rand Books, 1997.

———. "Participatory Research Zoning of the Río Plátano Biosphere in the Honduran Mosquitia." In *Natural Resource Management: Between Poverty Alleviation and Nature Conservation*. Hamburg, Germany: Gesellschaft für Agrarprojekte, 1999.

Nietschmann, Bernard. "Defending the Miskito Reef with Maps and GPS." *Cultural Survival Quarterly* 18, no. 4 (1995): 34–37.

———. "Protecting Indigenous Coral Reefs and Sea Territories, Miskito Coast, RAAN, Nicaragua." In *Conservation Through Cultural Survival: Indigenous Peoples and Protected Areas*, edited by Stan Stevens, 193–224. Washington, D.C.: Island Press, 1997.

Poole, Peter. "Indigenous Lands and Power Mapping in the Americas: Merging Technologies." *Native Americas* 15, no. 4 (1998): 34–43.

Toledo Maya Cultural Council and the Toledo Alcaldes Association. *Maya Atlas: The Struggle to Preserve Maya Land in Southern Belize*. Compiled by the Maya People of Southern Belize in conjunction with the Toledo Maya Cultural Council and the Toledo Alcaldes Association, with the Assistance of the Indian Law Resource Center, GeoMap Group-U.C. Berkeley, and the

Society for the Preservation of Education and Research. Berkeley, Calif: North Atlantic Books, 1997.

WWW Sites

Honduras This Week Online
Weekly newspaper in English often has articles about nature conservation in the Mosquitia region of Honduras. http://www.marrder.com/htw/

Patuca River Campaign
Describes a proposed dam project in the Mosquitia region of Honduras.
http://www.ben2.ucla.edu/~alexagui/patuca/index.html

Smithsonian Institution, National Museum of Natural History, Department of Botany.
Information about the Río Plátano Biosphere Reserve.
http://nmnhwww.si.edu/botany/projects/centres/platano.html

Chapter 8

The Ngóbe of Western Panama

John R. Bort and Philip D. Young

CULTURAL OVERVIEW

The People

The Ngóbe live in the three western provinces of the Republic of Panama: Bocas del Toro, Chiriqui, and Veraguas. Unlike in other groups, the Ngóbe way of life is endangered not because their population is declining but because it is increasing. With a population of about 125,000, they are the second largest indigenous group in Central America, outnumbered only by the Maya in Guatemala. The Ngóbe are often referred to as Guaymí by outsiders but call themselves Ngóbe and prefer to be identified by this name, which means "people" in their language. Little is known about their history before the arrival of Europeans in the New World, but they are probably descended from groups who fled from the devastating Spanish conquest of the more accessible and desirable coastal areas of Panama. The Ngóbe are first mentioned as a distinct group in 1682. Early descriptions of their culture and traditions indicate strong cultural continuity over the centuries. Culturally, the Ngóbe are closely related to the Bugle and Teribe populations in Panama and the Cabécar and Bri Bri populations in Costa Rica. All speak languages of the Chibchan language family, which also includes many native languages in northwestern South America.

Even though they have been influenced by the European world for 500 years, since the time of Christopher Columbus, most of the Ngóbe had relatively little contact with the outside world. Early contact led to "mestizoization" or adoption of nontraditional ways among some segments of the population. Descendants of these people have been absorbed into the general (ladino) population of Panama. Contact with the outside world for the more isolated segments of the population was infrequent and sporadic

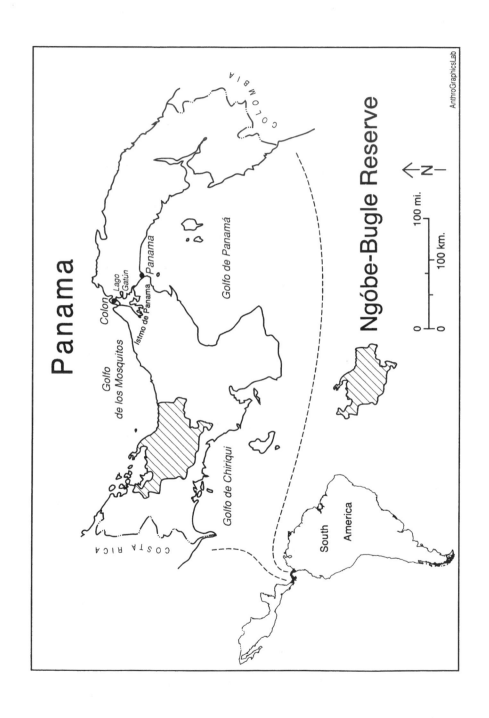

Panama

Ngóbe-Bugle Reserve

COLOMBIA

COSTA RICA

Golfo
de los Mosquitos

Colon

Lago
Gatún

Istmo de Panama

Panama

Golfo de Panamá

Golfo de Chiriquí

South
America

N

100 mi.

100 km.

0

0

AnthroGraphicsLab

well into this century. Because of this isolation and the fact that outsiders had little interest in mountainous, marginal lands, the Ngóbe were left alone to follow their traditional way of life. As a result, they have managed to preserve their language and many of their customs and to maintain a very distinct cultural identity.

The Setting

Today the Ngóbe occupy approximately 2,500 square miles of rugged mountainous territory in western Panama. On the Caribbean side of the isthmus, their lands stretch from the continental divide to the Caribbean Sea. On the Pacific, they are restricted to the mountains. In the past the Ngóbe occupied a far more extensive area which stretched all the way to the Pacific Coast and the Costa Rican border. As time passed, ladino cattle ranchers and coffee growers gradually forced them off the best lands.

There were no roads in Ngóbe territory until the 1970s. Even today very few roads penetrate the Ngóbe homeland; most are little more than rough dirt and gravel tracks. Even with four-wheel-drive vehicles, these roads are frequently impassable during the rainy months. Throughout most of the area occupied by the Ngóbe, travel is possible only on foot or horseback, and some areas are too rugged even for horses.

Because Ngóbe lands are located between eight and nine degrees north of the equator, temperatures are fairly constant throughout the year. Altitude varies from sea level to about 6,000 feet. Near sea level, daytime temperatures are usually above 80°F with high humidity (similar to the southeastern United States in July and August). As altitude increases, average temperatures become cooler; some of the higher areas experience temperatures as low as 55° to 60°F on occasion.

The Caribbean and Pacific sides of the isthmus have different climatic patterns: On the Pacific, there is a distinct dry season that usually begins in early December and extends until April during which virtually no rain falls. On the Caribbean slope, no distinct dry season occurs, but there are occasional periods when it will not rain for a week or possibly two. This dramatic difference in rainfall patterns influences the natural vegetation patterns as well as the crops most commonly cultivated by the Ngóbe.

The terrain throughout the area is very rugged with extremely few areas where the land is flat. The soils are heavily weathered and rather poor in nutrients. When vegetation is disturbed and the soils are exposed to the tropical sun and rain, erosion and leaching of soil nutrients occurs rapidly. If left undisturbed, the natural vegetation of the region is mature tropical forest. However, extensive areas have been cleared for agriculture and pastures, and few areas of mature forest exist today. Large areas are now either grasslands or covered with secondary growth forest.

Traditional Subsistence Strategies

The Ngóbe traditionally meet their subsistence needs by combining slash-and-burn agriculture and the raising of livestock. Major crops include corn, beans, rice, bananas, and root crops such as sweet manioc (tapioca), yams, and New World taro. Root crops are more important on the wetter Caribbean side of the isthmus where corn and beans in particular do not grow as well as they do on the Pacific slopes. On both sides of the isthmus, the Ngóbe also cultivate a wide array of minor crops, including some fruit trees, which add variety to their diet. Cultivation is done with a few basic hand tools including machetes, axes, and metal-tipped digging sticks.

The most important domestic animals are cattle, pigs, and chickens with a few turkeys and ducks for variety. To augment these food supplies, some hunting and fishing as well as the gathering of wild plants is done, but these are secondary activities. Many wild plants, mostly greens, are also eaten, but these make up only a tiny part of the diet. Many wild plants are also used as medicines. Deer and wild pigs are the most important large game animals hunted, but many smaller animals and birds are also taken. Most hunting is done with .22 caliber rifles or shotguns. Because of deforestation and heavy hunting, wild animal populations have declined in recent years, and hunting is of only minor importance today. Fishing is done with dams, nets, weirs, hooks, spears, arrows, and fish poison. The importance of fishing varies greatly from area to area. It is most important along the Caribbean coast and along major rivers, such as the Cricamola in Bocas del Toro and the Fonseca in Chiriquí, and of very minor importance elsewhere in the highlands.

Until the twentieth century, the Ngóbe were predominantly self-sufficient. Their economy was based on sharing, barter, and reciprocity. Some domestic animals and small quantities of crops were sold to obtain the modest amounts of money that were needed to purchase the manufactured items that the Ngóbe had come to depend upon and could not produce, such as metal tools, cooking pots, and cloth. On rare occasions, individuals traveled out of their home area to seek temporary jobs for very short periods of time on cattle ranches and coffee or vegetable farms in order to earn enough cash to purchase desired goods. This was a rare occurrence until this century.

Social and Political Organization

The Ngóbe live in very small villages called *caserios* which seldom include more than five to ten houses. The houses in a *caserio* are occupied by people who are related to one another, either by blood or by marriage. Kin groups, that is, the extended group of relatives, are the organizational basis of Ngóbe society. Kin groups regulate the behavior of their members,

Ngóbe children, Cerro Mamita, Chiriquí, 1964. Photo by Philip D. Young.

and individuals look to their kin to provide moral, social, and economic support and assistance. Kin groups also control access to land.

Marriages may be polygynous; that is, a man may have more than one wife. Women are not allowed to have more than one husband. The co-wives of a man may be sisters or they may be unrelated. After marriage residence in the village of the husband is preferred; however, residence in the wife's village may occur if land is in short supply in the husband's community. Traditionally, marriage is not simply a union between individuals. It is considered to establish a political and economic alliance between the kin groups of the married couple. Ideally, marriages involved symmetrical exchanges of women between kin groups. That is, a man from one group would marry a woman from another and his group, in turn, would provide a wife, often his sister, to a man in the other group.

Ngóbe oral traditions describe great caciques (chiefs or leaders) of the past who exerted a considerable influence over areas within the Ngóbe territory. This informal influence was based on a man's personal characteristics, such as generosity, wisdom in settling disputes, and prowess in a major ritual called the *krun* in the Ngóbe language or *balsería* in Spanish. Hundreds, even thousands, attended these ritual events, and great prestige was gained by participating in and hosting them. The major activity of the *krun* is a contest in which individuals or teams take turns hurling six-foot-long balsa wood sticks at the calves of an opponent's legs while the opponent dances with his back to the thrower and tries to avoid being hit. Only men engage in the stick throwing, but men, women, and children attend the event which lasts four days.

Early in this century, the Panamanian government imposed a system of appointed officials (*corregidores* or magistrates) who were responsible for keeping the civil registry (recording births and deaths) and acting as judges in disputes. Ngóbe who had learned to read and write Spanish were appointed to these positions. However, many Ngóbe continue to seek out leaders who have earned the respect of the community through traditional means to settle disputes.

Religion and World View

After 500 years of influence by the Catholic Church, a large proportion of the Ngóbe are nominally Catholic, but extremely few practice any Catholic rituals. In a few localized pockets, some Protestant evangelical groups have attracted small numbers of followers, but their influence is not very widespread. Most Ngóbe still retain a number of traditional beliefs and rituals. Good and evil spirits are believed to exist as are a god of lightning and a protector god. The Ngóbe still tell stories of the great culture heroes of the past and often attribute godlike qualities to them. Rituals such as placing burning pieces of termite mound next to crosses on opposite sides of trails leading into communities or individual houses are believed to ward off evil spirits which are thought to cause illness. The crosses appear to be of non-Christian origin and are usually made of a special wood called fragrant cedar. Rituals are also performed to protect houses from lightning strikes. The consumption of cocoa bean paste mixed with hot water during a nightlong vigil is believed to prevent injury by spirits. Some spirits are believed to be capable of disguising themselves as animals in order to ambush unwary travelers along trails at night and cause them to become ill. For this reason, traditional Ngóbe do not like to travel at night. Traditional religious practitioners called *sukias* also attempt to cure illness, make predictions about the future, and interpret dreams based on communications with spirits.

THREATS TO SURVIVAL

Demographic Trends

An explosive and continuing population increase has been driving many of the changes in Ngóbe society in recent decades. The total Ngóbe population was only 16,161 in 1930; by 1960, it had increased to 35,867; and in 1970, it had grown to 44,794. Even today reliable population figures are not available for all of the area occupied by the Ngóbe. However, the census of 1990 put the population at 121,769, which probably is a reasonably accurate figure. Approximately 109,000 live within the territory traditionally occupied by the Ngóbe; the rest live in the towns and cities of Panama. Some reside and work permanently on commercial banana plantations. Others, not included in the census, have moved to Costa Rica seeking lands to farm.

This dramatic population increase has had major implications for the sustainability of the traditional slash-and-burn agricultural system. By 1960 Ngóbe population density was about six people per square kilometer (15 people per square mile) which is believed to be about the maximum density sustainable for slash-and-burn agriculture in tropical areas. Most of their land is not well suited to more intensive forms of cultivation, and land shortages are now common. Individuals and whole groups of kinsmen are increasingly forced to seek alternatives or supplements to subsistence agriculture to feed their families. This usually means greater involvement in wage labor in locations distant from their homes.

Current Events and Conditions

More than ever before in their history, the Ngóbe are being confronted by outside influences. Most notable during the past thirty years are the increasing intrusion of the national political system and the global economic system. The decade of the 1970s was the period in which most of the forces with ongoing and increasing influence began to manifest themselves. Panama's national government under Omar Torrijos initiated a series of efforts ostensibly designed to benefit the indigenous population. However, to date, the Ngóbe have had little or no input into the various projects designed to help them, and some Ngóbe have protested. According to Ngóbe leader Julio Dixón, "We ask national organizations and Panamanian society in general to give us the right to choose our own destiny" (emphasis in original).[1] A well-known Ngóbe female leader expressed similar sentiments: "[W]e do not have the right to express our viewpoints about major community issues. What we have always had are imposed decisions without the slightest consent of those of us who, historically, have lived in these communities."[2]

During the oil crisis of the late 1970s, an oil pipeline was constructed across the isthmus from the Pacific to the community of Chiriqui Grande on the Caribbean. The pipeline was built to transship oil from Alaska to refineries on the East and Gulf coasts of the United States. A high-quality paved road paralleling the pipeline was constructed. For the first time, the province of Bocas del Toro was connected to Chiriquí Province and the rest of Panama. This road does not go through Ngóbe territory, but it does make the movement of goods and people into and out of Ngóbe areas far easier than in the past. Trade and travel patterns have been dramatically reoriented throughout Bocas del Toro as a result of the road.

Some access roads have also been extended into traditional Ngóbe territory. Most are relatively rough dirt tracks, but they do allow access by vehicles. One of the most spectacular efforts has been the construction of an access road from the Pacific lowlands to Cerro Colorado in the highlands, the location of a very large low-grade copper deposit. Since 1972 Cerro Colorado has been the site of exploration and test drilling by four different multinational mining companies. To date, a mine has not been developed because of the relatively low international copper prices and ample supplies of ore from mines in other countries. However, the development of a very large-scale open-pit mining operation deep in Ngóbe territory would have tremendous social, economic, and environmental consequences. The Ngóbe are certainly aware of the potential impact. As one Ngóbe spokesperson put it, "This mining project will affect the future of our community and will have negative consequences for the natural environment, the life and the social and political institutions of our community."[3]

More access roads are being constructed, and with each new road another part of the population is exposed to more influence from the outside. Some Ngóbe are in favor of roads because they supposedly facilitate travel and the movement of goods that they wish to sell. However, the roads are probably of more benefit to the merchants who sell products to the Ngóbe and Panamanian agroindustrial interests that depend on the Ngóbe as a source of low-cost agricultural labor.

Since the 1970s, the Panamanian government has extended its school system into nearly all of Ngóbe territory. Many schools are quite rudimentary but offer greatly improved access to primary education. Prior to the 1970s, some children received a few years of primary education when their parents sent them to live with Latino families in small Panamanian towns bordering Ngóbe territory. The children were treated as servants, but most learned Spanish, and some attended school. The percentage of boys who received any education in this manner was quite small, and it was extremely rare for girls to receive any formal education at all. The extension of the educational system changed this dramatically. Today the vast majority of children, both girls and boys, attend school for at least a few years, and many complete the primary grades. Increasing numbers are continuing on to high school, and a few go to trade schools and universities. This was unheard of a generation ago.

Children learn to speak Spanish in school and develop at least basic literacy skills. Interaction with Latino teachers and the educational curriculum increases familiarity with the Latino world and facilitates easier interaction with it. It also makes the introduction of outside influences easier than in the past when geographic and linguistic isolation buffered external influences.

The 1970s also ushered in major changes in political participation at the national level. Prior to 1972 all functionaries connecting the Ngóbe to Panama's political system were appointed by outside authorities. For the first time in 1972 the Ngóbe elected their own representatives to Panama's national assembly. At first scarcely understood, the idea of electing representatives was well established by the end of the decade, and competition for office was keen, in part because elected offices provided attractive salaries. By the end of the 1970s, the Ngóbe were also holding large meetings (called congresses) in their territory which brought together people from the different provinces to discuss matters of common interest. As Ngóbe political sophistication grew, a new level of nontraditional political organization began to emerge. This has been encouraged by the national government which wants to integrate more effectively the Ngóbe into the national polity. Toward this end, the national government has, since the late 1960s, recognized caciques in the three provinces with Ngóbe populations. Historically, the Ngóbe have had no recognized permanent leadership positions. Traditional leadership is found in kinship groups and is informal. Individuals exert influence because of their personal qualities, not because they hold a formal office or position. Modern chiefs and elected leaders are both alien ideas. As one Ngóbe man put it in 1978, "*Cacique* means a different thing to the people. A true *cacique* is one who is born knowing. These new *caciques* are not like that. Many people are waiting for such a man."[4] While a few are still making up their minds, by 1999, most Ngóbe recognize the provincial caciques as the legitimate authorities.

The gradual intrusion of external political models has begun to break down traditional patterns of authority. Disputes, which frequently occur over who has land-use rights, have been increasingly brought before officials appointed by the national government instead of being mediated in the traditional manner by an influential, usually elder, member of the community. The result has been the gradual undermining of traditional leadership and authority.

In 1997 the National Assembly of Panama officially established a Ngóbe *comarca* (reserve) with the passage of Law 10. This was the first time that any government had recognized or acknowledged that the Ngóbe had a legal right to the territory they occupy. Having a reserve has been a long cherished dream of many Ngóbe. A reserve with clearly marked boundaries has been seen as a way of stopping further theft of their lands by outsiders. However, the law establishing the reserve also mandates the creation of an internal political system different from the one that currently exists. The legislation specifies the development of a system that mimics the structure of the national political system. It also requires close coordination with the national system. It will probably be several years before this new system will be in place and functioning. However, when put in place, it is very likely that it will further erode traditional patterns of authority and leadership.

Environmental Crisis

Population pressure has created a serious environmental crisis that will probably become more severe in the future. Simply put, the long-term carrying capacity of the land has been exceeded. Land shortages are forcing people to clear and replant land more frequently than is desirable. Since the 1930s, fallow periods between crops have decreased from about twenty-five years to eight and sometimes only six years. With shorter fallow periods, the land is unable to recover its fertility. The result is a vicious circle of declining productivity. As fertility declines, more and more land must be cultivated to obtain the same harvest. As a consequence, the land is used more and more frequently and produces less and less. Many Ngóbe now have insufficient land and must resort to poorly paid wage work on outside farms, ranches, and plantations to earn money to purchase food. This too has become a problem because it is often difficult to find work during the months in which it is most needed.

Food shortages have become chronic for many and are especially severe in the months of June and July, just before the crops are ready to harvest. One Ngóbe expressed himself in a letter,

My brother, this year just past [1995] has been the worst of all the years for the Ngóbe. Almost no one was able to burn [the slash] because the rains fell early. There was much hunger and it continues still. Many have nothing. In general, this is how it is among the Ngóbe. . . . The situation is very difficult. Everything is going up in price and we Ngóbe are in a food crisis.[5]

Many children now suffer from nutritional problems. Many are underweight for their ages because they have experienced extended periods without enough to eat. They also often suffer from illnesses that are, in part, related to poor nutrition.

The need for cash income adds additional environmental stress to the already serious problems caused by the spiraling need to grow more food. A cash income is essential to all Ngóbe households in order to purchase things the people cannot grow or make themselves. Manufactured products, such as machetes and axes, pots and pans, cloth and kerosene for lamps, all must be purchased. Other than wage labor away from home, the only way to obtain money is to produce things that can be sold.

To sell crops or farm animals, precious land resources must be devoted to them, thus increasing pressure on the land. When the population was small, land was relatively abundant and raising cattle for sale was the most popular way to earn money. Cattle, as well as chickens, pigs, beans, rice, and corn, can all readily be sold to outside buyers. However, cattle need pastures that cannot then be used for crops. Today the Ngóbe continue to sell these farm animals and crops, and some now also raise coffee and cocoa as cash crops. What they sell today, however, is seldom a real surplus. What they sell at one time of the year may cause them to go hungry later.

Roads into Ngóbe territory have also encouraged more production of crops for sale. Bringing even small loads of crops out to market is slow and laborious if they must be carried or packed out on horses. Roads allow buyers to bring trucks into the areas and transport larger volumes rapidly. This ease of sale stimulates even more overuse of the land. Easy access to markets encourages significant numbers of families to sell a large proportion of a crop immediately after harvest to earn cash to make needed purchases of manufactured goods. This is also the time at which they will receive the lowest prices for their crops because so much is available. Later, just before harvest time when food supplies are running low, the same families often suffer because they cannot afford to buy food. Prices then are at their highest because of shortages in the market.

Sociocultural Crisis

The Ngóbe have been able to maintain their cultural identity and way of life because of the interplay of several factors. The isolation of their homeland has been important. In addition, the way in which they are organized has had an important influence on their interaction with the outside world. Because, until recently, they had no system of political organization above the level of small kin groups, it was impossible for external forces to influence more than a small number of people at a time. Each kin group is essentially politically autonomous, so influences are not readily transmitted from one kin group to another as they could be in systems with more centralized patterns of authority.

Patterns of access to land have also been important. The right to use land is based on kin group membership. An individual's kinship ties defined his rights. Traditionally, the right to use land could be inherited, but land could not be purchased or sold. Thus, it could not be alienated from the kin group, which owned the land collectively. This system of use rights (usufruct) strongly tied individuals to their kin groups and tended to ensure that customs were observed.

Traditionally, individuals and households depended on reciprocity among kin for economic and social security. If harvests were poor, or if a household experienced hardships for some other reason, food could be obtained from kin. The expectation, of course, was that when kin experienced periods of need, assistance would be provided if possible. This worked well when adequate land was available and everyone could plant enough crops to meet their projected needs. Today land shortages and periodic wide-spread food shortages are causing a breakdown of this system of reciprocal sharing.

Increasing participation in wage labor also takes time away from agri-cultural production. Wage work is often most available during periods when the planting or harvesting of subsistence crops needs to be done. The result is that, even in situations where enough land may be available, the need for a cash income can reduce subsistence production. Those who are away working for wages do not plant enough to meet their own subsistence needs let alone provide aid to others who may experience a poor harvest. This puts even more strain on the traditional reciprocal exchange system.

RESPONSE: STRUGGLES TO SURVIVE CULTURALLY

Individual Responses

As the Ngóbe population grew, population densities increased more rap-idly in some areas than in others, and individuals responded according to their individual circumstances. Today, virtually all parts of the Ngóbe homeland are experiencing overpopulation and land shortages. Everyone is struggling to grow enough food to meet their needs. At the same time, the need for cash has steadily increased, demanding even more adjustments in economic strategies. These adjustments have taken a variety of forms.

Agricultural Intensification and Production for Markets

The first and most logical way to obtain cash was to produce something for sale. Cattle, pigs, and chickens have been the traditional choice because they can be moved easily and there is a ready market in rural Panama. When land was abundant this was the option selected by most people. It required keeping a few more animals than would normally be raised for consumption, but virtually no change in traditional activities was required.

Raising more food crops than needed for consumption or producing crops specifically for sale has gone hand in hand with raising animals for sale. Corn, beans, and rice all can be readily sold as can coffee and cacao. With increasing land shortages, it has become more difficult to raise ani-mals or crops for sale because the land is needed to grow food for home consumption. However, some Ngóbe regard coffee as a cash crop that will produce enough income to more than offset the lost food production on the land.

Seasonal Wage Labor Migration in Panama and Costa Rica

A few Ngóbe began to obtain money by working for wages on cattle ranches and farms in the nineteenth century. Periods away from home were usually very short, lasting only as long as necessary to earn the money to meet immediate needs. During the twentieth century, many more Ngóbe began spending longer periods away from home as the need for money gradually increased. Wage labor has now become the most important source of cash because land shortages make it impossible for many people to meet even their subsistence needs by raising crops and animals, much less produce a saleable surplus. Now they depend on wages to buy some of the food they need as well as manufactured goods. It is unusual today to find a Ngóbe man who has not spent at least some time away from home working for wages. Many now spend several months a year away from home to earn the money they need. Often their wives and children accompany them and work for wages at such tasks as harvesting coffee.

The need to earn money has prompted many to travel long distances from home in search of work. Today large numbers of Ngóbe travel to neighboring Costa Rica to find jobs harvesting coffee. So many are seeking work that not enough jobs can be found in Panama.

Permanent Emigration

Some Ngóbe have dealt with the problem of land shortages and food scarcity by leaving their homeland altogether. Some now work and live permanently on the large banana plantations of western Panama. Others have moved to Panama's cities and towns in search of jobs. Not all have been lucky enough to find work, and some families live in abject poverty in urban slums. These migrants usually maintain contact with their relatives who have remained in their homeland, but over time it is not unusual for such contact to become infrequent or lost altogether. Many migrants eventually abandon their traditional customs, lose their cultural identity, and adopt the ways of Panamanian society. They and their children become part of the Latino world.

Group Responses: Political Organization

Group responses to the problems faced by the Ngóbe are becoming more common. This is most evident with such organizations as Acción Cultural Ngóbe (Ngóbe Cultural Action) and in the congresses that are now held on a regular basis. Acción Cultural Ngóbe publishes a newsletter called Drü. The newsletter provides information and editorials on topics of widespread interest among the Ngóbe people. It also encourages a sense of group identity among the Ngóbe living in their traditional homeland as well as those who now reside in other areas of Panama.

Regional congresses are now being held annually in each of the three provinces straddled by the Ngóbe homeland. These congresses bring together hundreds of people from all over the province to discuss matters of mutual concern. Even larger general congresses are held less frequently, usually every two or three years, which bring together people from all three provinces. The congresses have facilitated the flow of information between Ngóbe living in different areas and have focused attention on matters of common concern, such as the potential impact of a copper mine and relations with government agencies. They have also served as a source of information about the activities of the national government and international companies that may have an impact on the Ngóbe.

The Ngóbe have also organized to bring their concerns to the attention of the general Panamanian public. In recent years protest marches have been held in major cities, and the Interamerican Highway has been blocked more than once to draw attention to the desire of the Ngóbe for a reserve. These efforts were very successful in attracting the attention of the national news media and may have influenced the national government's decision to pass Law 10 which did create the reserve sought by the Ngóbe for almost thirty years.

The new reserve is still in the process of being organized, and its political structure is still to be developed. It will create a new organizational structure unlike anything in the past. However, even at this stage, there are signs that the reserve will play a very important role in the future of the Ngóbe. Territorial boundaries are being delimited, and the political subdivisions (districts) within the reserve are being reorganized and renamed to reflect a discrete and distinct Ngóbe identity. The reserve will also promote the development of a more centralized and coordinated political system than the Ngóbe have ever had. Only time will tell if this will help the Ngóbe deal more effectively with the Panamanian national government and help them address the problems they face.

FOOD FOR THOUGHT

Very rapid population growth and increasing influence from outside forces have combined to confront the Ngóbe with challenges unlike those faced in the past. The population has increased rapidly, and subsistence needs can no longer be met with the land available. This has forced greater involvement in wage labor which, in turn, has increased the influence of external forces on the society and weakened traditional economic and social patterns.

At the same time that population pressure is increasing the need to participate in Panama's national economy, more external influences are penetrating the previously isolated homeland of the Ngóbe. Access roads are connecting them to outside markets and facilitating travel in and out of the region. The extension of the Panamanian school system into the area has facilitated the introduction of influences from the outside but also has enhanced the abilities of the Ngóbe to meet the challenges of interaction with the outside world.

The recently established Ngóbe-Bugle reserve holds out both promise and threat to the Ngóbe. The legal recognition of the right of the Ngóbe to their homeland is a significant milestone in their long and often difficult struggle to determine their own destiny. The reserve assures rights to the land and prohibits the usurpation of land by Latinos, a common occurrence in the past. At the same time, the reserve could threaten traditional social and political patterns because it requires the Ngóbe to develop a political structure that parallels the Panamanian national system and is quite unlike their traditional system. It is difficult to predict how much this will alter the traditional system.

One view of the future for the Ngóbe in a rapidly changing world would be that they are doomed to become more and more like the general Latino population of Panama and eventually lose their cultural identity. This has happened to many other native populations. However, we should remember that, during 500 years of contact with the outside world, the Ngóbe have demonstrated remarkable adaptability and resiliency and have maintained their distinctive cultural identity and way of life. They have been resourceful survivors. As they move into their sixth century of interaction with the outside world, new challenges will have to be faced and changes will occur. Our optimistic view is that the Ngóbe will survive as a culturally unique and distinct people.

Questions

1. Why can population growth be considered a major cause of many of the problems faced by the Ngóbe today? How have the Ngóbe addressed their population problem? In what other ways might they address it?

2. How might improved access to education influence the Ngóbe in the future? Would literacy in their own language (in addition to Spanish) be useful to them?

3. What factors do you think have helped the Ngóbe to maintain their cultural identity despite 500 years of political domination? Do you think their culture is now in danger of disappearing?

4. How has involvement in a cash economy influenced the Ngóbe? How are changes in the global economy likely to affect them?

5. Why are new forms of political organization developing in Ngóbe society? What kinds of changes are they likely to cause? Do you think changes in their political organization will help the Ngóbe solve their problems?

NOTES

Unless otherwise noted, data and statistical information presented in this chapter come from the following sources: Philip D. Young, *Ngawbe: Tradition and Change Among the Western Guaymí of Panama*, Illinois Studies in Anthropology no. 7 (Urbana: University of Illinois Press, 1971); Philip D. Young and John R. Bort, "Ngawbe," in *Encyclopedia of World Cultures*, vol. 8, pp. 194–199 (Boston: G. K.

Hall, 1995); Philip Young and John Bort, "Ngóbe Adaptive Responses to Globalization in Panama," in *Globalization and the Rural Poor in Latin America*, ed. William M. Loker, 111–36. (Boulder, Colo.: Lynne Rienner, 1999).

1. César Picon, Jesús Q. Alemancia, and Ileana Gilcher, eds. *Pueblos Indigenas de Panama* (Panama: Edotora Sibauste, S.A., 1998), 256.

2. Ibid., 253.

3. Letter sent to Philip Young (and many others) from a Ngóbe spokesperson dated August 26, 1996, and signed "Secretary of International Affairs, Ngóbe-Bugle General Congress.

4. Philip Young, field notes, 1978.

5. Letter from a Ngóbe friend to Philip Young, dated February 9, 1996.

RESOURCE GUIDE

Published Literature

Bourgois, Philippe I. *Ethnicity at Work: Divided Labor on a Central American Banana Plantation.* Baltimore: Johns Hopkins University Press, 1989.

Gjording, Chris N. *Conditions Not of Their Choosing: The Guaymí Indians and Mining Multinationals in Panama.* Washington, DC: Smithsonian Institution, 1991.

Young, Philip D. *Ngawbe: Tradition and Change Among the Western Guaymí of Panama.* Illinois Studies in Anthropology no. 7. Urbana: University of Illinois Press, 1971.

Young, Philip D., and John R. Bort. "Ngawbe." *Encyclopedia of World Cultures*, vol. 8, pp. 194–99. Boston: G. K. Hall, 1995.

———. "Ngóbe Adaptive Responses to Globalization in Panama." In *Globalization and the Rural Poor in Latin America*, edited by William M. Loker, 111–36. Boulder, Colo.: Lynne Rienner, 1999.

WWW Sites

Ngóbe-Buglé Rural Community Development Project
http://www.fidamerica.cl/ngobe.htm.
(This site is currently available in Spanish only.)

A few colored photos of Ngóbe life
http://darkwing.uoregon.edu/~pyoung/ngpict.htm

Organizations

Acción Cultural Ngóbe (ACUN)
Apartado 1149, Zona 9A, Panamá
Republica de Panamá
Tele. (5076) 267–3777

Chapter 9

The Kuna of Panama

James Howe

CULTURAL OVERVIEW

The People

Today, a few thousand Kuna can be found in eastern Panama in the valleys of the Bayano, Chucunaque, and Tuira rivers, as well as nearby in Colombia. However, the greatest number, more than 34,000, live on the northeastern coast of Panama, on a great arc between the Colombian border and Mandinga Bay or the Gulf of San Blas, some 130 miles to the west.[1] The Panamanian government in 1938 designated this region, known traditionally to outsiders as the Coast of San Blas, as an autonomous territorial reserve or *comarca* (the Comarca of San Blas). In the early 1980s the reserve was officially renamed Kuna Yala.

Of the forty-nine villages in Kuna Yala, only eleven are located on the mainland. The remaining thirty-eight villages are situated on coral islands lying anywhere from a few yards to several miles offshore. The typical island village is filled from one side to another with large thatch-roofed wooden houses inhabited by extended families. The little space left is used for trees, kitchen gardens, narrow streets, a basketball court, two large halls dedicated respectively to village meetings and the celebration of female puberty, a school or schools, and in some cases one or two small churches. Since little can be grown on the island, people return to the mainland each day to farm, cut firewood, and (except for villages that now have aqueducts) fetch water.

The Kuna have existed as a distinct indigenous group for at least 400 years. At the beginning of the seventeenth century, outlying settlements on the eastern edge of the Spanish colony in Panama suffered fierce attacks from Indians whom the Spaniards called Bugue-Bugues. The eastern half

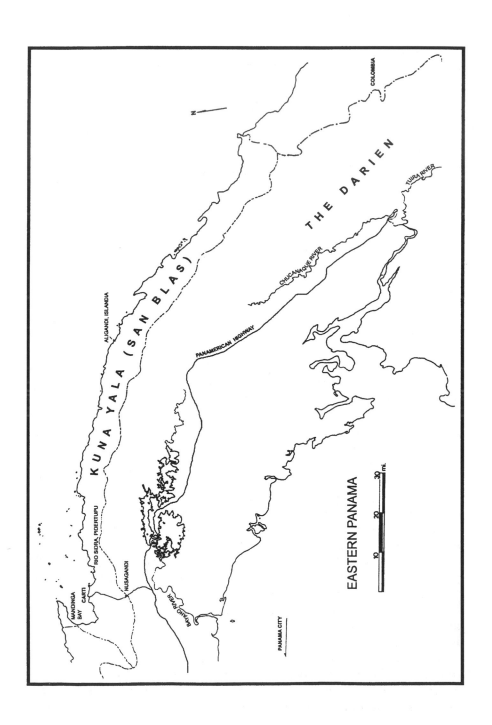

EASTERN PANAMA

COLOMBIA

THE DARIEN

TUIRA RIVER

CHUCANAQUE RIVER

PANAMERICAN HIGHWAY

KUNA YALA (SAN BLAS)

ALIGANDI, ISLANDIA

RIO SIDRA, PIDERTUPU

MANDINGA BAY

CARTI

NUSAGANDI

BAYANO RIVER

PANAMA CITY

N

10   20   30   mi.

of the Isthmus of Panama, known as the Darién, had once been heavily populated, but the initial Spanish conquest had destroyed the indigenous chiefdoms and entirely depopulated the whole eastern region. In the following century, the so-called Bugue-Bugues, today known as the Kuna, had apparently begun migrating back onto the isthmus and repopulating the region. Their attacks signaled the beginning of 200 years of conflict.

Panama, where the Atlantic and Pacific are separated by only a few land miles, the crossing point for silver bound from Peru to Spain, was a region of great strategic importance, attracting freebooters and military forces from Spain's European enemies. The Kuna, who often allied themselves with pirates, were repeatedly missionized and partly subdued by Spanish authorities, only to break free again. These struggles culminated in the late eighteenth century with a campaign to conquer or exterminate the rebel Indians, which probably would have succeeded had not its high costs persuaded colonial authorities to abandon the effort.

After Latin America achieved independence in the early nineteenth century, outside powers abruptly lost interest in the region, leaving the Kuna, their numbers seriously diminished, to lick their wounds. Already concentrated mostly in the northern half of the Darién, the Kuna began in the nineteenth century to settle on the northern shore, known as the Coast of San Blas, and then on small inshore islands where they could escape snakes, mosquitoes, and endemic disease. Throughout the century, the Kuna maintained mostly peaceful relations with coastal trading vessels and Colombian authorities in Bogotá but kept themselves largely independent of outside control.

This benign neglect ended abruptly in 1903, when Panama achieved independence from Colombia, and the United States began construction of the Panama Canal. For about a decade, however, the new and impoverished nation, lacking the resources to control the San Blas Coast effectively, approached the Indians primarily through Catholic missionaries. In 1915, finally ready to act on its own, the government established an administrative headquarters on the coast, authorized a colony with mines and banana plantations, and placed schools and police detachments in four Kuna villages. The presence of non-Indians, who had been coming into the area in pursuit of sea turtles and wild forest products such as ivory nut and latex, was encouraged in the area.

Then, in 1919, the government initiated a program to "civilize" the Kuna. The government's first action was to prohibit female puberty ceremonies, as well as the nose rings and bead bindings worn by Kuna women. Later all of women's dress, and eventually Kuna culture as a whole, was suppressed. After six years of resistance within the national political system, the Kuna finally rebelled and killed a number of the policemen who were oppressing them. The United States, which in that era reserved the right to intervene in major disturbances in Panama, brokered a peace settlement

139

Endangered Peoples of Latin America

between the Kuna and the national government that guaranteed the Indians the right to their own culture. In the 1930s the Kuna and the government hammered out further agreements protecting indigenous land rights. Thus, by the last quarter of the twentieth century, the time period covered in this chapter, the Kuna had, without exaggeration, accumulated 400 years of experience in resisting threats to their physical and cultural survival.

The Setting

The Kuna Yala Indigenous Reserve (the Comarca of San Blas) is characterized by diverse ecological zones. The reserve ranges in elevation from sea level to about 1,000 meters (3,000 feet) and receives from 2,500 to 3,500 millimeters (100 to 140 inches) of precipitation annually. The average annual temperature is approximately 24°C (75°F). According to the widely accepted classification scheme of L. R. Holdridge, the area encompasses three life zones: low-lying wetlands, very wet tropical forest, and wet premontane forest.[2]

The reserve is characterized by a diverse array of marine and terrestrial ecosystems. These include coral reefs, mangroves, lagoons, gallery and evergreen hardwood forests, and agricultural fields. Many species of endangered fauna also live within the reserve including several species of felines, crocodilians, and marine turtles, as well as the giant anteater, harpy eagle, and Baird's tapir. In addition, the reserve functions as a resting place for many species of migratory birds.[3]

Traditional Subsistence Strategies

The Kuna have, for a very long time, produced for both their own subsistence needs and the world market. They feed themselves through slash-and-burn agriculture, based on a staple of bananas and plantains, supplemented by manioc, corn, rice, and other crops. The Kuna meet their protein needs with fish from the sea, caught mostly on hook and line. Game animals, lobsters, sea turtles, conch, and freshwater fish are eaten only occasionally.

Since the late nineteenth century, the Kuna have sold several million coconuts a year, the product of palms planted on much of the coast and uninhabited islands. Throughout the twentieth century, coconuts have provided the income needed to buy steel tools, kerosene, cloth, and other manufactured items. However, a series of coconut blights, combined with shifts in the world market, have drastically cut production and increased Kuna reliance on other sources of income.

A few miles inland a low mountain range runs parallel to the coast. Dozens of small rivers and streams, only a few miles long but fed by heavy rains from April to December, run down from the mountains and enter the

Caribbean, in some places through mangroves, in others across sandy beaches. On the shore, coconut palms are planted everywhere they will grow; farther inland, Kuna farms are interspersed amid secondary growth and patches of tropical forest, until one reaches the zone of old forest well up the mountain slopes. On this side of the isthmus, tides are minimal; facilitating use of the hundreds of low coral islets along the coast as villages and work camps. The comarca, which the Kuna often refer to as "the long land," is in effect a narrow coastal ribbon from the mountain tops down to the shore, with its territorial waters and islands.

One of the most important ways of earning money is the sale of elaborately sewn blouses and blouse panels, called *molas*, for which the Kuna have become world famous. *Molas* began to be marketed in significant numbers after World War II, although up through the early 1960s women only sold used blouses that they had first worn themselves, and the prices paid scarcely sufficed to cover the cost of materials. By the 1970s Kuna women were selling thousands of panels a year, of which a considerable number were made for immediate sale. Today many households depend heavily on *molas* for cash income, especially in the region of western Kuna Yala most visited by tourists.

Migrant wage labor, which began in past centuries with young men who shipped out as sailors on trading boats, has greatly increased. In 1930 indigenous leaders made a special agreement with U.S. authorities in the Canal Zone to employ Kuna men to do much of the kitchen work on military bases. Building on this experience, the Kuna have established a niche in restaurants in Panama City and Colón, and quite a few have worked at banana plantations in western Panama. Kuna with high school diplomas, some in recent years with university degrees, have secured salaried positions as teachers, government functionaries, and now as professionals. The majority of Kuna migrants, however, have found jobs only at the lower end of the labor market.

Until recently, men went away for a year or more to work, and women and children stayed at home in Kuna Yala in the households of the women's parents. In the 1970s, labor migration increased dramatically, and some men began taking their families with them to the city and enrolling their children in urban schools. The 1990 census recorded more than 9,000 Kuna living in Panama City and Colón, a number that has undoubtedly grown since then.[4] Kuna migrants cluster in certain neighborhoods, and they have established several all-Indian communities on the outskirts of the two cities.

Social and Political Organization

Kuna villages appear to be strategically located to take advantage of both terrestrial and marine resources. Typically densely settled, island villages apparently were established earlier this century to avoid the pests that plagued mainland communities. Compared to other forest-dwelling peoples of Central America, the Kuna are a relatively well-organized people. Communities have gathering houses where villagers meet regularly to discuss community life and problems. As this chapter shows, this social and cultural cohesiveness has facilitated the ability of the Kuna to retain their cultural identity in the face of powerful outside forces, including the recent attempts of the Panamanian government to impose its own political structure on the Kuna.

Religion and World View

The Kuna give thanks for their existence and for the bounty of the world to a pair of deities, Great Mother and Great Father. They say that Father put Mother in place as the Earth, and, as her children, they must continue to care for the natural world as they do their own human mothers. Each village keeps up connection with Father and Mother by assembling several nights a week in a gathering house: a village chief chants to his followers about history, cosmology, and morality, and when he finishes, a secondary leader called *argar* interprets the chant in spoken Kuna, drawing out its lessons for the people. On other nights, village men meet in secular gatherings to make decisions and adjudicate disputes. Outside the gathering house, most men participate in elaborate female puberty rituals or in some of the numerous varieties of traditional curing.

THREATS TO SURVIVAL

Intrusions and Invasions

In the past, Kuna Yala was vulnerable mostly on its ocean side: the reserve's long mountainous terrestrial border was separated by miles of tropical forest from the nearest Panamanian town. By the 1960s, however, landless mestizo peasants from western Panama had begun migrating into the Bayano and Darién regions, cutting down the forest, raising crops, and converting the land into cattle pasture. The wave of in-migration and deforestation accelerated when the Pan-American Highway was extended across much of the Darién and a hydroelectric project was constructed on the Bayano River.

The colonists began to approach and enter Kuna Yala, especially after 1970, after a dirt road was opened from the Pan-American Highway up to the border of the *comarca* at its western end. Concerned Kuna discovered that a few colonists had already started clearing lands within the reserve, and that others had been living in the most remote parts of western Kuna Yala for some years. As the colonists replaced forests with cattle pasture throughout eastern Panama, they threatened the viability of the Kuna reserve's ecosystem as well as its territorial integrity.

During the same years, other intruders appeared in the east. Afro-Colombians infiltrated the valleys closest to the national border in search of gold and natural products of the forest. Drug smugglers, following a traditional contraband route down the San Blas Coast to the port of Colón, further destabilized the region.

In the 1990s, new and even more dangerous intrusions occurred, as guerilla war and social unrest in Colombia spilled over into adjacent parts of Panama. The largest guerilla group, the Revolutionary Armed Forces of Colombia (FARC), which had begun keeping camps in the Darién forests, was followed by right-wing paramilitaries, and even by apparently apolitical but well-armed "unknowns." The Panamanian national police, too weak to drive out the intruders, have so far mostly left them alone, and to date the situation remains tense.

Tourism

As a tourist attraction, Kuna Yala has many virtues: beautiful "desert" islands, excellent diving, a comfortable climate from January to April, an exotic and colorful indigenous culture, friendly people, outstanding artisanry, and a deep-water bay at its western end. Tourism, which began in the 1920s with occasional outings by boat from the Canal Zone, has become much more significant since the 1960s. Large cruise ships visit western Kuna Yala throughout the dry season, day trippers fly in by light plane, and smaller numbers of visitors stay for a night or two at a handful of inns and small hotels. So far only a few Kuna make money from guiding or accommodating visitors, but tourism is welcomed for the sake of selling *molas*.

Tourism, however, is a mixed blessing (see chapter 5). The Kuna worry about the influence of outsiders who dress in skimpy clothing or act inappropriately by local standards, and they regret that profits from tourism go to outsiders. Most of all, they fear that non-Indian interests, if they established themselves in Kuna Yala, could threaten Kuna autonomy and control of their own territory.

Even the commerce in *molas* has its negative side, in particular for the women who sew them. At one time, tourist guides tried to keep prices down, telling their clients not to pay more than a certain amount. Although prices have risen sharply in recent decades, the cost of materials is still high, and a good *mola* panel requires at least a week of intensive work to sew. Except in the primary tourist zone of Mandinga and Carti in western San Blas, women usually have to sell to Kuna middlemen. In some villages, they barter *molas* for goods with shop owners. In the international market, foreign traders take by far the largest share of the profit.

Kuna spectators at a commemoration of their 1925 rebellion. Courtesy of James Howe.

National law offers the Kuna some control over tourism and other activities by outsiders. The legislation recognizing Kuna self-governance (Law 16 of 1953) mandates that non-Kuna may not alienate land in the *comarca* without the approval in two successive sessions of its governing body, the Kuna General Congress, a council of village chiefs and delegates. The three elected leaders of Kuna Yala, who are called caciques or *sagla dummagan* (great chiefs), have no right to act in such matters without the consent of the General Congress, although outsiders often expect them to do so.

In the late 1960s these legal strictures were put to the test when two American entrepreneurs, Thomas Moody and W. D. Barton, obtained permission from the three caciques to explore sites for possible resorts. Both found suitable spots—Moody, an uninhabited island in western San Blas called Pidertupu; Barton, an island farther east which he renamed Islandia. Both men rented the islands from their Kuna owners, and both constructed small beach cabaña resorts. Neither obtained the required permission from the Kuna General Congress, which by 1969 was issuing formal objections to their presence. The General Congress, however, had no administrative or enforcement capabilities, and in this matter the government would not act on its behalf.

Moody developed good relations with the nearest Kuna community, Río Sidra, which received various favors as well as fees for cargo and tourists landing at the village airstrip. Barton, in contrast, ended up in heated disputes with his neighbor, Ailigandi, about alleged breaches of promise and offenses to Kuna sensibilities. Local men twice burned down parts of Islandia, and in 1974 the government finally ejected Barton.

By this time, a much greater crisis was brewing involving the government itself. The Instituto Panameño de Turismo (IPAT), founded in 1960, was given an expanded role soon after the 1968 military coup that brought General Omar Torrijos to power. In the early 1970s, as part of a master scheme to foment tourism in four regions of Panama, IPAT and its outside consultants devised a plan for a grandiose hotel of 686 rooms (twice the size of the largest hotel in Panama City), with casino, tennis courts, pool, beach, and marina, all to be built on an artificial island in western San Blas, as well as workers' quarters and an airfield capable of accommodating small jets nearby on the mainland.

In 1973 IPAT began a campaign to persuade the Kuna to accept the project, presenting it to several successive sessions of the Kuna General Congress, which usually meets every six months. The three caciques signed a document authorizing a feasibility study, though the head of IPAT publicly promised not to proceed with construction without the assent of the full General Congress. The three Kuna representatives to a national council of representatives, newly created in 1972, strongly supported the project, and rumors circulated that they were being paid by IPAT.

Opposition was slow to develop, but over a series of General Congress sessions doubts began to be voiced. Then, in early 1974, after the leaders of the village closest to the proposed site of the project began to take in its full scope, in particular the impact of the airport on their own airstrip and coconut groves, a mob confronted a party of surveyors who landed there and forcibly prevented them from deplaning. In the wake of the incident, IPAT revised its plans, reducing the size of the project and calling for implementation in stages. Nonetheless, in September 1975, the General Congress revoked permission for the feasibility study. The ultimate resolution of the crisis almost destroyed the Kuna reserve.

In the aftermath of this episode, the General Congress turned its attention back to Moody. Despite repeated resolutions denouncing his presence, Moody was protected by high-ranking government figures, including Manuel Noriega, who was then on the rise but not yet head of state. Finally, in June 1981, after Kuna authorities personally visited Moody to warn him of threats to his safety, a party of young men raided Pidertupu, slightly wounded Moody, and attempted unsuccessfully to burn the rain-soaked cabañas, after which the government finally evicted him. The Kuna had again countered a serious threat, though again, at great cost.

Although crises of this magnitude have not erupted again, serious difficulties concerning tourism recur periodically. During the 1990s, several small resorts were authorized, on the grounds that Kuna individuals held major interests in their ownership. Later, however, Indian lawyers determined that these Kuna were merely acting as fronts for non-Indian interests. Disputes concerning another resort called Iskartup have dragged on for almost a decade. Most ominously, during the mid-1990s, Panamanian entrepreneurs with strong government connections developed a plan to build a resort a few yards beyond the western limits of the reserve, where they could exploit the touristic possibilities of Kuna Yala without obtaining Kuna permission.

Government Threats to Kuna Yala

The government of Panama deals with the Kuna through a great variety of officials and agencies, including an appointed governor or *intendente* (who since 1980 has always been a Kuna), three Kuna legislators in a national legislative assembly, the three district representatives mentioned above, a Kuna judge and prosecutor, agents of the national police, school-teachers, paramedics in village clinics, and the representatives of various ministries and agencies. Political parties, which were suppressed in 1968, returned in the 1970s. For major issues concerning Kuna Yala as a whole, however, the government deals with the Kuna General Congress.

The Panamanian government, which has established a better record in dealing with its indigenous citizens than have many of its counterparts in Latin America, provides a number of important benefits and services to the Kuna. At the same time, as sponsor of many public and private projects and the body that can most authoritatively demand access to indigenous lands, the government itself has presented some of the gravest threats to Kuna autonomy. Like many other countries, Panama has favored a top-down model of development based on large-scale projects capable of bringing in revenue but also of harming local populations. Government functionaries give lip service to indigenous veto rights but clearly expect native leaders to say yes when asked, and they show little patience for Kuna democratic procedures. As a result, the General Congress and the government have repeatedly ended up locked in struggle.

In addition to the hotel project discussed above, official initiatives since the late 1960s have included two projects that would have led to conflict had they not been abandoned for other reasons, one a proposed oil pipeline with a terminus in western Kuna Yala, the other a sea-level canal to be excavated with nuclear bombs. On two occasions, one in the 1980s and the other in the 1990s, the government insisted on building a military base in eastern Kuna Yala. In the first instance the Kuna refused, leading to a protracted standoff. In the second, which concerned a naval base intended for interdicting drug shipments, the government wished to build at a protected site several miles into Kuna Yala, which would give its vessels extra time to meet incursions into Panamanian territory. The General Congress insisted, however, that the base be built on the border. The question has yet to be resolved.

Mining and oil drilling present special difficulties because the laws of Panama (and almost every other Latin American country) assign subsurface rights to the national government. In theory, therefore, the Kuna cannot exclude concessions made in their territory, though in practice it would be hard to establish mines without their consent. In the mid-1990s, the government granted mining concessions in a number of regions of Panama, including concessions for gold and other minerals encompassing three-quarters of the surface area of Kuna Yala. The Kuna vowed to oppose any mining, by force if necessary, and to date the concessions have not been implemented.

RESPONSE: STRUGGLES TO SURVIVE CULTURALLY

The Kuna have responded to threats and problems in a variety of ways, public and private. Among the most significant are a cooperative organized for the production and marketing of *molas*, a project to protect the threatened borders of the Kuna reserve, and the efforts of the Kuna General Congress to defend indigenous territory.

The *Mola* Cooperative

Males dominate Kuna politics, and it is usually the men who have organized against threats to cultural survival, with one very significant exception. In the late 1960s, when a number of Peace Corps volunteers were working with the Kuna, one of their projects, which was initially supposed to teach women how to make baby clothes, was reorganized to produce and market *molas*. The project soon had branches on eight islands as well as a retail store in Panama City.

In 1971, when the government of Omar Torrijos expelled the Peace Corps from Panama, the *mola* cooperative faced a severe crisis and a sharp drop in membership. The remaining members, however, began to rebuild the project on their own, and in 1974 they secured official recognition as a handicrafts cooperative. In 1978 a grant of $30,000 from the Inter-American Foundation made it possible to organize new programs and workshops, and by 1985 the cooperative had grown to include seventeen branches and 1,500 members. Today, in addition to an elected leadership, the organization has professional managers based at a store and headquarters in Panama City, as well as its own website.

The *mola* co-op assists its members in a number of ways. It buys materials in bulk at favorable rates. It secures a better-than-average return to producers for their work, approximately 75 percent of the purchase price, and it is now increasingly marketing *mola* work abroad. Although the co-operative represents less than a quarter of Kuna *mola* producers and *mola* production, it has had a wide impact on gender roles throughout Kuna Yala, making it possible for women to travel and conduct business without male supervision, to choose their leadership from among their own female membership, to communicate useful information and raise consciousness in workshops and meetings, and to gain a voice in the Kuna General Congress. Thirty years after its inception, the co-op continues to thrive and grow.

The PEMASKY Project

In the early 1970s, when peasant colonists began to threaten Kuna Yala, a young man named Guillermo Archibold began to travel to the spot in western Kuna Yala where the newly made dirt road crossed into the *comarca*. To establish a Kuna presence at the border and find a way to make productive use of the surrounding land, Archibold and other volunteers began to clear forest and plant crops. A Kuna labor organization, the Asociación de Empleados Kunas (AEK), contributed $70,000 and official sponsorship. Their efforts, however, only served to demonstrate that traditional Kuna agriculture would not work on mountain peaks.

In 1982 the United States Agency for International Development (USAID), which had financed the road, awarded a grant to the Centro Agronómico Tropical de Investigación y Enseñanza (CATIE) in Costa Rica to help the Kuna create a plan for a large forest reserve, which would involve ecotourism, environmental education, cooperation with visiting scientists, and status as a biosphere reserve. In 1983, having secured primary funding from the Inter-American Foundation, Archibold and his collaborators formally launched El Proyecto de Estudio para el Manejo de Areas Silvestres de Kuna Yala (Project to Study Forest Areas of Kuna Yala), or PEMASKY. With further grants, including an unsolicited award from the MacArthur Foundation, total funding eventually passed a million dollars.

The project was off to an encouraging start. In addition to securing offices in Panama City, PEMASKY built a large camp with dormitory buildings at a spot called Nusagandi, where the road enters the reserve. Scientists conducted baseline studies of the surrounding forest in conjunction with Kuna staff, who also undertook technical training of various sorts. During the mid-1980s, the project hosted visits at Nusagandi from numerous scientists, journalists, and development specialists, many of whom published glowing reports holding PEMASKY up as a model for cooperation between indigenous groups and environmental organizations.

Ironically, by this time, the project was already on the verge of collapse. PEMASKY had simply grown too fast, outstripping the managerial expertise of the Kuna staff. The model used for the management plan was inappropriate for a society in which traditional agriculturalists and medicinalists knew a great deal more about the natural environment than did young men with school learning, and neither staff nor outside advisors had thought ahead sufficiently about the implementation stage and the fresh funding it would require. As it turned out, the plan was never completed, and when the initial funds ran out and foreign advisors withdrew, the project faded away.

The end of PEMASKY as a viable organization, however, and its failure to meet its most ambitious goals concealed significant successes. Between 1985 and 1987, teams of volunteers came up from the coast to work with surveyors. They cut a boundary trail, which eventually extended for more than 150 kilometers (93 miles), and the project staff managed, without violence, to dislodge all of the colonists already within the reserve. Surveying and trail cutting continued through the 1990s up to the present.

In the field of environmental education, staffers and their associates produced a coloring book called *Anmar Napguana Mimmigana* (We the children of mother earth), as well as a thoughtful volume on environmental issues for Kuna adults, *Plantas y animales en la vida del pueblo kuna* (now available in English translation, *Plants and Animals in the Life of the Kuna*, edited by Ventocilla, Herrera, and Nuñey). Numerous presentations by PEMASKY staff to the General Congress and local village gatherings greatly raised environmental consciousness among the Kuna as a whole, building on their traditional devotion to Great Mother.

Finally, a number of Kuna nongovernmental organizations (NGOs), several of them staffed by PEMASKY veterans, have appeared since the project's demise. These include Napguana (the Earth); Fundación Dobbo Yala; Koskun Kalu; Fundación Osiskun, dedicated to the marine environment; DESOSKY, concerned with sustainable development; and an umbrella organization called IDIKY. PEMASKY itself, which continues today on a reduced scale, has given birth to many vigorous children.

The General Congress as Defender of Kuna Yala

The Kuna say that more than anything else, it is their General Congress that should *yar bin urwe*, "fight for the land." As a thoroughly democratic body, composed of several hundred delegates from forty-nine constituent villages, the Kuna General Congress discusses important current issues, especially those dealing with Kuna autonomy and the preservation of their territory. If danger threatens, it is the General Congress that should forge a consensus and lead the resistance.

The General Congress, however, meets except for extraordinary sessions only twice a year, each time for three days. In the interim between meetings it has no means to enforce its decisions nor any permanent officers other than a general secretary. As a deliberative body, it has often been slow or inconsistent or divided among different opinions. Because the General Congress and the Kuna as a whole fear giving too much power or independence to their three caciques, they keep them on a tight leash, which limits their capacity for good as well as evil. As a result, efforts to counter outside threats have as often as not been time consuming, wasteful, and divisive.

This was certainly true in the case discussed above in which the government attempted to force a hotel project on Kuna Yala. After Kuna opinion turned decisively against the project, ominous newspaper articles appeared insisting that the hotel would be built regardless. The General Congress cancelled permission for the project feasibility study in 1975, and in March 1976 it voted to repudiate the three Kuna representatives on the national body of district representatives, who were widely perceived as sellouts. The representatives, however, managed to separate the elderly caciques from a delegation sent to the government, and within a few weeks the *comarca* had been partitioned into three districts, each one headed by one representative and one cacique, a move that effectively ended Kuna autonomy. A few days later, the General Congress elected a new set of caciques, whom the government refused to recognize. It was not until 1977 that intense negotiations yielded a compromise by which the partition was rescinded and the new caciques-elect were named as successors to the old caciques, who soon retired.

Just as the Kuna were beginning to recover from this debacle, in 1981, the attack on Moody's resort Pidertupu occurred. The people of the nearest village, although warned in advance that his cabañas would be burned, were very upset that Moody himself had been hurt, and they mistakenly shot and killed an out-of-uniform Kuna national guardsman sent to the site of the incident. Bad feelings between the home communities of those involved in the shooting persisted for years.

The General Congress now has administrative offices in the city, but it still lacks a real staff or enforcement powers, and it struggles to reach consensus on major issues. The Kuna have for two decades been rewriting the constitution and enabling law of the *comarca*, but the national legislative assembly has yet to ratify the changes.

FOOD FOR THOUGHT

Problems of other sorts also concern the Kuna. They worry about uncontrolled social change, both on the islands and in the city; about a lessening commitment to agriculture and traditional institutions; and about the damage they themselves are doing to the natural environment through activities such as commercial lobster fishing. They have often been distracted from these concerns, however, by the endless struggle to preserve Kuna Yala from appropriation or exploitation by outsiders. Thus, although the

Kuna have so far countered all major threats to their land and autonomy, they continue to pay a high price.

Questions

1. How should a country like Panama balance the needs of its indigenous peoples with those of other segments of the national population?
2. What does it mean for a group like the Kuna to recognize that the national government is the legitimate authority in the country, is the greatest potential source of help, and yet is also the organization with the most power to do harm?
3. Control of their own territory is both the greatest strength of the Kuna and their point of greatest vulnerability. How does this paradox influence their efforts to defend themselves?
4. The manufacturing and sale of *molas* to tourists have provided important and necessary income to the Kuna. Has this "commodification of culture" helped sustain or destroy Kuna cultural identity?
5. The Kuna have attempted to control the development of tourism in their reserve in order to ensure that they enjoy the economic benefits of tourism. To what extent have they been able to do so? Do you think that the expansion of tourism within the reserve is a threat to Kuna cultural identity.

NOTES

1. Government of Panama, *Censos Nacionales de Panama, Censo de 1990* (Panama City: Government of Panama, 1990).
2. Brian Houseal, Craig MacFarland, Guillermo Archibold, and Aurelio Chiari, "Indigenous Cultures and Protected Areas in Central America," *Cultural Survival Quarterly* 9, no. 1 (February 1985): 10–20.
3. Ibid.
4. Government of Panama, *Censos Nacionales de Panama, Censo de 1990*.

RESOURCE GUIDE

Published Literature

Howe, James. *A People Who Would Not Kneel*. Washington, D.C.: Smithsonian Institution Press, 1998. Salvador, Mari Lyn, ed. *The Art of Being Kuna: Layers of Meaning Among the Kuna of Panama*. Los Angeles: UCLA Forlwer Museum of Cultural History, 1995.

Tice, Karin. *Kuna Crafts, Gender, and the Global Economy*. Austin: University of Texas Press, 1995.

Ventocilla, Jorge, Heraclio Herrera, and Valerio Nuñez, eds. *Plants and Animals in the Life of the Kuna*. Austin: University of Texas Press, 1996.

Wali, Alaka. *Kilowatts and Crisis: Hydroelectric Power and Social Dislocation in Eastern Panama*. Boulder, Colo.: Westview Press, 1989.

Two Kuna-published magazines, *Abisua* and *Onmaked*, are available only in Panama.

Film

The Spirit of Kuna Yala, an interesting film by Andrew Young and Susan Todd, is carried by distributors for school showing.

WWW Sites

Kuna General Congress
http://www.peoplink.org/partners/pa/id/kuna-eng.htm

Mola Cooperative
http://www.peoplink.org/products/pa/cm/global.htm

Chapter 10

The Tz'utujil Maya of Guatemala

James Loucky

> To us it's all rock. We don't have time to just gaze at it.
> —Elderly Tz'utujil man to author at the top of a trail
> overlooking Lake Atitlán[1]

CULTURAL OVERVIEW

The People

The name Maya evokes images of ancient cities, long abandoned and over-grown by jungle. Yet today there are 7.5 million Maya living in Guatemala, southern Mexico, and Belize, as well as in a growing diaspora across North America. With nearly thirty distinct language groups, the Maya together represent the second largest indigenous population in the Americas. They have also faced some of the worst conditions of poverty and exploitation in the hemisphere. Yet the Maya have demonstrated tremendous tenacity in the face of encroachment and repeated cycles of conquest that continue to this day. They also maintain strong cultural cohesion despite considerable linguistic heterogeneity. Their close connection to the land, shared subsistence base, and deeply ingrained and encompassing world view help explain the remarkable endurance of the Maya.

About 60% of Guatemala's 11 million inhabitants are Maya. Most are concentrated in the western highlands, a mountainous region that has been inhabited for several thousand years. Corn (maize) and other subsistence crops domesticated in the Mesoamerican region continue to be cultivated using centuries-old technologies and indigenous knowledge. Many Maya also engage in a variety of nonagricultural activities and wage labor, and today increasing numbers have migrated to cities and north to the United States.

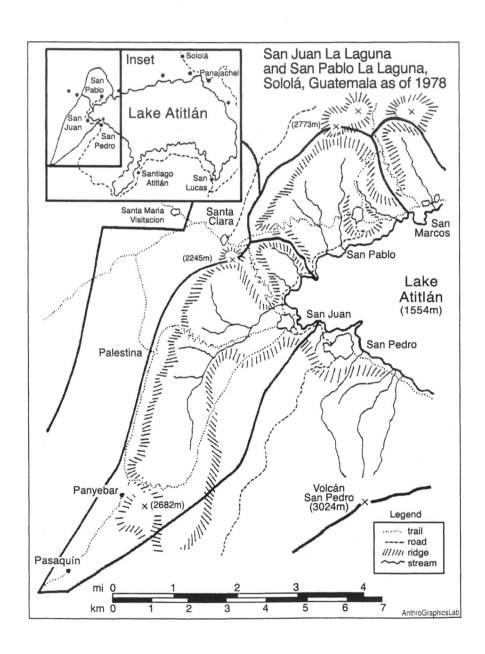

Inset

• Sololá

• Panajachel

San Pablo

San Juan

San Pedro

Lake Atitlán

• Santiago Atitlán

San Lucas

San Juan La Laguna and San Pablo La Laguna, Sololá, Guatemala as of 1978

(2773m) ×

Santa Maria Visitacion

Santa Clara

(2245m) ×

San Pablo

San Marcos

Lake Atitlán (1554m)

San Juan

San Pedro

Palestina

Panyebar

× (2682m)

Pasaquín

Volcán San Pedro (3024m) ×

Legend

.... trail
- - - - - road
////// ridge
〜〜 stream

mi 0   1   2   3   4

km 0   1   2   3   4   5   6   7

AnthroGraphicsLab

Situated on the western shores of Lake Atitlán, in the central highland area of Guatemala, are the Tz'utujil Maya ("tz' " is pronounced much like the "ts" in the contraction "it's"; "jil" is similar to a soft pronunciation of the word "heal"). They call themselves *vinuk* (the people), and their name refers to the "flower of the maize plant." While neither the most populous of Mayan groups nor occupying the largest extent of land, the Tz'utujil people have experienced most of the major demographic, economic, and political changes that have affected other Mayan groups. Thus, they represent a good case for understanding the contemporary pressures on, and responses of, the Mayan population as a whole.

The Setting

Whereas the lowlands were the epic setting for the classic Mayan civilization, most of the contemporary Mayan population is found in the highlands. Extending from Chiapas, Mexico, to present-day Guatemala City, this mountainous region contains hundreds of settlements ranging from tiny dispersed hamlets to concentrated villages and towns linked by a network of trails and roads, mostly unpaved. Often there are only a few nonindigenous residents, most of whom are teachers and government personnel. Fertile volcanic soils cover some of the area, and the natural vegetation is mainly oak-pine forest and chaparral. However, virtually all arable land has been converted to subsistence and export crops, and steep terrain and overuse of the land have led to serious environmental degradation. Combined with varied timing and levels of precipitation, conditions for most of the highland Maya today are characterized by agricultural uncertainty and periodic scarcity of food and other crucial resources.

Intermediate between the Pacific coastal plain and higher elevations lies an ancient volcanic basin holding magnificent Lake Atitlán. Ringed by volcanoes and one mile in elevation, the lake has long been a major tourist destination. Promoted as a "land of eternal springtime," the Atitlán region has moderate temperatures throughout the year. Cycles of life are governed primarily by cyclical rainy and dry seasons. As throughout the highlands, vertical ecology and micro-geographic diversity result in a wide spectrum of economic and cultural variation in a relatively small area. The lake itself is a principal source of water for irrigation, fishing, and transportation by small launches and canoes to other lakeside communities.

Traditional Subsistence Strategies

The highland Maya have long relied on rainfall farming of corn, beans, and root and vine cultigens, usually combined in fields referred to as *milpa*. In years past, fields were left fallow for sufficient time to allow regeneration of soil fertility. Where there are sources of water, such as springs and streams as well as along lakeshores, small irrigated garden plots (*tablones*) allow more intensive growing of vegetables and nontraditional cash crops. Increasingly milpa has been converted to the cultivation of coffee, which is destined for distant markets. The Maya also have a long history of producing nonagricultural goods, including textiles, wood and fiber products, and mats, for both domestic use and sale. The extensive marketing system of highland Guatemala is known internationally.

Tz'utujil communities remain focused on the land, despite their location on the shores of the lake. Corn is grown on hillsides that have been cleared and planted using machetes, hoes, and digging sticks. Many Tz'utujil have planted coffee or invested considerable labor in building and maintaining irrigated terraces and raised plots, with the goal of earning more money from cash crops than from the corn that could be grown on the same land. Households with little or no land engage in craft production as well as in local day labor and seasonal wage labor. In addition, a host of household maintenance activities are conducted, including collecting firewood, cooking, and socializing children. Attending to these activities is critical for the success of agricultural and money-producing pursuits.

Social and Political Organization

The household, the principal social and economic unit of the Maya, operates on the basis of cooperation between sexes and among generations. Division of male and female labor corresponds roughly to work done in the field and work done in and near the home. Nonetheless, there is a considerable overlap of gender roles, particularly in times of need. Tz'utujil children are socialized early to the necessity of work, and they begin performing simple tasks such as errands and the care of younger siblings from the age of four or five. They learn that their contributions help meet tangible needs, and they are effectively socialized to accept the values of responsibility and interdependence which help ensure family integrity.

Most Tz'utujil live in nuclear families composed of husband, wife, and children, although three-generation extended families are common until a couple inherits or acquires a house site and land which enable them to establish a separate household. Marriage usually occurs within the village. Villages themselves were traditionally governed by a civil-religious hierarchy known as the *cofradía*, made up of men serving year-long positions chosen on the basis of community respect.

Religion and World View

Maya have long believed that physical locations, animals, and natural phenomena have spirits associated with them, which can be accessed through shamans and which are sometimes observable to other people,

Tz'utujil Mayan children returning from helping in the fields. Courtesy of James Loucky.

particularly at dusk or at night. Individuals are also thought to have animal guardian spirits. Traditional healers, midwives, and diviners are still largely revered. Currently, religious beliefs are an integrated mix of Mayan and Christian elements. Most religious ceremonies are tied to the Catholic saints' calendar, although the connection may be only nominal for many participants. *Cofradías* persist in some communities; in others, the most important religious leaders are Catholic priests or Protestant pastors.

THREATS TO SURVIVAL

> Don't you understand that we're poor? Hurry up. I'm working. I'm thirsty, too.
> —Tz'utujil mother encouraging son to finish making a fiber bag for sale[7]

Demographic Trends

The invasion of the Mayan homeland by the Spaniards in the sixteenth and seventeenth centuries ushered in tremendous upheaval and death. The population was decimated by violence and disease, including smallpox, measles, and influenza. The demographic collapse of the Tz'utujil was typical. The population had declined nearly 90% by 1780, and only recently did the number of Tz'utujil regain its preconquest level. Today there are over 70,000 Tz'utujil in five lakeside towns as well as in the mountains to the west and on the Pacific coastal plain to the south. With the falling of mortality rates, population growth has been explosive, especially in the latter half of the twentieth century. Although infant and child deaths are still common, there has been a gradual decrease in mortality associated with a wider understanding of risk factors and slowly improving health services. A growing awareness of higher child survival, accompanied by a shift out of agriculture, where child labor is particularly valuable, is beginning to be reflected in smaller family sizes.

Heritage of Conquest

Many Mayan customs and institutions were attacked or destroyed during and after the Spanish conquest. Combined with the "great dying," the Spanish instituted the *encomienda* system which provided huge land grants to friends of the Spanish crown, along with rights to the labor of the native residents. Previously scattered populations were concentrated into settlements to ensure easier control of labor and potential unrest. Conversion to Christianity was often ruthlessly enforced. A profound racial and cultural division separating Maya from Spaniard began to be engendered during the pervasive ethnic and genetic mixing that occurred during and following the conquest. Those of mixed descent are known in Guatemala, as elsewhere throughout Central America, as ladinos. While oftentimes poor, ladinos nonetheless have continued to enjoy greater economic privileges and higher status in the social hierarchy that emerged.

The Maya hardly benefited from Guatemala's independence from Spain in the 1820s. Instead, conditions generally worsened as Indian autonomy and resources were eroded further. Privileged Hispanicized citizens (ladinos) moved into Mayan territories to occupy positions of political authority and economic power. Even the so-called liberal reforms of the late nineteenth century were damaging since they enabled a series of despotic governments simultaneously to abolish communal lands (local level lands managed by Mayan communities) and to impose harsh edicts that ensured forced labor from the Mayan highlands to the coffee plantations spreading across wrested Indian lands. Among the most notorious were the so-called vagrancy laws which required Indian males to perform between 100 and 150 days of unpaid labor a year. Some of these laws were not abolished until the 1940s. Similarly destructive was the introduction of distilled alcohol, particularly cane liquor (*aguardiente*), which became an unfortunate avenue of relief or oblivion for many Maya despondent over the conditions of turmoil and suffering. Loans, alcohol, and "company stores" were among the means by which ladino overseers and store owners entrapped many Maya in the vicious cycle of debt servitude.

Current Events and Conditions

Recent developments involving the Maya of highland Guatemala are closely associated with the progressive loss of land, which undermined agriculture as a secure means of livelihood while at the same time fueling further conflict, culminating in a thirty-year civil war that has only recently subsided. Indigenous farmers did what they could to oppose the accumulation of land, wealth, and power by the growing non-Indian elite. However, their passive and active resistance was usually no match for the violence of plantation owners and their private armies, the outright occupation of communal lands, the defrauding and falsification of titles, the abuse by local ladino authorities, and the forced sale of remaining fields as children went hungry and died. The average size of landholdings declined throughout the twentieth century, and Guatemala today has one of the most extreme divisions of wealth in all of Latin America. While 1% of the population controls about 65% of the land, over 40% of the rural population is now completely landless.

To cope with the shortage of land and money, the Tz'utujil have intensified their agricultural and other forms of labor. As landholdings shrank and agricultural yields declined, local land conflicts festered between neighbors as well as between towns. Growing internal divisions of wealth have also exacerbated factionalism, much of it expressed in terms of religious differences. Decreasing ability to meet basic needs locally has also resulted in more permanent displacement. Many Tz'utujil youth have headed to towns, particularly Guatemala City, which has mushroomed in size with the influx of rural migrants. They work in a variety of factory jobs, including in export-processing plants known as *maquiladoras*, similar to those that have been set up on the U.S.–Mexico border and elsewhere throughout Latin America. Some strive to continue their education and training; others engage in a variety of informal sector work such as street vending and day labor. Whether in village or city, however, most Tz'utujil Maya remain at the lower levels of a long-standing racial and economic hierarchy.

Inequality and subordination are thus the two most fundamental and unchanging realities characterizing Maya history to the present day. However, as conditions worsened, their awareness of the roots of impoverishment grew. While laboring on plantations, people found themselves working alongside poor from other communities. Following reforms within the Catholic Church, beginning in the 1960s, priests and other religious personnel embraced liberation theology which, concerned with social inequality, promoted social justice among the poor and the oppressed. Growing media exposure also introduced news of other struggles, including the successful revolution in nearby Nicaragua. At the same time, increasing tourism increased contact with people from Europe and the United States who were wealthier and enjoyed far more civil and human rights.

During the 1970s, efforts to achieve greater social and economic gains peaceably included community-based campaigns for potable water, better health facilities, and land reform. As more Mayan youth completed school, they sought access to teaching, health, and municipal positions previously monopolized by ladinos. Tragically, this political opening was short lived. Determined to maintain the status quo of extensive landholdings and associated power, and fearing indigenous activism, the ruling elite became further entrenched. Military force was used to intimidate and repress. Ostensibly this was directed against a growing guerilla movement composed of Maya and non-Maya who, frustrated by the assassinations of anyone working publicly for political change, had come to see no alternative but underground organization and even armed struggle. As the military repression grew, it became more indiscriminate. By the early 1980s, massive scorched-earth campaigns, in which whole villages and adjacent agricultural lands were destroyed; widespread torture; and disappearances had left between 150,000 and 200,000 dead. The vast majority of victims were Mayan civilians. Hundreds of villages were annihilated, and hundreds of thousands of men, women, and children fled to the mountains or cities, into Mexico, and as far away as the United States and Canada. An institutionalization of military control in the highlands followed, including requirements for all Indian males to serve in civil patrols, highway checkpoints, and relocations of "subversive" groups into closely monitored "model" villages.

In the Tz'utujil region, the message voiced by those opposed to the succession of military governments resonated with most, given local experience with social and economic injustice. Some people gave moral or tangible support to the revolutionary group operating in the nearby mountains. Many others, however, felt caught in the middle. Little good came from the government, but there was also uncertainty about the motives and prognosis for the guerillas, who included urban ladino leaders who perceived the Mayan culture as an anachronistic impediment to a proletarian revolution. Regardless, the Guatemalan army regarded this as a largely subversive region, and all Tz'utujil communities were targeted to some degree. In the largest town, Santiago Atitlán, several hundred people were "disappeared" (kidnapped, tortured, and killed by the military and paramilitary death squads) over a ten-year period. In the next largest community, San Padre la Lagoon, a death squad operated with impunity for several years. Everywhere people were fearful and suspicious. A gradual calm returned by the 1990s, marked by the successful removal of troops from Santiago Atitlán following a massacre of thirteen civilians by soldiers in 1990. Strong local insistence on the right to be left alone corresponded to growing indigenous political leverage at the national level and strong international pressure for peace. A peace accord between the government and the guerilla forces was finally signed in 1996.

Environmental Crisis

The combination of population growth throughout the highlands and the wide disparity in landholdings has had profound ecological effects. Farmers who have small landholdings have been compelled to change their farming systems significantly. They have reduced the length of the fallow period and overtilled fields, leading to declines in soil fertility and greater erosion. Along with this has come growing dependence on costly chemical fertilizers to keep shrinking plots of land viable. With the decline in the number of people who can still depend on subsistence farming to meet their food needs, the economies of virtually all communities have become reliant on alternative crops for export as well as on nonagricultural economic alternatives and trade. Nonsustainable cropping techniques and toxic pesticides are often associated with these recently introduced crops.

Growing population pressure is also visible in extensive deforestation. Wood remains the principal fuel for cooking and heat. In addition to firewood cutting, both legal and illegal timbering have denuded many slopes. One result is a significant loss of habitat for indigenous wildlife. For example, the national symbol, the iridescent green and red quetzal bird, is highly endangered as a result of the widespread destruction of the last remaining cloud forests in which they live.

The Atitlán basin is a microcosm for seeing many of the environmental problems that persist throughout the highlands. Fragmentation of landholdings has increased pressure to boost productivity through the application of chemical fertilizers and pesticides. To generate maximal income, much land has been converted to producing crops for export, most notably coffee. Once self-sufficient in the production of food for home consumption, all Tz'utujil communities must now buy corn (the most important household food staple) that is produced outside their communities. The annual harvest for most households today is sufficient to meet family nutritional needs for only four or five months. Erosion and deforestation are evident especially at higher elevations. Rising populations and an increase in the use of imported products have greatly increased pollution, particularly of solid waste. Where household waste and garbage traditionally has been taken to the fields to act as a natural fertilizer, today the prevalence of manufactured products has resulted in the widespread scattering of plastic and other nonbiodegradable waste.

Picturesque Lake Atitlán is also far less pristine than it appears. The water quality has declined with the runoff of agricultural effluents and human waste, which only rarely is confined to sewage facilities. The water level has declined rapidly in recent years, presumably in part from overuse through the widespread adoption of gasoline-powered pumps for irrigating cash crops. The fishery itself has never recovered from a short-sighted development scheme in the 1960s, in which carnivorous black bass were introduced in hopes of promoting tourism through sports fishing. Instead, a centuries-old traditional fishery, based on traps and vegetation enclosures, was destroyed when native species were devoured by the introduced bass.

Sociocultural Crisis

Recent decades have witnessed fundamental social transformations in highland Guatemala associated with changing economic orientations, political turmoil, and the ascendancy of global telecommunications and international consumer brands and cultural symbols. Thirty years ago, fairly tight-knit Mayan communities comprised households who either planted enough corn to meet family needs or augmented milpa farming with seasonal labor on plantations or the sale of cash crops and crafts. In the period since, regional, national, and international processes have combined with population growth to result in a shift from subsistence to commercial agriculture, from production for household use to a more monetized life. The altitude and volcanic soil of much of the highlands are ideal for growing high-grade coffee, and in many areas virtually all suitable land has today been converted from corn to coffee. Increasingly, quality as well as quantity of land has led to greater social differentiation. Communal landholdings (land controlled and managed by the community) has been replaced with the buying and selling of private property by individuals which now occurs even across municipal boundaries.

Along with the decline of milpa farming as the universal occupation and varying access to land, the gap between richer and poorer Maya has widened through the diversification of economic activity. Greater accumulation of wealth is possible not only for those with a land base to expand, but also for those entering relatively secure teaching and government jobs and for those with capital to invest in commercial activity. With the growing significance of outside markets, a small number of men in each community have acquired trucks and, as a result of the profits associated with commerce, have become far more wealthy than most others. Large multiroom residences now stand out among small adobe houses.

Just as changes in the larger economy involving region and nation have ushered in changes in the local economy and greater social stratification, transformations in larger government and church institutions have been reflected in changes in political and religious organization in the villages. Traditionally, community service through the civil-religious hierarchy functioned to help unify by defining sociocultural identity, as well as to foster respect for the local authority system based on seniority and to confer prestige. Conscription into Guatemala's armed forces increased the reluctance of young men to accept unpaid community service, at the same time that the national government undercut local autonomy by channeling power through appointed authorities, often ladinos. Participation in national political parties in turn became a primary means for individual, if not collective, gains. At the same time, factionalism has increased, largely associated with the proliferation of Catholic and Protestant congregations. Boundaries of "community" have thus been eroding from above as well as from below.

Given the military apparatus that has dominated Guatemala for virtually its entire history, continuing Mayan ambivalence toward government and its largely ladino functionaries is not surprising. Their changing world became tragically apparent during the growing and then violent conflict that engulfed the highlands during the late 1970s and early 1980s. Even innocent activities like organizing health efforts and advocating bilingual education became politically suspect, leaving a legacy of caution and diminishing further communal sentiment.

Ideological developments have accompanied these profound political-economic shifts. While values of responsibility, hard work, and thriftiness persist, growing access to outside markets has altered the range of images available to people. Whereas fatalism was understandable in the face of insecure harvests and malnutrition, Maya are increasingly and perhaps inadvertently more oriented toward the future. Television and other media provide models that encourage consumption, individualism, and competitiveness. Higher levels of schooling, made possible as children's work has become less critical than it was in subsistence agriculture, boosts greater proficiency in Spanish at the same time as it encourages greater assimilation to the national culture and entry into wage labor, increasingly outside of home communities.

All Tz'utujil communities have experienced these social changes in various degrees. Coffee has been planted widely, providing sufficient earnings to stimulate higher levels of consumption, ranging from new construction to vehicles to longer schooling of children. *Cofradías* have disappeared in some towns and are on the wane elsewhere. Growing orientation to the outside has been accompanied by expressions of shame of their own culture. First evident in the 1970s, this was marked by the shedding of hand-woven clothing and the rejection by youth of the wisdom and moral authority of their elders, including shamans. Widespread intrusion of external values has also come through the growing numbers of tourists to the lake region, the availability of a wide array of material goods, and the reruns of U.S. television shows and movies (from *The Three Stooges* to *Rambo*). Frequent travel to previously infrequented places has become commonplace with multiple bus and boat connections each day. Growing numbers of younger men and women have emigrated to Guatemala City to work in assembly plants or in the service sector, returning mostly only for visits such as during the annual town fiesta.

RESPONSE: STRUGGLES TO SURVIVE CULTURALLY

It is like mushrooms, which spring up on their own.
— Maya leader Demetrio Cojtí on Mayan cultural resurgence[3]

The Maya of highland Guatemala have faced multiple threats to their cultural integrity in recent years: continuing loss or fragmentation of land, deforestation and degradation of topsoil, monetization of nearly everything, and mass tourism. A new phase of social and economic transformation followed in the shadow of the trauma of counterinsurgency. While each community is distinct, certain common ways of dealing with the changing world have emerged. Some continue to sell remaining land; others contribute migrants to cities, and almost all are intensifying their investments in coffee and other export commodities. Paralleling the vast changes in livelihoods across the highlands are fundamental transformations in community relations and identity. Perhaps the most significant basis for Mayan cultural survival is the contemporary affirmation of the continuity of their ethnicity. The Mayan past has long been glorified in Guatemala at the same time the Mayan present was denigrated and repressed, but Maya today are everywhere reclaiming their past while also asserting their crucial and varied roles in the present.

Economic Strains and Strengths

The history and habitat of poverty have led indigenous Guatemalans to make heavy commitments of time to a wide range of economic activities in order to utilize fully the resources available to them. Through a highly organized household economy, family workloads are allocated among everyone but the very young. Even socialization of children and the care of siblings represent a cultural system for ensuring child and family survival. As both population growth and loss of land to outsiders have required new economic ventures—and undercut self-sufficiency—new pressures are being brought to bear on Mayan families. Interdependence is still a primary organizing principle for a full range of household maintenance requirements and for some production activities. However, as the emphasis shifts to export production, commerce, and emigration, the perceived utility of children is increasingly seen as a future investment linked to higher levels of schooling. It is not at all certain, though, that further education necessarily leads to expected occupational gains; today, for example, there are far more youth qualified to teach or do accounting than there are positions available.

Erosion of shared patterns of land tenure and work also represents a threat to community solidarity. Where houses and harvests traditionally drew on unpaid extended kin and communal labor (labor that is allocated and shared among members of the community), these tasks are today almost exclusively arranged on the basis of daily wages. However, new cooperative ventures have arisen to help offset this trend. The agricultural, coffee, and weaving cooperatives that exist in many communities allow access to bulk purchases of supplies as well as larger or more secure markets. As relative peace has replaced the bloody years of civil war, numerous international agencies and community development initiatives have entered highland communities. They provide a valuable source of investment and expertise for a variety of indigenous economic and educational ventures. Yet their varied understanding of historical and contemporary social and cultural dynamics, gender relations, and implications of income differences within and between communities poses a further challenge to maintaining unified communities.

Cultural Revitalization

From the Spanish conquest through the recent terror, the highlands of Guatemala have been a region of refuge for the indigenous population in their struggle to resist domination. Mayan history reveals numerous examples of resistance, from outright rebellions to more passive means of surviving without full subjugation. Most social and religious practices today reveal syncretism, as Maya strive to retain indigenous heritage by selectively incorporating and modifying what is thrust upon them. Even religious conversion and ethnic conversion, or "ladinoization," are increasingly seen as survival strategies. Neither did the recent horrors of counterinsurgency eliminate Mayan consciousness. Scorched-earth campaigns spread great fear, but Mayan roots remained intact. In fact, the war seems only to have intensified Mayan commitment and helped redefine strategies. As earlier, current resistance is based less on revolutionary idealism than on continuing pragmatism. There is also growing recognition that, ultimately, demography is destiny. The proportion of indigenous survivors in Guatemala is higher than in all other areas of the Americas except the Andes and the highland Oaxaca. Today the Maya represent 60% of the population of the country.

Coinciding with global panindigenous activity, the 1990s has seen a remarkable Mayan renaissance. Central to current developments are identity questions, while common to activities in all communities is the sense that the Maya have been an excluded people. Longstanding state and ladino power contribute an increasingly regional and national character to the

Mayan struggles, but there really are a multiplicity of Mayan movements rather than a single voice. What it means to be a Maya is today being discussed and re-created in every community. Rituals are being reintroduced or reinvented, including the introduction of Mayan elements into the Catholic Mass. Since language is a critical marker of identity, Mayan languages are being consciously used at home and in the community, in names and signs, and through an increase in the number of publications printed in Mayan languages.

Today there are over 500 Mayan organizations, ranging from local associations geared to meeting specific needs relating to education, health, and cultural practices, to higher level coordinating bodies. Mayan proposals for political reform and participation are being implemented as identity and cultural rights accords at the national level. These address such areas as bilingual education, sacred sites, rights of indigenous women, officialization of languages, and even greater economic independence and territorial autonomy. Expanding ventures by Maya outside of their local communities is reflected in increasing assertions regarding the national and even transnational character of Mayan peoples today, as they are found in urban centers and even as far away as the United States.

Tz'utujil Developments

Rapid political economic changes in the Lake Atitlán region have both substantiated and transformed the sense Tz'utujil have about themselves and their communities. The communities around the lake are a discrete cultural and ecological area, and they are among the most sought-after destinations of international travelers. They are also at a pivotal point in an uncertain developmental trajectory. They are increasingly integrated into national and international arenas through extensive coffee production and out-migration, as well as tourism, and it is recognized that the present and future are vastly different from the past. Yet there are also growing efforts to reclaim Tz'utujil history in order to provide guidance during the current flux. Elders are again being sought out to explain traditional norms of conduct as well as their underlying principles. Since the oral tradition presents an antecedent and then a consequence to reinforce an important value, proverbs and myths are being collected. The Tz'utujil language is also being explicitly used in ceremony, for names on signs, and in school instruction.

Particular efforts are being made to halt the extensive environmental degradation experienced by the lake and surrounding lands in recent years and restore the land and water. Trees are being planted, partly to provide shading for coffee, partly to offset the continuing harvest of firewood. Reed beds along shore have been rerooted. New reports state that a tiny number of flightless grebe found only on Lake Atitlán may have narrowly escaped extinction. Ecotourism now goes hand in hand with cultural tourism. Further conservation efforts include organic farming of coffee and other crops. Still, local factionalism and longstanding boundary disputes between villages persist, complicating long-range planning and more effective restoration possibilities.

FOOD FOR THOUGHT

The Maya of highland Guatemala provide valuable lessons for understanding how indigenous people confront powerful forces of economic change, ecological degradation, and violent repression. Following a lengthy impoverishment and the recent slaughter of thousands of civilians, a relatively peaceful transition is under way. Today a variety of Mayan cultural revitalization activities are occurring in nearly every community, while at the same time new production activities are stimulating higher levels of consumption, less perceivable economic value of children, and widening disparities in wealth. The Tz'utujil Maya represent a case of people responding to a combination of factors over which they have limited control, including outside market forces, shifts in national political climate, expansion of landholdings and lakeside homes by outsiders, and international tourism. Whether they ultimately will achieve greater empowerment and local control or experience further dependence and social decomposition remains to be seen.

Questions

1. With thirty different languages, can Guatemala become a model for a truly multicultural nation? Can heightened awareness of being one people with a long past overcome the linguistic, religious, ethnic, and wealth differences among the Maya?
2. Can the peaceful transition in Guatemala be sustained, given the memories of tens of thousands of Maya killed so recently.
3. What does the growing migration of Maya to cities and across borders mean for their future as a people? Can Mayan identity be sustained through the turmoil associated with globalization and transnational development?
4. How does tourism and ecotourism impact the Maya, either positively or negatively?
5. Women and children are central to the transmission of culture. How are their activities and roles changing today?

NOTES

The information presented here is based primarily on the author's ethnographic fieldwork in the Tz'utujil communities of San Juan and San Pablo beginning in the mid-1970s.

1. Author's fieldnotes.
2. Ibid.
3. Ibid.

RESOURCE GUIDE

Published Literature

Canby, Peter. *The Heart of the Sky: Travels Among the Maya*. New York: Kodansha International, 1994.

Carlsen, Robert S. *The War for the Heart and Soul of a Highland Maya Town*. Austin: University of Texas Press, 1996.

Carmack, Robert M., ed. *Harvest of Violence: The Maya Indians and the Guatemalan Crisis*. Norman: University of Oklahoma Press, 1988.

Fischer, Edward F., and R. McKenna Brown. *Maya Cultural Activism in Guatemala*. Austin: University of Texas Press, 1996.

Gonzalez, Gaspar Padre. *A Mayan Life*. Rancho Palos Verdes, Calif.: Yax te' Press, 1995.

The first English-language novel by a Maya author, it is available through http://www.yaxte.org/.

Watanabe, John M. *Maya Saints and Souls in a Changing World*. Austin: University of Texas Press, 1992.

Videos and Films

The Cakchiquel Maya of San Antonio Palopó (1991). Discovery Channel, Peoples of the World series (Tracy Ehlers, anthropologist).

Daughters of Ixchel: Maya Thread of Change (1993). University of California Extension, Center for Media and Independent Learning, 2000 Center St., Berkeley, CA 94704 (Kathryn Vigesaa and John McKay, filmmaker).

Todos Santos Cuchumatan: Report from a Guatemalan Village (1982) and *Todos Santos: The Survivors* (1989). Distributed by First Run/Icarus Films, 153 Waverly Place, New York, NY 10014 (Olivia Carrescia, ethnographic filmmaker).

WWW Sites

A great deal of information about the Maya with links to many other resources can be found on several WWW sites. Three of the best include:

University of Georgia, Department of Crop and Soil Sciences
http://mars.cropsoil.uga.edu/trop-ag/the-maya.htm

Jaguar Books
http://www.criscenzo.com/jaguar/maya.html

Indigenous Peoples Literature—Newsgroup
http://www.indians.org/welker/maya.htm

Organizations

Guatemala News and Information Bureau
  3181 Mission, Box 12
  San Francisco, CA 94110
  (415) 826–3593 publishes quarterly "Report on Guatemala"

National Coordinating Office on Refugees and Displaced of
  Guatemala
  1830 Connecticut Ave., NW
  Washington, DC 20009

SOUTH AMERICANS

PACIFIC OCEAN

COLOMBIA

N

● Awa

● Quito

E C U A D O R

PERU

0   km   100

KEY
----- International boundary

Area ➔

SOUTH
AMERICA

Chapter 11

The Awa of Ecuador

Janet M. Chernela

CULTURAL OVERVIEW

The People

The term Awa refers to approximately 10,000 native Amerindian speakers of the language Awapit who are situated on both sides of the Colombian-Ecuadorian border. In 1987 about 3,000 of these indigenous people, or 30% of the total population, were located in one continuous area within Ecuador. The remaining 6,000 to 8,000 Awa resided in scattered communities, interspersed among newer settlers in Colombia.[1]

This chapter is concerned with the Awa and the formation of the Awa Reserve in northwestern Ecuador. The Awa Reserve, which, formed in 1987, combined Ecuadorian indigenous legislation with forestry legislation and administered and managed by the indigenous Awa as stewards of their own lands, was one of the first of its kind. The United Nations Conference on Environment and Development (UNCED) with its Agenda 21 would not be written for five more years, and the conceptual linkage between indigenous peoples and environmental sustainability had not yet entered the language of international policy. The case of the Awa, therefore, is a remarkable one. It continues to provide an example of environmental preservation, economic sustainability, and local autonomy of indigenous peoples. To date, the Ecuadorian Awa ethnic and forest reserve remains one of the few that may be deemed a success.

The Setting

Lying within the southern extension of a bioregion whose core is the Chocó area of Pacific Colombia, the region inhabited by the Awa contains

Awa traditional house. Courtesy of Janet M. Chernela.

some of the widest biological diversity found anywhere in the world. The area presents an extraordinarily large number of distinct habitats, including humid tropical forests, low montane forests, upper and lower páramo zones, and high montane forests. Among these are two of the most endangered ecosystems of the world: tropical wet forest, including one of the world's few remaining true cloud forests, and the ecologically distinct páramos. The area includes over 300,000 hectares (741,000 acres) of pristine tropical montane wet forest, estimated to have one of the highest concentrations of endemic species in the world. The various ecosystems that make up the area contain large numbers of both migratory animals and endemic species of plants and animals, including endangered tropical ungulates, carnivores, primates, and avian species. Over 500 bird species have been identified within the area; a full 30 of these are endemic to the region. More than 400 species of epiphytes have been identified, including numerous orchids and bromeliads. This rare wealth of biota includes the only species of bear found in South America, the spectacled bear (*Tramaretos ornatus*), declared endangered by the international conservation community.

A combination of factors, including high rainfall, extreme variability in topography and climatic conditions within a relatively limited geographic area, and proximity to the equator, account for this high concentration of species diversity. The region comprises an altitudinal range from 50 meters (164 feet) in the southwestern tropical lowlands to 4,850 meters (15,900 feet) in the upper montane region. The area also includes numerous intermediate ranges with uniquely characteristic biota. The average annual temperature varies from 12°C (53°F) in the higher elevations to 24°C (75 °F) at the lower elevations, while precipitation in the highest regions ranges from some 2,000 millimeters (78 inches) annually and to a high of 8,000 millimeters (315 inches) in the lowlands.[2]

Traditional Subsistence Strategies

Traditional Awa subsistence practices combined hunting, gathering, and fishing with plant cultivation. Today, the Awa continue these activities with some changes and have added to them income-generating activities such as animal husbandry. Like many inhabitants of humid tropics elsewhere, the Awa practice a form of shifting agriculture in which the forest is cut into small parcels (from 0.5 to 2 ha [1.25 to 5 acres] in size), cultivated for two or three cycles, and left to lie fallow for more than seven years. The Awa variety of swidden cultivation is known as slash and mulch to distinguish it from the more common slash and burn. Burning, employed elsewhere in the neotropics to release nutrients locked in the standing forest, is not possible due to the dampness of the vegetation. Instead, the Awa cut the moist vegetation cover and leave it to decay. Within a period of days a shallow humus layer, which forms on the rotting mulch, provides favorable conditions for the planting and sprouting of seeds, such as corn. When the forest cover is removed, the heavy rainfall leaches out important nutrients, leaving the soils infertile. Yields quickly decline after one or two harvests. Awa agricultural techniques may be regarded as a means of coping with the conditions of high rainfall and quickly eroding soils.

The complex composition of Awa gardens is characterized by a mixture of plant varieties with differing resistance qualities, nutrient requirements, climate tolerance, and rates of maturation. There is both diversity within and among species. In addition to growing different crops in the same garden, intraspecies variation is high. For example, the Awa plant at least five varieties of plantains and an undisclosed number of manioc varieties. The technique, known as intercropping, mimics the floristic diversity of the standing forest and is widespread among native lowland South Americans. This strategy of polycultures has proven more successful than monocultures in the tropics where the risks of any single crop loss to disease or predation are high.

The main staples of contemporary Awa gardens are the plantain, a crop domesticated in Asia and imported to the Americas, and maize, a New

World domesticate. Gardens also contain a number of New World tuberous crops including manioc (*Manihot esculenta*) (tapioca) and two high-carbohydrate, yamlike tubers (*Colocassia* and *Xanthosoma*). Additional plants, including beans, sugarcane, fruit trees, medicinal plants, and fish-stunning plants, are intercropped among others.

Planting schedules are complex. Each crop has a distinct maturation cycle, and Awa families maintain several gardens in various stages of maturation. For example, corn is harvested from five to eight months after planting, depending upon the variety, and manioc is harvested between six and nine months after planting. The cultivation of plantains and sugarcane involves a lengthier process. Plantains mature from nine to twelve months after planting, while sugarcane requires a full annual cycle between planting and harvesting. In some cases, the timing of plant introduction is closely related to the rainfall regime. Although there is no true dry season, some plants, such as maize, must be planted in January and August when rainfall is at its lowest. Likewise, manioc is susceptible to rotting when soil conditions do not allow adequate drainage.

Many fruit-bearing trees and shrubs are interspersed among crops in the gardens. These include hot peppers (*Capsicum spp.*), chirimoya (*Annona sp.*), (sweetsop or custard apple) tomato (*Lycopersicum*), tree tomato (*Cyphomandra*), lulo or naranjilla (*Solanum quitoensis*), peach palm (*Bactris gasipaes*), papaya (*Carica papaya*), madrono (*Rheedia chocoensis*), guayaba (*Psidium guajava*), inga, (*Inga edulus, I. spectabilis*), tamarind (*Tamarindus indica*), mango (*Mangifera indica*), borojo (*Boroja patinoi*), avocado (*Persea americana*), and anchiote (*Bicha orrelana*). A number of important trees bearing edible fruits have been selected and improved for quality by Amerindians over centuries or millenia. One of these, planted by the Awa, is the peach palm. Its densely clustered fruits are rich in oils, protein, Vitamin A, and other essential nutrients. The wild variety has far less flesh on its fruits than has the improved domesticated variety. In the shifting agriculture practiced by the Awa, a plot of land is harvested for two or three cycles, then a new garden is cut and the former is returned to secondary forest. The planted trees, which long outlast the food crops, enhance the biodiversity of the subsequent secondary forest, providing fruit after the last crops are harvested and attracting game, such as deer, that feed on the fruit. A number of researchers argue that arboreal species are deliberately planted by indigenous gardeners in order to enrich the soil for future vegetation. These include a number of leguminous species, including inga, a tree valued for its tasty fruit as well as the nitrogen-fixing properties of its root system. The former garden sites that appear to be abandoned may continue to play an important role in food production as well as species diversification and soil enrichment.

Population density tends to vary with altitude; the lower elevations are more sparsely populated than the higher elevations. The Awa living in lower elevations depend more on game and fish than those living at higher elevations. Awa hunt in both primary and secondary forests. Secondary or so-called abandoned forests may serve to attract game. Among the animals hunted are the large agouti (*Dasyprocta punctata*), paca (*Agouti paca*), collared peccary (*Tayassu tajasu*), brocket deer (*zamaa americana*), iguana, and a number of large birds.

Before the introduction of the shotgun, animals were hunted using a blowgun and poisoned darts. Two types of poison were used in dart venom: one was extracted from the skin of the frog (*Dendrobates histrionics*) and the other from the latex of the *Maraceous Perebea sp.* The blowgun has been replaced by the shotgun, and, after a period of overexploitation by indigenous peoples and new settlers, hunting is now regulated within Awa territory.

Fish is also a food source of greater import at lower elevations. Together with catfish (*Bagre spp*), the common freshwater characins constitute the majority of fish captured and eaten. Besides spear fishing, and fishing with a hook and line, the Awa employ a variety of fish traps said to be introduced by them and generally in use throughout the Chocoan lowlands. These include fish fences in which are set guillotine-type devices and funnel traps with capture chambers. The Awa understanding of plant-animal interactions is revealed in a number of their fish-collection practices that demonstrate a close awareness of feeding habits. Capture techniques, for example, utilize the fruits favored by a specific variety of fish or animal as an attractant to traps. In addition to baiting traps with fruit, the Awa are reported to build capture platforms in fruiting trees. These practices illustrate that the Awa have observed the importance of fruit in the diets of fishes, something that was not known to Western scientists until recently.

The Awa also use the plant product barbasco (*Lonchocarpus sp.*) in fishing. When beaten, the plant produces a milky discharge. During the brief dry season, the Awa mash and beat the leaves, stems, or roots and submerge them in low streams. The discharged liquid stuns fish, causing them to float to the surface (an action similar to that of rotenone) where they are easily captured in small nets and baskets. Prior to 1990 both Awa and neighboring non-Awa employed dynamite to capture fish. This practice resulted in drastic reductions in fish populations, and the Awa have since prohibited it.

The Awa maintain domestic animals but invest in the activities associated with them minimally. These animals, including chickens, pigs, ducks, and guinea pigs, roam the environs of houses and former gardens, feeding on available food. Occasionally wild fowl are captured and kept for eating. With the exceptions of pigs and cattle, both of which are raised to be sold for cash, most animals are raised as food.

According to a conservation biologist with two decades of experience among the Awa, the Awa production system exhibits the zoning principles contained in the modern concept of a biosphere reserve.[3] Each core of protected forest or household production unit forms a portion of the system, providing important services to to other productive areas such as microwatershed protection, erosion prevention, and nutrient provision. In zones of protected forest, the Awa harvest forest products on a sustainable basis. Along with other features, the complex macrosystem contains zones of intensive agroforestry that combine agriculture and animal husbandry practices; buffer zones of low-intensity slash-and-mulch horticulture well adapted to the regenerative capacity of the soil and the high rainfall; and fallows of different ages, including those recently returned to secondary forests, enriched by human contribution. Some conservation biologists assert that this combination of permanent, semipermanent, occasional, and annual plants is an excellent example of sustainable agriculture and agroforestry.

Social and Political Organization

The extended family household is the fundamental unit in Awa social and political life, and settlements are dispersed at some distance from one another. According to a consultant to the Awa for two decades, each semi-isolated extended family household once functioned as an independent and self-reliant economic, social, and political entity (personal communication). Family household clusters were united through kinship ties into some eight loosely allied larger social groupings. Marriage is permitted among members of the same society who live in different residential clusters. The household cluster continues to be the elementary building block of Awa society even in the context of more formal organizations that have been recently established.

Prior to 1986 there were no Awa organizations larger than the residential cluster of households. During their visit to the Awa in the 1970s, two anthropologists found no coercive political controls, no foci of power, and no formal structures of rank or status among the Awa that differentiated individuals.[4] All political, economic, and social decisions were made at the household level. Invidious distinctions between individuals, including displays of prestige or power, were not positively valued.

Religion and World View

The Awa recognize a cosmology that explains their origins as a people. In addition, they possess a body of oral literature, passed down from generation to generation, which recounts adventures of figures with supernatural qualities. These are often transformations of forms that Westerners would place in the realm of "nature." The Awa hold to a theory of interaction among all living entities. Within this body of theory, the individual is responsible for consequences and is vulnerable to consequences that are beyond his or her control. Theories of health and illness are based upon a conceptualization of the body into internal and external forces and entities. Penetration by external disease-bearing agencies is treated by a specialist shaman who must remove the harmful agents in order to return an ill person to health. It is the role of the shaman to protect the body from foreign objects and to remove them once embedded. Shamans rely on a large corpus of knowledge of different types of curing methodologies. These include a wide repertoire of forest plants with medicinal qualities, as well as incantations and fumigants. In recent years the number of healing specialists has diminished, and the extensive knowledge accumulated and passed on by shamans over generations is now threatened with disappearance. One important shaman, for example, respected by Awa and Western scientists alike for his treatment of snakebite, had no apprentices when visited by a botanist less than a decade ago. It is not unusual to find a decline in shamans among indigenous peoples that accompanies western education and increased contact with non-indigenous populations. Shamanism is based upon an intricate body of knowledge that must be learned with extreme dedication and sacrifice. Shamanic students apprentice themselves for a period of years to experienced shamans, during which time they are required to abstain from many ordinary tasks and foods. Practicing shamans themselves are vulnerable to dangerous supernatural threats and must undergo protective measures to avoid these. The difficulties associated with becoming a shaman, together with new values placed on bilingualism and western medicinal practices compromises the traditional medicinal specializations.

THREATS TO SURVIVAL

The Awa have been described as an independent people who have zealously guarded their autonomy from outsiders and their lands from invasion. These attributes continue to characterize the Awa in spite of the many historic alterations to their lifestyle and increased interaction with outsiders. Their attitude was formed by several decades of threats to their land and their livelihood, including pressures from ranchers, gold miners, lumberers, and landless migrants. Ranchers invaded Awa territories from the highlands to the east, while lumbering companies entered from the lowlands to the west. Along with miners and settlers, they appropriated lands claimed by Awa communities. Disputes and disagreements resulting from counterclaims for the same lands were common.

Pressures on land reached a culmination in the 1950s when a railroad line and roads brought an abrupt influx of newcomers into the Awa territory. While the road provided the Awa with access to markets, it also greatly accelerated penetration into their territory. One of the most profound impacts following the opening of the region by roadways was the drastic depletion of game, caused by unsustainable exploitation practices. The greater number of people and the narrowing food base resulted in competition for increasingly scarce resources. In the last forty years, several animal populations have become severely depleted, including formerly important food sources such as wild pigs and large rodents. Endemic species such as the military macaw and the spectacled bear became threatened. Numerous additional animal populations are also in decline, including the oppossum (*Didelphis*), two-toed sloth (*Choeleopus*), three-toed sloth (*Bradypus*), anteater (*Tamandua*), tapir (*Tapirus bairdii*), nine-banded armadillo (*Dasypus*), prehensile-tailed porcupine (*Coendu*), black howler monkey (*Allouatta palliata*), and black spider monkey (*Ateles seniculus*). Currently, the Awa are attempting to restore animal populations to their former sizes, and there are some indications that populations of some species are on the rise.

In order to preserve their lands, and their control of them, the Awa have become internally organized into a federation with several levels of representation. The federation, in turn, participates in national-level indigenous organizations as well as global networks. In the context of overarching hierarchical institutions, the Awa have maintained their strong traditional egalitarian values.

RESPONSE: STRUGGLES TO SURVIVE CULTURALLY

Since the early 1980s Ecuador's Ministry of Foreign Relations has demonstrated concern over its northwestern border with Colombia. Fearing that without a government presence the region could become a refuge for guerilla movements, narco-trafficking, small-scale mining, and other undesirable activities, it took a number of measures during that decade to regularize a formal Ecuadorian presence in this frontier zone. The ministry recommended surveillance of the region, a precise demarcation of the little-known border, the issuance of citizenship documentation to all residents, and the demarcation of an indigenous reserve. In 1983 the ministry formally expressed concern for the "preservation [of] . . . 'Awa' . . . native culture, presently in danger of extinction."[5] With encouragement from international funding sources, a coalition of government agencies, international indigenous advocacy organizations, and the Confederation of Indigenous Nationalities of Ecuador (CONAIE) formed to meet the stated goals. Attempts made by this coalition to demarcate Awa territory between 1983 and 1989 encountered difficulties. Demarcation efforts were punctuated with disputes and disagreements owing to counterclaims for the same lands. In some areas, such as Guadalito, lumber companies continued to log the forests in spite of Awa attempts to halt their activities. A number of mining companies, such as one in Mataje, had become installed and could not be moved. Ranchers and colonists settled on Awa lands, then refused to leave. Solutions eventually were achieved through negotiation and compensation in which indigenous organizations and public agencies worked jointly to remove outsiders from the demarcated area and compensate them. Between 1984 and 1986, the Ecuadorian government and the Awa, with assistance from international, nongovernmental agencies, such as Cultural Survival, a North American, indigenous advocacy organization, accomplished several major objectives. The most important among these was the issuance of citizenship cards to over 1,100 adult Awa and the demarcation of Awa territories.[6]

The consortium also functioned to present proposals to international funding agencies and to receive financial assistance from these sources. In less than a decade, collaboration among the Awa, the national Indian association, and governmental agencies resulted in the demarcation of indigenous lands and numerous projects in organization, resource management, health, and education. Among the projects were the construction of meeting facilities and medical stations, initiatives in sustainable resource management, and education, including a bilingual training program for Awa teachers and a curriculum geared to the Awa.

New forestry legislation prompted the framers of the Awa reserve to incorporate the guarantees of forestry legislation into a new and original land title. The Ecuadorian forestry law of 1981 guaranteed that forested land in the categories "protective," "regenerative," or "in permanent use" would be protected by the national government. Prior to that legislation, lands not visibly in use could be expropriated, and tropical forest Indians wishing to title their lands were often forced to clear forests rather than risk losing forested lands to competitors. Although "forest reserve" would provide the Awa with more titled land than an Indian reserve, forested lands are state owned. The national Indian organization, aware of land disputes under way in the eastern tropical forests, opposed application of the forest reserve form of land title to Indian lands. After months of negotiations, the communities and the commission agreed to combine two pieces of legislation, one regarding forest reserves and the other Indian communities, in order to create a unique Indian/forest reserve. In 1989 the government created the "Awa Ethnic and Forest Reserve" (Reserva Etnica Forestal Awa) and officially recognized Awa territorial rights. The final demarcation produced a land claim of approximately 120,000 hectares (296,400 acres) for a population of about 1,800 people.

With outside pressure on lands increasing, the Awa perceived the need for links to existing national-level indigenous organizations and for spokespersons to negotiate with the state and international agencies in support of their interests. This meant the creation of a political structure capable of uniting all Awa and allowing for representation of all constituent units. Following the experiences of other indigenous groups in Ecuador, such as the large and well-organized Shuar of southern Ecuador, the Awa, in 1983, began to create a federation based upon a model of regional centers. In their 1997 *Diagnostico de la Zona de Esmeraldas, Territorio Awa del Ecuador*, written by a planning group of the Federation of Awa Centers of Ecuador (Federación de Centros Awa del Ecuador, or FCA), Awa spokespersons described the formation of the federation this way:

Before [the existence of the Federation] the Awa obeyed the oldest member of the family. Problems that arose were treated at the level of each family, and it was unusual for people of different families and different communities to sit down together to discuss their problems and to seek common solutions. As long as the problems that confronted people were related to Awa life and the environment in which we lived, this system of family organization functioned well. But when groups of organized settlers together with lumbering and mining firms began to threaten the Awa territory, people realized that another kind of organization was necessary that would unite all the Awa in order to defend our lands, our forests, and our culture.[7]

In order to deter the Awa from establishing their own reserve, members of the federation were accused falsely of carrying out narco-trafficking and guerilla activities. Numbers were arrested and jailed.

The work of organizing wasn't easy. We were accused of being guerrillas, narco-traffickers, and everything else. We were called Colombians and told that we had no right to our lands. Many of our companions were imprisoned, beaten and threatened so that they would stop organizing among the Awa . . . Finally, the strength of the Awa organization succeeded in blocking the entrance of these companies.[8]

In 1986, after numerous setbacks, all the Awa communities united to form the FCA.

The FCA comprises fifteen regional centers. Each center includes all the inhabitants of an area and is governed by locally elected councils. The FCA holds workshops in each center in order to assess needs and gather input from members in each locale. This bottom-up form of representation is regarded as crucial by the Awa. Representatives from each center, who walk for as many as four or five days, attend FCA assemblies. The FCA, in turn, maintains representation in the national indigenous organization, thus linking each Awa regional center to a national indigenous network. It is only through the formation of the FCA that the Awa achieved control of their lands. Spokespersons continue to explain the necessity of the FCA: "The future of the Awa depends upon the organization of the Federation from the basic level of each Center. This we all know. It was through our organization that we succeeded in demarcating and titling our territory, addressing, and resolving innumerable internal and external problems."[9]

During the first decade of its existence, the FCA worked with the Ministry of Foreign Relations in proposing and receiving financial support from international funding agencies to implement resource management programs in the area. Besides the U.S. organization Cultural Survival, the Awa received assistance from the MacArthur Foundation, the World Wildlife Fund, and various Belgian and British foundations. Today the Awa federation has an independent legal identity, as has each community in it.

The FCA's first project was the creation of a "green belt" around the territory. The belt was intended to define clearly the boundaries of the reserve to outsiders. Within the green belt, the Awa federation worked jointly with the indigenous confederation of Ecuador, technicians from the Ministry of Agriculture, and international botanists. Besides providing income to Awa communities through cash-producing crops such as cocoa, coffee, coconuts, and native fruit trees, the belt provides a visible ring of cultivation, delimiting Awa territories, and discouraging encroachment by new settlers. "The belt sends the unmistakable message to all the world that the Awa will not permit others to destroy our lands."[10] Moreover, the FCA monitors its borders and removes intruding miners and loggers by force when necessary. "Today we are respected; the [mining and lumbering] companies don't try to enter our territory because they know that the Awa People will not permit it. We earned this respect through our struggle, through our organization of the Federation."[11]

The FCA's bylaws and regulations are decided by community consensus and are subject to ongoing review by the membership. This last is critical to maintaining ground-level support and compliance of members to these regulations. In ten years, the Awa have changed the regulations somewhat, after discussion and approval by the assembly, according to problems raised by Awa communities. Regulations regarding natural resources, for example, are reviewed regularly. According to Awa spokespersons, the FCA

entered an accord among the communities regarding certain rules and regulations for the management of the natural resources of our territory. The purpose of these regulations is to assure that the different natural resources that exist within our territories are not depleted, not by ourselves nor by our children or grandchildren. These natural resources are the basis of life for the Awa; it is from the forests and the rivers that we get our food, medicines, materials for house construction, and much more.[12]

After review and debate, the membership agreed once again that it was necessary to maintain these rules in order to maintain natural resources. Outsiders are prohibited from entering the Awa territory to fish, hunt, or prospect. Although miners, lumberers, and ranchers have tried to befriend individual Awa, any negotiations or proposals for transfer must be discussed during group meetings. The Awa have refused offers from timber enterprises, and the FCA prohibits the cutting of timber by outsiders. Moreover, the Awa themselves are regulated in their use of wood and wood products. Removal of wood for sale is permitted only in cases of urgency, and then felling is limited to two trees by authorization of the center directive. Hunting and fishing are regulated and limited to consumption by the Awa. It is prohibited to sell fish or meat to outsiders. Regulations for the management of natural resources of the Awa territory include prohibitions on fishing with dynamite or poisons. As part of the ongoing effort to sustainably harvest resources, communities inventory and monitor animal populations. The Awa identify the times of year in which the animals reproduce and prohibit hunting during these times. Recent programs by the Awa to preserve habitats appear to be successful. The 1997 report documents the return of several important species. A number of animal populations are currently on the rise, including several species of monkey.

The successful effort to control exploitation contrasts with the prevalent devastation of the surrounding areas. In 1950 80% of the coast was covered with forest; now only 7% is. Of the remaining forest, about one half lies within Awa territories; its preservation may be attributed to Awa land-use practices. By refusing to accommodate timber companies and mining concessions, the Awa have kept deforestation at bay and have limited impact.

The Awa are aware of the importance of their efforts.

The geographic and climatic conditions result in the very special qualities of the Awa Territory . . . We know that the forests within this portion of our territory are unique. The contiguous primary forests of the Awa Territories of Ecuador and Colombia form the largest protected area of tropical Chocoan forest in the world. Elsewhere along the Ecuadorian coast, forests have been destroyed by lumberers and settlers. The Awa Territory holds the only remaining reserve of these natural resources. We have conserved them.[13]

FOOD FOR THOUGHT

Formerly Awa social networks were composed almost exclusively through kin relations or residential proximity. Today, an elaborate internal federation overlies the informal network of kinship that unites households. For the acephalous Awa, organization has been an important experiment. Through it the Awa have attempted to preserve the egalitarian underpinnings of their society, while at the same time utilizing the bureaucratic models of internal specialization and organization that allow communication, representation, and decision making among constituent communities. The success of the FCA is due in part to its recognition of traditional organization: the elementary building blocks of the federation are the very household clusters at the center of traditional Awa society, now organized into "centers." Each center has its own decision-making process and participates in the decision-making apparatus of the Awa federation. The federation, in turn, articulates with broader external national and international entities and networks.

Traditional Awa society lacked formal structures for decision making. The Awa of 1970 had no organized leadership nor wide-reaching formalized organization. When, in 1986, the Awa communities of Ecuador formed the FCA, they created mechanisms for a structured organization of representation. The first organizational challenge for the Awa, therefore, was internal organization. Such organization involves the incorporation of all Awa into local, juridical identities, themselves organized into a hierarchy of increasingly inclusive membership groups with juridical and practical identities. Moreover, groups at every level are linked through mechanisms of representation. At the highest level, the Awa as a confederation are represented in the union of indigenous peoples of Ecuador. A certain amount of autonomy has been lost as a degree of interdependency has been achieved. However, the Awa have maintained the egalitarian qualities of their society in spite of a system of regulation and a structure with roles of leadership and differential responsibility. The second organizational challenge for the Awa is the articulation of the emergent Awa federation within larger constituencies, both governmental and nongovernmental. First working closely with government agencies, the Awa have more recently opted for an independent presence.

The Awa case is an exception to the general prevalence of development models in which decisions are initiated at a national or international level, are subject to a government's or an agency's broader policy goals, and are not necessarily matched to the specific needs of the peoples targeted to benefit by them. Far from being the passive recipients of "assistance," the Awa themselves spearheaded the self-representation and coalition building that allows them their own linkages to resources.

Questions

1. In what ways do you think the formation of the Awa Federation has affected life at the community level? How have things changed for men? Women? Children?

2. Has the Awa Federation changed or maintained Awa culture?

3. Are there lessons from the Awa example for other cases described in this volume, such as the Río Plátano Biosphere Reserve participatory mapping and management project described in Chapter 7?

4. Why do you think the Awa have been so successful in managing and maintaining their traditional territories?

5. What does the Awa example tell us about notions of indigenous or native peoples "living in harmony with nature?"

NOTES

I gratefully acknowledge Flor Pascal, Coordinator; Manuel Taicuz, Julian Cantuncuz, Felipe Cuajivoy, Alfonso Pay, Julio Cesar Pascal, Amilcar Cuasaluzan, and Luis Hernando Nastacuaz, members of the Equipo de Planificacion Awa; Federación de Centros Awa del Ecuador; and authors of the 1997 report *Diagnostico de la Zona de Esmeraldas Territorio Awa del Ecuador*. I also wish to thank Jim Levy, whose twenty years of work among the Awa is a model to us all.

1. Jorge Orejuela, "Traditional Productive Systems of the Awa (Cuaiquer) Indians of Southwestern Colombia and Neighboring Ecuador," in *Conservation of Neotropical Forests: Working from Traditional Resource Use*, ed. Kent Redford and Christine Padoch, New York: Columbia University Press 1992; Jorge Orejuela, "La Reserva Natural "La Planada" y la Biogeografia Andina," *Humboldtia* 1, no. 1 (1987): 117–48.

2. Ibid.

3. Ibid.

4. Judith Kempf and Jeffrey Ehrenreich, "Field Report: The Coaiquer," *Newsletter of the Latin American Anthropology Group* (Washington, D.C., American Anthropology Association, 1980), 7–10.

5. Theodore McDonald, "Anticipating *Colonos* and Cattle in Ecuador and Colombia," *Cultural Survival Quarterly* 10, no. 2 (1986): 33–36.

6. Ibid.

7. Equipo de Planificacion Awa, Federacíon de Centros Awa del Ecuador, *Diagnostico de la Zona de Esmeraldas, Territorio Awa del Ecuador* (Ecuador: Federacíon de Centros Awa del Ecuador (FCA) and World Wildlife Fund, Ecuador, 1997).

8. Ibid., 9.

9. Ibid., 18.

10. Ibid.

11. Ibid., 11.

12. Ibid., 25.

13. Ibid.

RESOURCE GUIDE

Published Literature

Chernela, J. "Sustainable Development and Sustainable Control: Political Strategies of Indian Organizations in a Proposed Biosphere Reserve in Ecuador and Colombia." In *Human Ecology in Amazonia*, edited by Leslie Sponsel, 245–261, Tucson: University of Arizona Press, 1995.

Clay, Jason W. *Indigenous Peoples and Tropical Forests: Models of Land Use and Management from Latin America*. Cultural Survival Report 17. Cambridge, Mass.: Cultural Survival, 1988.

Davis, Shelton. "Working Toward Native Resource Control." In *Native Resource Control and the Multinational Corporate Challenge: Aboriginal Rights in International Perspective*, ed. Sally Swenson, 5–6. Boston: Anthropology Resource Center, 1982.

Ehrenreich, J. "Lifting the Burden of Secrecy: The Emergence of the Awa Biosphere Reserve." *Latin American Anthropology Review* 1, no. 2 (1989): 49–54.

———. "Shame, Witchcraft, and Social Control: The Case of an Awa-Coaiquer Interloper." *Cultural Anthropology* 5, no. 3 (1990): 338–45.

Macdonald, Theodore. "Anticipating *Colonos* and Cattle in Ecuador and Colombia," *Cultural Survival Quarterly* 10, no. 2 (1986): 33–36.

Orejuela, Jorge. "Traditional Productive Systems of the Awa (Cuaiquer) Indians of Southwestern Colombia and Neighboring Ecuador." In *Conservation of Neotropical Forests: Working from Traditional Resource Use*, edited by Kent Redford and Christine Padoch. New York: Columbia University Press, 1992.

Redford, Kent, and Christine Padoch. *Conservation of Neotropical Forests: Working from Traditional Resource Use.* New York: Columbia University Press, 1992.

Sponsel, Leslie. *Indigenous Peoples and the Future of Amazonia: An Ecological Anthropology of an Endangered World.* Tucson: University of Arizona Press, 1995.

Videos and Films

Out of the Forest: The Kayapo (1989). Disappearing World Series. Films for the Humanities.

WWW Sites

Indigenous Knowledge and Development Monitor
http://www.nuffic.nl/ciran/ikdm

Indigenous Knowledge Listserve
indknow@u.washington.edu

Chapter 12

The Otavaleños of the Ecuadorian Highlands

Rudi Colloredo-Mansfeld

CULTURAL OVERVIEW

The People

The Otavaleños are a Quechua-speaking indigenous group, one of many ethnically distinct Andean Indian societies in the highlands of Ecuador. Numbering about 70,000, they have a unique reputation among native groups for their cultural pride—signaled in part by their distinctive outfits—their business acumen, and their international travel. They, in fact, do suffer the problems of other indigenous groups, including discrimination against their language and culture, land shortages, poor schools, and a lack of potable water, electricity, and other crucial services. However, throughout the twentieth century, they slowly overcame many of these disadvantages by making the most of their subsistence farming resources and expanding the local textile trade into an international ethnic-arts business. Their success has now created new problems. Overcompetition and increased economic inequality are undermining important social institutions, and population pressure and continued disparities in land distribution hurt agriculture. In the face of such challenges, the Otavaleños have developed new political and economic strategies that hold the promise not only to preserve, but also to revitalize, key elements of the indigenous Otavaleño culture.

The Setting

Covering an area the size of Oregon and with a population of about 12 million, Ecuador is South America's most densely populated nation. Although no longer officially tracked by the national census, ethnic identities divide the politically and culturally dominant mestizos from a variety of significant minority groups including multiple indigenous peoples (who alone account for approximately one-third of the total population), as well as Afro-Ecuadorians, Asian-Ecuadorians, and others. Two high, parallel ridges of the Andes run the length of the country from its northern border with Colombia to Peru in the south, creating three regions—the coast, the Andean highlands, and the upper Amazonian rain forest—each with a distinctive political and economic identity. Home to expansive plantations, the coastal plain has historically been the most economically dynamic region (exporting more bananas than any other region or nation in the world), and its largest city, Guayaquil, is the center of commerce. In contrast, the upper Amazonian rain forest to the east of the Andes was peripheral to the economy until the 1970s when large-scale, commercial exploitation of the petroleum reserves began. This oil exploration and extraction has seriously threatened Amazonian native peoples, even as it led to an economic boom in the capital city Quito. Located in the inter-Andean valley, Quito is not only the nation's political center, but also the cultural center of the Hispanic landed elite who for centuries have dominated the highlands' most fertile lands with their haciendas or large estates.

The majority of Otavaleños live and work in about seventy-five communities that range in size from 200 to 3,000 inhabitants and stretch across a broad valley in Imbabura Province, about 100 kilometers (62 miles) north of Quito. In the midst of this region lies the small, provincial market town of Otavalo. Home to the region's weekly market, banks, civil offices, and minority (but politically dominant) white-mestizo population, Otavalo also hosts a swelling class of indigenous merchants and small-scale manufacturers. After decades of migration, additional Otavaleño communities exist in the provincial capital of Ibarra, Quito, Bogotá, Amsterdam, and elsewhere, accounting for an expatriate population of between 5,000 and 10,000 people.[1]

Traditional Subsistence Strategies

Farming, weaving, selling, and wage work have long anchored the economy. Taking advantage of a vertical ecology that ranges in altitude from 2,000 to 4,000 meters (6,560 to 13,123 feet), the Otavaleños plant diverse crops, including potatoes, oca (a tuber similar to a potato), quinua (a traditional Andean grain rich in protein), peas, beans, and, most important, maize. From the margins of their fields and the areas that fringe gullies and streams, they gather mora (a fruit that resembles raspberries) and other wild fruits, as well as medicinal herbs. In order to meet their needs, households must also earn cash, often by performing low-paying manual and domestic work.

The greatest opportunities for advancement have come through the handicraft industry. Textile manufacture and trading have long been a dis-

Belt weaver displaying his wares before a sales trip to Ecuador's central Andean highlands. Courtesy of Rudi Colloredo-Mansfeld.

tinctive feature of the economy, documented first in colonial chronicles and, later, in the diaries of U.S. President Abraham Lincoln's ambassador, who described the bustle and diversity of the Indian market over a century ago. Since the 1960s, local weavers have continually innovated their craft, developing new products for tourists, including wall hangings, backpacks, and sweaters.

Social and Political Organization

Households, the core economic and social unit of Otavaleño society, usually consist of a married couple and their children. Earlier in the twentieth century, extended families, called *ayllus*, structured the wider public and economic life of rural communities. Reckoned through both the mother's and father's sides, these kinship ties created a social group that could be tapped into for help with planting and harvesting, fulfilling ceremonial obligations like weddings, and managing civic affairs. Though still important, *ayllus* have weakened over the past thirty years. Migration, exhausted subsistence resources, and erratic job markets have fragmented the economy and undermined the social institutions that have long held Otavaleño society together.

Religion and World View

The Roman Catholic Church is the greatest institutionalized influence upon the spiritual lives of the Otavaleños, although, in recent years, a number of Protestant sects have gained significant numbers of converts. Work and celebration annually unfold in a rhythm marked by Christian holy days. Weeding takes place around Christmas and harvesting around Easter. The final storing of the cornstalks happens toward the end of June at the time of the region's most important fiesta, the feast of Saint John, which people also sometimes call by its Quechua name, Inti Raymi (the feast of the sun). Church ritual also marks significant life cycle events, consecrating them through baptisms, confirmations, weddings, and funerals. More than marking individual milestones, these ceremonies formalize interfamilial social bonds through the institution of *compadrazgo*, or co-parenthood. In the case of a baptism, for example, the parents and the godparents who sponsor a child's initiation into the church become *compadres* and enter into a lifelong obligation of assistance to each other as well as to the baptized child. *Compadre* obligations help organize wide networks of households and families.

THREATS TO SURVIVAL

Demographic Trends and Environmental Problems

A middle-aged man with four children stood up at a community meeting and spoke in support of a development project that might have improved the value of his land: "Divided up, divided up, our land is in pieces. What will we give our children?"[2] A walk through the fields on the slopes of Mount Imbabura above the indigenous farming and weaving communities shows why he is concerned. A once vital zone of agricultural production, the area supports a bleak patchwork of small subsistence plots—sometimes little more than two meters (six feet) wide—and spindly cornstalks widely placed in tired, gray soil. These are the material traces of two broad historical processes that have shaped Ecuador's highland economy: rapid population growth and failed land reform policies. The nation's population grew from 8.1 million in 1980 to 12.8 million in 1998 and currently has the second highest annual population growth rate (2.2%) in South America.[3] Furthermore, recent research has shown that populations are growing faster in predominantly indigenous areas like the province of Imbabura where the Otavaleños live.

Such expansion would challenge subsistence agriculture practices under the best of circumstances. Unfortunately, indigenous peoples frequently farm under the worst. Through centuries of coercion and mistreatment, large landowners dispossessed native highland communities of much of their land. By the 1950s, just 6% of the population owned 80% of the land; 389 estates accounted for half of that figure.[4] The vast majority of the rural population—90% of the landowners—farmed holdings that averaged about two hectares (five acres) and accounted for only 16% of the land.[5] Such severe inequalities led to a major land reform initiative which was passed into law in 1964. Seeking to abolish exploitative labor practices that bound Indians to haciendas (large estates) through debt peonage and to redistribute underutilized land holdings to peasant farmers, the law had mixed consequences. While the reform swept away the last vestiges of formalized, unpaid exploitation of hacienda laborers, little land changed hands. In 1974, for instance, small farmers (those with less than ten hectares [twenty-five acres]) still accounted for 87% of the landowners and used 18% of the land—a slight improvement. However, the average parcel size dropped to 1.9 hectares (4.7 acres).[6] Again and again, in the years following land reform, indigenous peasant communities found their claims to land stalled in interminable legal proceedings.

Unable to expand significantly the amount of land available for farming, the Otavaleños have seen their fields divided into smaller and smaller plots. Inheritance practices speed the breakup. Following deeply held cultural norms, each individual man and woman in rural Otavaleño society inherits roughly the same amount of land as his or her siblings. Although a married couple farm their land together, they retain individual rights to their fields, and a husband and wife will see to it that each child receives a fair proportion of their separate holdings. Some sibling sets come to agreements that leave fields intact. However, many are forced to break fields up into ever narrower allotments leaving individuals with a series of micro-holdings spread out through two or more communities. Under such circumstances, the costs of subsistence farming (primarily the time it takes to get to and work one's fields) increase as its overall contribution to the family budget decreases.

Along with diminishing plot size, declining yields pose another threat to subsistence farming. Many informants have indicated that "the fields do not give as they did before." Farmers cite several factors that have decreased productivity. First, with growing involvement in the tourist economy and urban labor markets, people have less time to farm. Consequently, rather than multi-cropping potatoes, beans, maize, and quinua on the same plot, households narrow their crops to just maize and beans. This reduction means that households can cut down the number of trips they make to weed and harvest crops that mature at different rates. As they do so, though, they eliminate nutritious foods such as quinua that require extensive labor to separate the tiny grains from the chaff and wash the bitterness from their husk. The land's productivity also declines the absence of sheep and cows that once provided the primary fertilizer for fields. Now with less time to care for them and fewer fields on which to pasture them, households rarely keep more livestock than a few pigs and some chickens.

In sum, long central to their economy and their sense of identity as native Andeans, agriculture has rewarded Otavaleño labor less and less. Land shortages and falling yields decrease the viability of subsistence production. Ironically, such decreases come at a time when instability in other segments of the Andean economy make farming resources all the more necessary.

Economic Cycles and Indigenous Peoples

Since the 1960s, the Otavaleños, like almost all of Ecuador's native peoples, have migrated to urban areas in significant numbers, finding work with transportation cooperatives, on construction sites, and in big city marketplaces. The rapid expansion of oil production and revenues led to a building boom in Quito during the late 1970s, creating relatively high-wage jobs where people learned new skills. Contrary to expectations, though, the expanding urban economies caused a *decrease* in permanent migration of native peasants to the cities and an increase in temporary migration.[7] That is, as people found new opportunities to earn higher wages, they renewed their investments in houses and fields back in rural sectors.

In 1982, however, oil prices fell sharply, and Ecuador's financial markets collapsed, precipitating an economic crisis that endured into the late 1990s. Native people bore the brunt of these shocks as construction work and other nonsalaried positions were among the first casualties of the faltering labor market. In indigenous areas north of Quito, the failure of urban wage markets had sharper, more immediate consequences for Otavaleño men than for women. Careers built on construction skills and urban contacts derailed, cutting men off from advancement and knocking out a much-needed source of income for many households. Unlike other Quechua peoples, however, the Otavaleños still had an important avenue for their ambition. The handicraft textile market flourished in the 1980s, although this growth spawned its own problems.

From the beginning of the trade in ethnic arts and handicraft textiles, Otavaleño merchants looked for ways to satisfy the growing demand well beyond their local market. An anthropologist wrote in the early 1960s that it was not uncommon to see Otavaleño traders in the streets of Bogotá, Colombia, or in the airport in Lima, Peru. Later, working with peace corps volunteers, weavers developed whole new categories of products, like wall hangings and sweaters. By the 1980s, entrepreneurs had further diversified these to encompass over twenty new craft goods made specifically for the tourist market.

Such innovation illustrates the creativity of Otavaleño craftspeople. It also demonstrates a key problem that producers face. Intense competition and technological innovation erode the profits that can be earned with any one class of goods and lead to rapid product cycles. For example, once the mainstay of textile production, the poncho nowadays gets made only by a dwindling number of older weavers. The craft was the first victim of the electric power looms that native weavers invested in over thirty years ago. Where automation does not flood the market, scores of rival hand weavers will. Many have turned the treadle looms once used for poncho making over to the task of making *tapices* (wall hangings). These are especially prone to copying because all merchants can see which designs sell well in Otavalo's stores and open market and then make them on their own looms (or pay other weavers to make popular designs for them). Thus, the weaving of wall hangings gives way to the weaving of panels for bags, and these in turn may yield to making cloth for sweaters or some other good. Those who do not innovate often find themselves reduced to the status of piece-work weavers, supplying wealthy merchants with high quantities of standard designs and receiving low wages in return.

The Case of Belt Weaving, 1978–1998

The work there, in Quito, became a little "more-or-less" [hard to find]. I returned. Indigenous men must defend themselves with their own work in their own homes. . . . [My brother-in-law] said "work here" and he taught me belts and then I made my own designs. With belts, one can earn a little, and little by little, advance.[8]

This young man, in early 1994, offered a biographical glimpse into the kinds of connections that exist between national labor markets, weaving careers, and artisan practice. Indigenous women in Otavalo and elsewhere in the Ecuadorian Andes wear *fajas* or colorfully woven belts that are about ten centimeters (four inches) wide and three meters (ten feet) long. The belts, which are laboriously created on a narrow backstrap loom, were one of the last subsistence crafts, produced by men for their wives, mothers, and daughters. In 1978 an entrepreneurial nineteen-year-old weaver from the community of Ariasucu on the rural fringe of Otavalo developed a way to make the belts on a more efficient, upright, wooden treadle loom. Soon he could weave as many in a morning (three to four) as could have once been made in a week, and he developed a successful belt-making business by hiring other weavers, adding looms, and traveling to sell the belts in cities where indigenous women had migrated.

The commercialization of *faja* production, however, began in earnest after the collapse of urban wage markets in the mid-1980s. In the wake of the economic crisis, many industrious men from Ariasucu found themselves out of work and back home with few opportunities. They learned the skills of the trade by starting out as piecework weavers in the few established shops in their community. Eventually, they abandoned the original shops, fixed up their fathers' looms (or bought a new one for themselves) and ran their own operation. By 1992 half of Ariasucu's 135 households had become involved in belt making in one fashion or another, with some of the later shops expanding at an impressive rate to include up to ten paid weavers besides the original proprietor. Designs, too, multiplied with teenage boys manipulating nine-pedal looms to produce intricate diamond and sun patterns. Through innovations and expanded sales, belt weavers improved their standard of living. In the early 1990s, the weavers bought televisions, radios, gas stoves, and other goods at double the rate of households that did not specialize in the new trade.

The economics of belt making then soured, and they did so over a very short period. To be sure, profit margins had declined throughout the 1990s as inflation ratcheted up the costs of thread, and competition kept people from raising prices. Yet skilled weavers could still sell all their wares and make reasonable earnings through early 1994. Later that year, however, even the best belt makers with the greatest market knowledge began to return home with unsold product. As one discouraged weaver said, "There was no way to sell. Those with shops, those resellers say, 'your countryman was just here. I can't take anymore.' In vain did I travel."[9]

One of the finest weavers, who continued to find outlets for his wares, saw his profits on two months of belts drop from around $100 to $10. Faced with the flood of product coming from two large, neighboring communities as well as their own, Ariasucu's belt weavers began to drop out of the trade and look for other opportunities. While a highly specialized craft, belt weaving suffers from the same general problem that afflicts subsistence farming and urban labor markets. Too many people are scrambling to make the most of too few resources and opportunities.

RESPONSE: STRUGGLES TO SURVIVE CULTURALLY

Political Strategies

This is not a workers' strike.
This is not a teachers' strike.

This is not a students' strike.
THIS IS AN INDIAN UPRISING.[10]

So shouted the marchers who confronted soldiers during the indigenous uprising of 1990. Deep frustration about the pace of land reform, in particular, had galvanized Indians for action at a national level. The uprising began when indigenous leaders and activists occupied the Santo Domingo Church in Quito in June 1990 to protest the failure of the legal system to process land claims. With impressive solidarity, native peasants from throughout the highlands left their fields, hearths, and workplaces by the thousands in order to block highways with tree trunks and boulders, march on provincial government offices, and support the Santo Domingo occupation. The protest forced the government to begin negotiations, which focused attention on seventy-two stalled land claims identified by the Confederation of Indigenous Nationalities of Ecuador (CONAIE). Yet, the bargaining went beyond community efforts to recover their fields to press demands for the constitutional recognition of indigenous culture, the expansion of bilingual education, and other protections for native peoples.

While these events resulted in few immediate changes, they deeply shook the complacency of the dominant white-mestizo society which has long assumed that indigenous cultures had no future in the modern nation-state. June 1990 proved them wrong, showing not only the Indians' cultural strength, but also their capacity for high-stakes political mobilization. Indeed, for indigenous people, this event brought new effectiveness to a society that was fragmenting through growing class differences, urbanization, migration, and reduced involvement in subsistence agriculture. According to an indigenous woman lawyer from near Otavalo, who is a leader of CONAIE, the uprising was a "sacrament of dignity, a symbol and path to liberation."[11]

Intensifying a nascent indigenous movement, the 1990 protest set the tone for native politics in the subsequent decade. Mass demonstrations and strikes have continued, most notably to protest the 500th anniversary of Christopher Columbus's "discovery" of America in 1992 and to block the implementation of land reforms laws in 1994 that would have weakened peasant communities' ability to maintain communal land holdings. Indigenous leaders, moving out of the streets and into the halls of power, have been elected to political office at all levels, including the national legislature in 1996, where Luis Macas, the former president of CONAIE, took a seat as a member of the Pachakutik movement—a political alliance that takes its name, in part, from the Quechua word for "world transformation."

In and around Otavalo, the national indigenous movement has both reinforced native people's pride and raised the profile of local political groups, including the Imbabura Federation of Indigenous People and Peasants (FICI), who have led provincial struggles for land redistribution and governmental reform. Yet, the movement has had little material impact on most peasant artisans. Indeed, many rural Otavaleños pursue an alternative politics, led by community councils, in order to change the factors that many feel severely limit their ability to get ahead—badly operated bus co-operatives, the lack of potable water and electricity, and a dearth of community meeting houses.

Once shunned by Otavaleños, officially sanctioned community councils now hold the key to rural development. When first mandated by national law in the 1930s, the councils posed a threat to the decentralized leadership of peasant communities. In a society where senior members of *ayllus* (extended families) and the holders of religious offices mediated conflicts and organized communal tasks, elected councils seemed at best redundant or, at worst, an unwanted intrusion of state power in local affairs. Through time, however, traditional leadership positions have weakened. Growing opportunities in the ethnic arts trade induced men and women to spend money on weaving implements and craft inventories, not the costs that come with fulfilling religious offices. Furthermore, dispersed by migration, *ayllus* no longer interact regularly and consequently fail to structure rural obligations and opportunities the way they once did.

In contrast, councils have strengthened, in large part due to their role in competing for development programs. Frequently, participation in an electrification project or water pipeline extension program depends not on state planning but on council politicking. Community presidents build out their sector's infrastructure by exploiting insider contacts, while at the same time motivating (or badgering) hundreds of volunteers to mobilize for *mingas* or communal workdays. With good timing and collective effort, councils can leverage the meager investments of state agencies or non-governmental organizations into community-wide improvements.

Yet there is a downside. Too often, council politics leads to factionalism, unhelpful competition among sectors, and piecemeal solutions to regional problems. In the absence of a province-wide implementation of water and electricity projects, for example, the community-led efforts have left small, poor neighborhoods on the margins of larger communities without services. More generally, hostilities crop up both within communities and between them when a small group of people seems to be accumulating benefits at the expense of others. Individuals may then seek to undermine councils and other political authorities. This is evident in the remarks of one man from a neighborhood bordering Ariasucu:

If I had some conflict, I would not go to the political officer, nor to the council, I would go to the National Commissioner directly. I go and get a lawyer and a warrant. Here the political officer is an enemy and the council is even more of an enemy and if the National Commissioner will not play, I go to the mayoralty in Ibarra.[12]

Such scheming can plunge communities into cycles of recrimination, thwarting all constructive efforts for change.

In the past, regional peasant organizations like FICI have stepped in to mediate these conflicts. As the national movement strengthens organizations like FICI, one of the indirect benefits may well be a political mechanism that will achieve greater cooperation among powerful community councils.

Economic Strategies

Participants in one of the strongest handicraft markets in Latin America, the Otavaleños have used economic channels as much or more than political channels to cope with the difficulties brought on by Ecuador's fiscal crisis. Over the past twenty years, textile entrepreneurs have worked hard to formalize and expand wholesale, retail, and export occupations. Indeed, perhaps more than any other Latin American native group, the Otavaleños have succeeded in maintaining their control over reselling—opportunities that offer the greatest chance for profits in the trade. In contrast to political strategies, these efforts are not collective. Nonetheless, their cumulative consequences have transformed the market town of Otavalo and the power of native-owned businesses within the provincial economy.

Refuting the stereotype of traditional artisans who weave goods only for their own use rather than sale, the Otavaleños have long marketed their wares to nonlocal buyers and pride themselves on their market expertise. Since the 1970s, successful entrepreneurs have purchased and remodeled houses throughout the northern side of the town of Otavalo, opening up their ground floors as retail shops or bulk-selling wholesale outfits. As these operations grow, their proprietors expand into other market niches: exporting sweaters to Europe; supplying younger or part-time merchants with inventory on consignment; importing crafts from Peru, Bolivia, and elsewhere; or establishing branches of their operation abroad in places like Amsterdam. The most successful go on to diversify their investments. Restaurants, hotels, and even health food stores have opened up under indigenous ownership.

Such active selling and investing ensure that much of the profits from the trade circulates within the indigenous society, although not to everyone. In fact, the consolidation of larger retailing and wholesaling operations in recent years has widened the gap between the haves and have-nots in Otavalo. Moving to new town homes, doing business via telephone and fax, traveling to sell abroad, and driving around in imported pickup trucks at home, members of the rising, native merchant class anger those peasant artisans who have been bypassed by the region's new wealth. The rural poor say that the wealthy have rejected their culture and "live like mestizos." Worse, prosperous natives are accused of mimicking the old elite by adopting their prejudices. "They go to Europe and sing of Andean life and native culture. But, when they come home they call us *indio sucio* (Dirty Indian)," observed one impoverished peasant artisan (personal communication/field notes).

During their visits to their old communities where they show off their new cars and clothes, many merchants could certainly be charged with arrogance. However, even those who have moved to the city cannot be accused of trying to blend in with the dominant mestizo culture. In comparison with poorer peasants, successful merchants are more likely to wear formal, explicitly indigenous outfits; spend large amounts of money on festive gatherings of *ayllu* members; and give Quechua names to their children. Cumulatively, these and other practices demonstrate the vitality of a modern, urbanized native Andean identity. Matching the political confidence of the indigenous movement, the economic accomplishments of the Otavaleños testify to the ways in which indigenous societies can strengthen themselves through engagement with the global economy.

Social Strategies

Because of its uneven distribution, the prosperity of the textile trade has not alleviated the insecurity of the poorest peasant artisans. Indeed, for all the economic innovation and political mobilization of the past twenty years, peasants still fall back on traditional social tactics to weather crises. In the 1970s, when entrepreneurs showed signs of being able to expand their operations greatly both at home and abroad, anthropologists in the region predicted the decline of *compadre* relations. They argued that the costly baptisms, confirmations, and weddings that formalized these bonds would lose out to investments in the textile trade. Instead, the new tourist arts economy of Otavalo has intensified spending on *compadrazgo* for three reasons.

First, both the Otavaleño society and economy largely operate in the absence of strongly centralized institutions. Banks, courts, government agencies, and even the police serve indigenous people haphazardly at best, corruptly at worst. In the absence of formal safeguards against failed crops, broken contracts, theft, indebtedness, and other economic risks, people prefer to do business with those with whom they share obligations of mutual support. Second, through the internationalization of the business, the artisan economy has become extraordinarily complex. Both neophytes and veterans depend on their social networks to learn of opportunities and to structure the credit that enables them to enter or expand new markets. Third, growing class stratification within Otavaleño society has made "vertical ties," those between rich and poor, all the more important. Those without resources seek out powerful allies to provide an entrance into the handicraft world, to intercede with authorities, or to offer emergency loans.

Meanwhile, entrepreneurs and successful migrants need their poor *compadres* to take care of their fields and perform mundane weaving tasks, which take too much time away from more profitable activities.

For all these practical reasons, *compadrazgo* endures. Yet, these ritualized bonds cannot be explained purely in material terms. Paced by the vibrant music of five-piece bands that belt out the latest soap-opera ballads, fueled by cauldrons of toasted cornmeal soup, and punctuated by carefully presented dishes of salty, garlic, roasted *cuy* (guinea pig), *compadre* fiestas celebrate more than strategic social bonds. They rejuvenate families and neighborhoods. The parties, which last for days, satisfy men and women's "anxiety to dance," while expressing the cultural exuberance of a tough, resourceful, and creative people.

FOOD FOR THOUGHT

More than simply adapting to economic change, the Otavaleños have sought it out. Artisans and merchants have actively engaged international markets for their wares and have pursued opportunities in Central America, North America, Europe, and Asia. Such entrepreneurship takes place in relation to a declining subsistence agricultural economy in the Imbabura countryside and erratic labor markets in Ecuador's cities. The uncertainties of these occupations have been amplified by integration into a global economy in which the collapse of oil prices, or new lending policies of the World Bank, or even changes in global consumer fashions can eliminate jobs or markets that have sustained households. Given the Otavaleños' long history of resilience, these new risks probably do not threaten the survival of their culture. Nevertheless, they have also sharpened social problems and have raised broader issues about the political and economic place of native peoples in the world economy.

As profits have flowed in from international sales, social inequality around Otavalo has dramatically increased. Do wealthy, indigenous entrepreneurs have any special obligations to promote the development of their home communities? If so, why should one moral standard prevail for successful capitalists within an ethnically subordinate community and another prevail among those in the dominant society? Far from being merely abstract ethical issues, these matters regularly crop up in conversations around Otavalo where people complain about the arrogance of some merchants while praising the goodness of others.

Although the Otavaleños garner praise from mestizo and foreign observers for the strength and unity of their culture, migration, occupational diversification, and stratification have deeply eroded the commonalities of experience. A monolingual, Quechua-speaking, poncho-weaving farmer has little sense of how to sell sweaters on the beach in California. Conversely, young merchants literally cannot believe that some households live without electricity. Can traditional rituals and practices bridge such differences? How effective are newly "invented traditions" in instilling shared values and perspectives?

Finally, the 1970s and 1980s were a time of migration, sharp rises and even sharper falls in income, and the development of urbanized tastes and skills within the indigenous society. And yet paradoxically, after deep integration within the national, Hispanic culture and economy, the native peoples organized a powerful indigenous movement. While white-mestizos have always believed that greater involvement with the modern economy would spell the end of Indian society, the opposite has happened. Why? What is it about the experience of working in manual wage work, selling handicrafts, and struggling to find viable incomes in liberalized marketplaces that leads to intensified commitments to Indian culture and politics? The answer to this question has as much to say about the consumerist, "Americanized," urban cultures as it does about those of modern, native peoples.

Questions

1. Is the state obligated to push through land reform, even if peasant agriculture is not commercially viable in national or international markets?
2. Should an artisan community try to reduce competition among its members, even if it means it will cut down the overall sales of their goods?
3. Do successful indigenous businesspeople have a special obligation to promote the development of their community?
4. Do shared consumption practices—including meals, family gatherings, and building homes—offer the same sense of community and culture as a common livelihood, such as agriculture?
5. Does the rise of a native movement signal the rejection of modern goods, values, and practices?

NOTES

1. Lynn Meisch, *Otavalo Weaving Costume and the Market* (Quito, Ecuador: Editiones Libri Mundi, 1987).
2. Author's fieldnotes.
3. United States Bureau of the Census, *Comparative International Statistics. Statistical Abstract of the United States* (Washington, D.C.: U.S. Bureau of the Census, October 5, 1998), 827.
4. Osvaldo Barsky, *La Reforma Agraria Ecuatoriana*, 2d ed. (Quito, Ecuador: Corporación Editora Nacional, 1988), 43.
5. Ibid.
6. Ibid.
7. Peter Peek, "Agrarian Change and Labour Migration in the Sierra of Ecua-

dor," in *State Policies and Migration*, ed. Peter Peek and Guy Standing, 121–146 (London: Croom Helm, 1982).

8. Author's fieldnotes.

9. Ibid.

10. Ibid.

11. Nina Pacari, *Levantamiento indígena, Sismo Etnico en el Ecuador*, CEDIME (Quito: Ediciones Abya-Yala, 1993), 186.

12. Susana Andrade, *Vision Mundial: Entre el cielo y la tierra: Religión y desarrolo en la sierra ecuatoriana*, CEPLAES (Quito: Ediciones Abya-Yala, 1990), 54. Stamford, CT: JAI Press.

RESOURCE GUIDE

Published Literature

Colloredo-Mansfeld, Rudi. *The Native Leisure Class: Consumption and Cultural Creativity in the Andes*. Chicago: University of Chicago Press, 1999.

Korovkin, Tanya. "Commodity Production and Ethnic Culture: Otavalo, Northern Ecuador." *Economic Development and Cultural Change* 47, no. 1 (1998): 125–54.

Meisch, Lynn A. 1998. "The Reconquest of Otavalo Ecuador: Indigenous Economic Gains and New Power Relations." *Research in Economic Anthropology* 19, edited by Barry L. Isaac, 11–30. Stamford, CT: JAI Press.

Salomon, Frank. "Weavers of Otavalo." In *Cultural Transformations and Ethnicity in Modern Ecuador*, edited by Norman E. Whitten, Jr., 420–449. Urbana: University of Illinois Press, 1981.

Weismantel, Mary. *Food, Gender, and Poverty in the Ecuadorian Andes*. Philadelphia: University of Pennsylvania Press, 1988.

Video

Weaving the Future, by Mark Freeman, is available from Documentary Educational Resources (DER), 101 Morse Street, Watertown, MA 02172, *Docued@der.org*.

WWW Sites

Abya Yala Net Site
http://abyayala.nativeweb.org/

The Abya Yala Net site contains information on this project which is supported by the South and Meso American Indian Rights Center (SAIIC) in collaboration with Native Web. The site includes information on indigenous peoples of Mexico, Central America, and South America as well as links to other sites about native peoples of the Americas.

Otavalo WWW Site
http://otavalo.com.ec/

The people of Otavalo maintain their own WWW site in English and in Spanish. This site contains information on local tourist attractions, locally owned tourist businesses including hotels, and locally produced textiles.

Organizations

The Confederation of Indigenous Nationalities of Ecuador
    Av. Granados 2553 y 6 de Diciembre
    Casilla 17–17–1235
    Quito, Ecuador
    ccc@conaie.ec.

Chapter 13

The Quechua of the Peruvian Andes
Paul H. Gelles

CULTURAL OVERVIEW

The People

The central Andean highlands cover the better part of the largest mountain chain in the world and are home to the greatest concentration of indigenous peoples in the Americas. They live at over 10,000 feet above sea level (f.a.s.l.), in thousands of hamlets, towns, and cities spread over a rugged and vertical terrain. Found in warm fertile valleys, on steep mountainsides, and on frigid high plains, indigenous peasant communities control vast territories in the highlands of Ecuador, Peru, and Bolivia. The millions of indigenous Quechua and Aymara people who live in these communities are tied to and affected by national and international political and economic forces. At the same time, members of this cultural majority have beliefs and rituals that are locally generated and distinctly Andean, providing important meaning and identity for their lives. Ignored and denigrated by dominant sectors in the Andean nations, these beliefs and ritual practices have long been a fundamental component of local systems of agricultural and pastoral production, of those activities that sustain life.

Together with terracing, llama and alpaca herding, and the vertical control of different ecological niches, irrigation facilitated the development of pre-Columbian states in the rugged environment of the central Andes. With the great population decline that followed the Spanish invasion, close to three-quarters of the pre-Columbian terraces were abandoned, as were thousands of irrigation canals. Over the last century, the rapidly growing highland population has put pressure on communal resources, engendering attempts to recover some of the lost infrastructure.

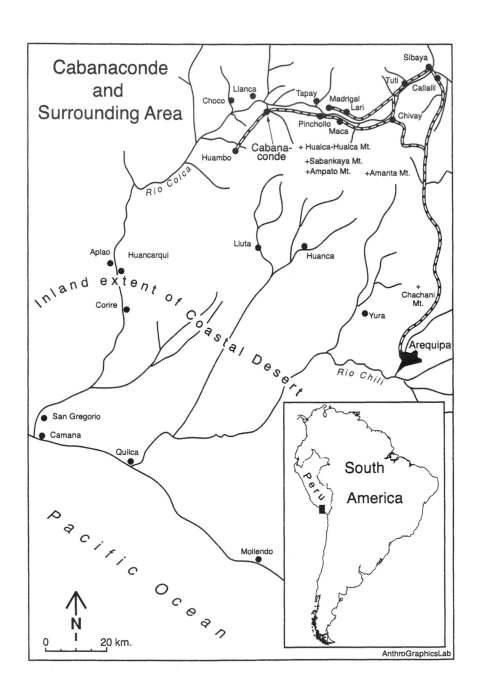

Cabanaconde and Surrounding Area

Sibaya
Llanca
Choco
Tapay
Madrigal
Lari
Tuti
Callalli
Pinchollo
Maca
Chivay
Cabana-conde
+ Hualca-Hualca Mt.
Huambo
+Sabankaya Mt.
+Ampato Mt.
+Amanta Mt.
Rio Colca
Lluta
Huanca
Aplao
Huancarqui
Inland extent of Coastal Desert
Corire
+ Chachani Mt.
Yura
Arequipa
Rio Chili
San Gregorio
Camana
Quilca
Pacific Ocean
Mollendo
South America
Peru

N
0   20 km.

AnthroGraphicsLab

Two women from Cabanaconde talking and drinking *chica* (corn beer). Courtesy of Paul H. Gelles.

The Setting

Cabanaconde, a large and growing community of some 5,000 bilingual
Quechua and Spanish speakers, is flanked by mountains on one side and
a precipitously deep canyon on the other. While the community sits at
10,500 f.a.s.l., nearby Mount Hualca-Hualca is almost twice that high
(19,500 f.a.s.l.). Here snow melt courses down the Hualca-Hualca River
to the community and is the lifeblood—or as the Cabaneños put it, the
"mother's milk"—of the agricultural fields and the townspeople. All agriculture in Cabanaconde is irrigated, and because it produces a valuable
commodity for subsistence and trade—Cabanita maize, which is famous
throughout the southern Andes for its taste and quality—irrigated land is
the central source of wealth in the community.

The productive potential of the Hualca-Hualca River basin and Cabanaconde's warm valley led at least two pan-Andean empires, the Wari and
the Inka, to colonize this hydrological system and the people dependent

207

upon it. During Inka rule, Cabanaconde's warm valley was the seat of the Cavana nation and was more important politically and in productive terms than neighboring valleys. There was considerable intensification of agriculture in Cabanaconde during Inka rule, and the rich volcanic soils and temperate climate that favored the production of maize allowed for greater population density. Here, and in hundreds of other areas, the Inka state invested in its periphery, expanding pre-Inka canals and terraces.

While the Cavana polity continued to be extremely productive during the early Spanish colonial period, this was not to last. Diseases, civil wars, and exploitation in the nearby mines of Caylloma led to a population decline, which reached an extreme in the late seventeenth century. From the 1570s until the 1680s, the number of "Indian" tribute payers decreased from 1,345 to 256, over 80%. With the population loss, the Cavanas were unable to maintain their pre-Columbian infrastructure, and dozens of canals and thousands of hectares of terraced fields were abandoned. Since the early part of this century, the Cabaneños have attempted to rehabilitate part of this lost infrastructure.

These attempts are part of other significant changes taking place in Cabanaconde. A road linking Cabanaconde to the city of Arequipa was built in 1965, which increased migration and participation in the market economy. Improved transportation changed community life dramatically. Today buses arrive and leave daily, and there is a continual flow of people, goods, and ideas between the community and its colonies in Arequipa, Lima, and Washington, D.C., which in 1987 had populations of approximately 1,000, 3,000, and 150, respectively. The associations formed by migrants in these cities are a part of community life; they channel resources back to the community and intervene decisively in communal conflicts with outside interests.

Traditional Subsistence Strategies

Cabanaconde is an economically differentiated community, and people there have conflicting interests. Different types of assets—land and cattle holdings, social networks, god parenthood (*compadrazgo*) ties, migrant remittances, access to market opportunities—vary greatly from family to family. Competition, factionalism, and envy, therefore, are part of community life and play an important role in the political processes of the community.

Lying on the arid west slope of the Andes, the territory of Cabanaconde is environmentally diverse and supports an extraordinary amount of wildlife; however, there is little hunting or fishing. Instead, Cabaneños depend on domesticated plants and animals. Cabanaconde has production zones ranging from 6,500 to 14,500 f.a.s.l., reaching from tropical orchards deep in Colca Canyon to high pastures, where alpaca, llama, sheep, and cattle herds are kept. The bulk of agricultural production takes place in the fields surrounding the town, between approximately 9,500 and 10,800 f.a.s.l., where Cabanita maize, famous for its taste and quality, is grown.

All agriculture in Cabanaconde is irrigated, and about three quarters of the 1,200 hectares (2,964 acres) of irrigated lands in the main fields is dedicated to maize. The Hualca-Hualca River picks up water from supplementary sources—since 1983 this includes the Majes Canal—as it winds its way down from the snow melt of looming Mount Hualca-Hualca. Annual rainfall is extremely variable, and periodic drought occurs in this area of the Andes.

Irrigation water in Cabanaconde and throughout most of the Andes is a type of common pool resource—understood to be a type of property relationship in which a particular resource (in this case water) is controlled by an identifiable community of interdependent users. This property management system usually excludes outsiders, and members of the local community regulate use. In the case of Cabanaconde, the access of *comuneros* to irrigation water is managed and controlled by a village-wide water users' association called the irrigators' commission.

Social and Political Organization

The official political structure of Cabanaconde, like many highland communities in Peru, consists of the municipal council (*concejo municipal*), the governor (*gobernador*), the Peasant Community (*Communidad Campesina*), and an irrigators' commission (*comisión de regantes*). Today, while these different political institutions often cooperate on projects of mutual interest, they also compete over local resources, personal loyalties, and funds from government and nongovernmental organizations.

The most respected and democratic institution in communal life is the Peasant Community, which can legally act as a corporate person to defend communal interests from internal or external threats. Individuals are inscribed as community members (*comuneros*) of the Peasant Community. In return for attending communal assemblies and carrying out communal work service, the (*comunero*) gains access to the common pool resources of the community. These common pool resources, which are managed by long-standing rules within the community, include irrigation water, grazing lands, medicinal herbs, and firewood. Other benefits, such as fiesta celebrations sponsored by the community, are also enjoyed by the *comunero*.

Religion and World View

During pre-Columbian times, and throughout the Spanish colonial period, Andean peoples and polities throughout the Central Andes traced their origins to sacred features of the landscape, such as mountains, lakes, and springs, which also often happened to be a source of irrigation water.

209

This peculiarly Andean definition of ethnicity continues to find expression in contemporary highland communities. As providers of fertility and life as well as of disease, death, and destruction, mountains and other features of the sacred landscape, as well as Catholic saints, serve as protector spirits and emblems of local identity. The ritual offerings, libations, and religious celebrations that are directed toward these deities are key features of social life, ethnic identity, and agricultural production.

THREATS TO SURVIVAL

Population Growth, Water Politics, and the Peruvian State

For the people of Cabanaconde and millions of other indigenous people in the Andes, water is life. A key element of production, water is also a source of great meaning and conflict. By exploring the Majes conflict and the Cabaneños' response to it, we gain insight into how state policies and other political forces condition Cabanaconde's relationship with its resources, and how Cabanaconde resists and, in turn, conditions these outside forces.

The population of Cabanaconde began to recover in the mid-nineteenth century and has more than doubled over the last century. As of 1987, there were at least 600 households and some 4,000 people in the community. This demographic expansion and the rampant partitioning of land holdings have been factors in permanent out-migration. Most important for our purposes here, since at least the turn of the century, the Cabaneños have attempted to expand their irrigation commons and rehabilitate some of their lost agricultural land. The Peruvian state, however, has lent little support to these efforts and, in some cases, has worked against the attempts of the Cabaneños and other highland peoples to expand the productive potential of their agricultural infrastructure because of negative stereotypes regarding highland peoples and the coastal-oriented nature of development that predominate in Peru. As in many other culturally diverse societies, state officials in Peru ignore the potential of indigenous technologies and models of resource management. This is because of the alleged superiority of "modern" Western cultural forms and organization and because the power holders and dominant cultures of these nations regard indigenous peoples as racially and culturally inferior.

Today, popular and national cultural discourses present the Spanish-speaking, white, Western-oriented minority as the model of modernity, the embodiment of legitimate national culture, and the key to Peru's future. Many of the negative stereotypes directed toward *indios*—that they are backward and unproductive—are extended to the mountains and their systems of production. These prejudices of a dominant cultural minority are diffused throughout Peru's educational system, civic ceremonies, language policies, and even its water policies.

The Majes Conflict

In March 1983, every night after the town was well asleep, the "eleven heroes"—as the people of Cabanaconde would later call them—met in the parched, water-starved fields outside of town and, picks and drills in hand, ascended the almost dry riverbed of the Hualca-Hualca River basin. When they arrived at Tomanta, the moonlit cement casing of the Majes Canal stood out against the clear Andean night like a wide, white sidewalk—or a white scar, a permanent reminder of the abuses and broken promises incurred by the Peruvian state and the billion-dollar Majes project as they gouged through communal territory to channel highland water to the coast. For over five years, the project had usurped resources and wreaked havoc on the social and ecological fabric of the community. And now, as the worst drought in thirty years devastated the community, Majes still refused to provide the promised water. While the remaining plants withered under the intense Andean sun, a virtual river was streaming by the community, sequestered in a thick cement canal and destined for cash crops on the coast. Enough was enough. Two stood guard, while the others, laughing and cursing, went at it again. They had already been at it several nights and were making little progress. It would have to be dynamite, they decided. Dynamite it was, and the rest is history.

As illustrated in this vignette, an important source of water, as well as of contention, is the large canal built by the Majes Consortium through communal territory in the late 1970s. Many of the maps elaborated by this billion-dollar development project neglect to show that in the path of the proposed canal lay more than a dozen communities and tens of thousands of peasants. This is symptomatic of the low regard that Majes and the Peruvian state had for the inhabitants of Cabanaconde and the Colca Valley.

The role of the state is clear. As early as May 6, 1967, the Ministry of Development and Public Works by way of Arequipa Board of Rehabilitation and Development stated that Cabanaconde "is being considered for three thousand hectares" to favor the irrigators there. Various other government agencies convened later that year. An entry in the Books of the Irrigation Commission states that the community is "[s]oliciting some three thousand liters [per second] of water from the Main Canal of Majes to be used in the irrigation of the fields now being cultivated and in the expansion of new lands." This same entry, dated November 10, 1966, reports that the Ministry of Development and Public Works, the Board of Rehabilitation of Arequipa, the National Fund for Economic Development, and the national office of the Agrarian Reform were going to study the springs of the entire area so that if the Majes Canal affected the town's resources, Cabanaconde could claim damages.

Promises were made but not kept. Until 1983 there were no benefits from the project, except an improved road and poorly paid, temporary, and dangerous jobs. The project instead brought widespread social and environmental problems to Cabanaconde. Workers from the project, who came from other highland regions and from the coast and who were housed in a large encampment near the community, abused the local townsfolk. Many workers would not buy products from women accompanied by their husbands, and there were incidents of prostitution and rape. Although the improved road provided the means for greater mobility up and down the valley and to and from Arequipa, the community was also subjected to economic, cultural, and political forces it had never experienced before. More money began to flow into the community, and stores were opened to meet the needs of a boom economy. Many Cabaneños lamented the changes and abuses the project brought. "Everything became money, money, money," as one man put it.[1]

Harder to express are the profound social and cultural changes the community experienced, including the way in which local society defined itself. "Criollo" views, disparaging toward the "simple" and "backwards ways" of the Cabaneños, became widely felt. As the president of the community ruefully expressed, "The workers would come rolling into town. They were from all over—Cuzco, Puno, the coast—all over. They'd come in, saying in Spanish, 'son of a bitch, it's hot! Hey, give me a case of beer,' and pretty soon all the boys in town were walking around, saying 'hey, son of a bitch'."[2] Less respect for elders, an increase in vandalism, and the breaking down of social mores were other consequences of Majes. The local culture was denigrated, and several rituals, such as *torotinkay* during the sowing, disappeared. The workers even instituted a new saint in the community.

The social impact was paralleled by an ecological one. Economic dependence on income generated by the project increased as the community's resources suffered. During a series of drought years, when the volume of river water was already extremely low, the project used large amounts of water from the river for its operations without the community's permission. Project roads damaged canals and terraces. The underground tunnels built by the project also affected subterranean sources of water. Because of the drought and Majes' insensitive use of the little river water that remained, the cultivated area decreased dramatically. A petition sent by the Irrigators' Commission to the Ministry of Agriculture on March 18, 1980, states that the devastation caused by "the last droughts" and the water supplied to Majes had "horrific results . . . our agricultural fields have diminished by 80 percent."

Abuses were tolerated, in part, because of the irrigation water and ex-

212

tended land base the community expected to receive from the project. Throughout 1979 and 1980, the Majes project continued to promise enough water, 1,000 liters (227 gallons) per second, to recover thousands of acres for the community. But it soon became clear to the community that Majes had no intention of carrying through with their promises. The first hint of resistance became manifest.

In March 1980, a commission made up of the president of the Peasant Community, the president of the Irrigators' Commission, and the mayor of Cabanaconde again requested water from the Majes Canal in the form of an offtake valve and assistance in improving the waters of Hualca-Hualca. They stated that "the District of Cabanaconde has been forgotten" and that "everyone will unite as one man" if their demands went unanswered. Later that month, a memorandum was sent to the Ministry of Agriculture and to the president of the republic, "clamoring for one thing alone, which is water." In August 1981, a letter to the Majes Consortium stated that, if it did not recompense the community for its water, "the agriculturists will stop the services they provide . . . the higher authorities are fooling us." More ominously, "the townspeople will take action to the last consequences if an immediate solution is not arrived at." Yet no water was allotted to the community. In September 1981, the books of the Irrigators' Commission refer to the drought of that year as "a frightful crisis."

In January 1983, the mayor of Cabanaconde sent another letter, this time to Fernando Belaúnde Terry, the president of Peru:

Cabanaconde is the most populated district of the Province of Caylloma . . . The ratio of man/land is unequal, and all community members are small holders, a situation which generates the massive exodus of the population . . . the current capacity is only 80 liters per second, insufficient for 1200 hectares. We irrigate every 100 days . . . This generates poverty, undernourishment, infant and adult mortality, alcoholism and illiteracy . . . Cabanaconde has been forgotten by the Majes Macon Project, whose canal crosses our jurisdiction and which has destroyed our natural resources, such as land and water, making even graver the already precarious economic situation of this community.

The letter asked President Belaúnde to authorize an offtake valve from the Majes Canal; money, machines, and technical assistance to reconstruct another canal; the construction of a cement reservoir in Joyas; and the settlement of families in the Pampas de Majes (the target area of the project). The communal authorities and several hundred people signed the letter. Their numerous cries for help—the many delegations and various pleas the community had sent to the consortium and to the regional authorities, the letters written, and the articles printed in Arequipa newspapers—fell on deaf ears. With the remaining plants withering in the most serious drought in thirty years, the possibility of famine became real.

RESPONSE: STRUGGLES TO SURVIVE CULTURALLY

Peasant Resistance

In March 1983, the Cabaneños opened the Majes Canal in a classic case of peasant resistance. The now renowned "eleven heroes" of the community, some of whom were authorities of the Irrigators' Commission and the Peasant Community, went nightly to drill a hole in the thick cement casing of the canal where it crossed the Hualca-Hualca River. Finally, they used dynamite. People in town soon began to comment that the volume of the Hualca-Hualca River had increased, and an assembly was hurriedly called. The entire community swung into action.

A permanent guard kept watch in the church tower, ready to sound the bell should the police arrive. A trumpeter was stationed at the entrance of the town, and barricades were built on the road. The eleven heroes left the community or slept in the orchards deep in the Colca Valley. A committee made up of local authorities traveled to Arequipa to report what had been done, and they were immediately arrested. But the Cabaneños had skillfully published several news clips in Arequipa newspapers in the weeks before they opened the canal, decrying the drought, the way Majes had lied to the community, and the lack of government support. This was done to assert the Cabaneños' rights to the water and to ensure that their actions would not be confused with those of terrorists.

A police contingent was sent to the community, but when they arrived the entire community confronted them. The community claimed collective responsibility for the opening of the canal and demanded that the water not be withdrawn. Several large machines of the consortium were taken hostage. A few days later, the subprefect of the region, the mayor of Cabanaconde, and other important authorities met in the plaza of the community. The subprefect agreed to provide a legal transfer of the waters within the briefest time possible, promising that there would "be no repression against the townspeople." But when he asked that the machines be returned to the Majes Consortium, his request was denied by the community. The mayor demanded that 68 gallons per second be given to the community. After he agreed to the conditions set by the community, the subprefect received an ovation. People still talk excitedly and proudly about how the entire community took responsibility, and how they were ready to fight to the end for the water.

The communal authorities, with help from the migrant associations of the community in Arequipa and Lima, continued to negotiate with the regional authorities, explaining that they were not terrorists, but were dying of hunger. Fearing further conflicts, Autodema (Autoridad Autónoma de Majes)—the administrative unit of the Majes Canal—finally agreed to cede 150 liters (34 gallons) per second to Cabanaconde. The Cabaneños also demanded that the state's water tariff, instituted several years earlier, be rescinded.

In August 1983, the hole was patched and a valve was installed at Tomanta. The next day the entire community went to Tomanta in a procession, with a band at its head. An entry in the Books of the Irrigation Commission reads, "After the blessing by the priest the two valves were opened in the presence of the president of the Irrigators Commission and the townspeople." With this victory, the Cabaneños became heroes in the region. The other communities of the left bank of the Colca Valley threatened to take similar action "or call in the boys from Cabanaconde," as several Cabaneños proudly said.[3] These other communities were soon given access to the "Majes water." When the abandoned fields were later recovered with the "Majes water," the eleven heroes were given choice plots.

Land Recovery

Once the flow of 150 liters (34 gallons) per second from the Majes Canal was secured in 1983, attempts to increase the cultivated area began almost immediately. Canals in the lower part of the agricultural lands were extended through communal labor, and abandoned terraced fields in the area of Auquilote were distributed through lottery. To decide which families could participate in the lottery for the 36 hectares (89 acres) being recovered, the Peasant Community held a communal assembly. As the name of each community member was read, the public decided who met the established criteria: full-time and responsible farmer, household head with dependent children, permanent resident in the community, and small landholder. More than 200 people qualified. The thirty-six lottery winners quickly organized into an association, elected a president, and began to rehabilitate their lands through cooperative labor. Many of the newly recovered fields yielded good harvests in 1988 and 1989.

Auquilote was the first step in recovering more than 1,000 hectares (2,470 acres) of agricultural land in Cabanaconde, this plan was predicated on an increase of water from the Majes Canal. The Majes Project Administration promised an additional 350 liters (80 gallons) per second if the community could provide a suitable plan for the use of the water. Release of the water was also contingent on the community's signing away their rights to Huataq, an important spring in the high pastures of Cabanaconde's communal territory. The reason for Majes' generosity comes to light: by releasing 350 liters (80 gallons) per second to Cabanaconde, they retain the 600 liters (136 gallons) per second of Huataq for the Majes Canal and for the powerful Arequipeños who currently use the Huataq water.

Nevertheless, since 1990, Cabanaconde's efforts to recover its lost infrastructure and agricultural have been extremely successful. As of 1997, the community had recovered more than 800 hectares (1,976 acres); another

740 will be brought into production in the next few years. By the year 2000, the community will have essentially doubled its agricultural lands. After a century of efforts, the Cabaneños' courageous actions and astute maneuvering have provided them with a relatively large and growing land base.

FOOD FOR THOUGHT

The colonial categories and racist attitudes that were instituted in Peru during the colonial period have survived with incredible virulence. National power holders who determine the state's policy toward Andean communities live an urban criollo lifestyle in coastal cities with Western life ways, and they generally disdain *indios*. The Majes Canal and development policies that favor the coast are thus part of a larger cultural politics in Peru, one in which the human and natural resources of the highlands are viewed as inferior to the criollo coast—this marginalizes Andean communities in many subtle and not so subtle ways.

Today, because of the Cabaneños' resolve, the state-sponsored Majes Canal is used not only for capital-intensive agriculture on the coast but also to recover part of Cabanaconde's lost infrastructure. By the way Cabanaconde challenged the Majes project, it recovered abandoned terrace fields and democratically divided these for the greater prosperity of the townspeople—a dramatic case study of open resistance to Peru's coastally oriented political economy of development.

The understanding of water, ethnicity, and power developed here can be applied to the politics of community, irrigation, and development in other culturally plural countries. This is especially the case in the Andean nations of Bolivia and Ecuador, as well as in Guatemala and Mexico in Mesoamerica. In these countries, pre-Columbian empires flourished and established extensive farming systems and infrastructure (e.g., raised fields, terraces, and irrigation works). Today, indigenous peoples continue to constitute a large percentage, often the majority, of the population.

Questions

1. How is development conditioned by the particular cultural politics and ethnic conflicts in nation-states?
2. How do development organizations and the bureaucracies of these states interface with indigenous communities?
3. What is the nature of this interface, both politically and culturally?
4. What form, if any, does local resistance take in response to state intervention in resource use?
5. How do indigenous technologies, and the cultural rationales that underwrite them, fit into this resistance?

NOTES

Data and information included in this chapter come from Paul Gelles, *Water and Power in Highland Peru: The Cultural Politics of Irrigation and Development* (New Brunswick, NJ: Rutgers University Press, 2000). Quotations come from various administrative *Books of the Irrigation Commission, Cabanaconde.*

1. Author's personal communication.
2. Ibid.
3. Author's personal communication/field notes.

RESOURCE GUIDE

Published Literature

Gelles, Paul H. *Water and Power in Highland Peru: The Cultural Politics of Irrigation and Development.* New Brunswick, NJ: Rutgers University Press, 2000.

Mitchell, William P., and David Guillet, eds. *Irrigation at High Altitudes: The Social Organization of Water Control in the Andes.* Washington, D.C.: Society for Latin American Anthropology and the American Anthropological Association, 1994.

Shozo Masuda, Izumi Shimada, and Craig Morris, eds. *Andean Ecology and Civilization.* Tokyo: University of Tokyo Press, 1985.

Starn, Orin, Carlos Iván Degregori, and Robin Kirk, eds. *The Peru Reader: History, Culture, and Politics.* Durham NC: Duke University Press, 1995.

Urban, Greg, and Joel Sherzer, eds. *Nation-States and Indians in Latin America.* Austin: University of Texas Press, 1991.

Van Cott, Donna Lee, ed. *Indigenous Peoples and Democracy in Latin America.* New York: St. Martin's Press, 1994.

Videos and Films

Q'eros: The Shape of Survival, Berkeley: University of California Center for Media and Independent Learning, John Cohen, 1979.

Transnational Fiesta: 1992, Berkeley: University of California Center for Media and Independent Learning, Paul H. Gelles and Wilton Martínez, 1993.

WWW Sites

Cultural Survival
http://www.cs.org

Cultures of the Andes
http://www.andes.org

Native Web
http://www.nativeweb.org

Glossary

Barrio. Neighborhood.

Calpulli. Territorially based kin group.

Campesino. Peasant.

Caudillo. Political strong man.

Class. Social category of modern societies used to rank the population into distinct levels based on wealth.

Compadrazgo (godparenthood). System of crosscutting upper and lower classes through a ritual kinship relationship.

Creole. Person of mixed European and African ancestry.

Curanderoa. A man or woman who cures diseases.

Degradation. Human-induced reduction in the quality of the environment or natural resources, such as water, air, and soil, that reduces the capacity of these resources to support life.

Ejido. Term used mainly in Mexico for a collective landholding, usually owned by indigenous or peasant communities.

Ethnicity. Regional or national identity based on heritage, religion, or language.

Gender. Way members of the two sexes are perceived and expected to behave.

Globalization. Integration of the world economies through various means.

Haciendas. Large Latin American landed estates often but not always used for the cultivation or raising of commercial agricultural commodities, such as cattle, for local markets.

Glossary

Indigenous. Human population originating in, or native to, an area or environment.

Ladino (similar to mestizo). Spanish term used throughout Central America to refer to a person of mixed Spanish and Indian ancestry.

Latin America. Includes the countries of Mexico, Central America, and South America.

Maquiladores. Factories often located in border zones or free trade zones.

Mestizo (similar to ladino). Originally referred to a person of mixed blood, usually of Indian and Spanish heritage.

Milpa. A cornfield.

Plantations. Similar to haciendas but organized for the production of export commodities such as sugar and cotton for global markets.

Quinceañeras. Young girl's 15th birthday party.

Shaman. Religious practitioner and healer.

Swidden (similar to slash-and-burn agriculture). System of shifting agriculture dependent on cutting down and burning a small patch of forest, planting crops for a few years, and then allowing the plot to lie fallow (unused) for a number of years until the forest has grown back.

Syncretism. Fusion of elements of two or more distinct cultural traditions, such as religions, belief systems, philosophies, or music.

Index

About the Contributors

DAVID BARTON BRAY is chair and associate professor of environmental studies at Florida International University, Miami.

JOHN R. BORT is associate professor of anthropology at East Carolina University, Greenville, North Carolina.

JANET M. CHERNELA is associate professor of anthropology and sociology at Florida International University, North Miami.

KATE CISSNA is a Ph.D. student in anthropology at the University of California, Santa Barbara.

RUDI COLLOREDO-MANSFELD is assistant professor of anthropology at the University of Iowa, Iowa City.

MARÍA L. CRUZ-TORRES is assistant professor of anthropology at the University of California, Riverside.

DAVID J. DODDS is a postdoctoral fellow at the Center for Institutions, Population, and Environment, Indiana University, Bloomington.

PAUL H. GELLES is associate professor of anthropology at the University of California, Riverside.

PETER H. HERLIHY is associate professor of geography at the University of Kansas, Lawrence.

JAMES HOWE is professor of anthropology at the Massachusetts Institute of Technology, Cambridge.

JAMES LOUCKY is associate professor of anthropology at Western Washington University, Bellingham.

About the Contributors

SCOTT S. ROBINSON is professor of anthropology at the University of Mexico, Mexico City.

SUSAN C. STONICH is professor of anthropology and environmental studies at the University of California, Santa Barbara.

JORGE VARELA MARQUEZ is the executive director of the Committee for the Defense and Development of the Flora and Fauna of the Gulf of Fonseca (CODDEFFAGOLF), Honduras.

PHILIP D. YOUNG is professor emeritus of anthropology at the University of Oregon, Eugene.

232